20TH-CENTURY COMPOSERS

Richard Strauss

Richard Strauss

by Tim Ashley

Φ

for Peter

Phaidon Press Limited
Regent's Wharf
All Saints Street
London N1 9PA

First published 1999
© 1999 Phaidon Press Limited

ISBN 0 7148 3794 6

A CIP catalogue record for this book is
available from the British Library.

Library of Congress Cataloging
In Publication Data available.

Printed in Singapore

Frontispiece, The Presentation
of the Rose from *Der Rosenkavalier* in the 1979 Munich
production, with Lucia Popp
as Sophie and Brigitte
Fassbaender as Octavian

Contents

Preface

I first heard the music of Richard Strauss when I was fourteen. Up to
that point, he had been no more than a name. One day, in a local
shop, I found a record of the Dance of the Seven Veils and Salome's
closing monologue coupled with the Awakening Scene from *Die
ägyptische Helena* ('The Egyptian Helen'). The singer was Leontyne
Price, the conductor Erich Leinsdorf. On impulse, I blew a week's
pocket money on it. I was unprepared for what I heard. It was heady
stuff, in which beauty and danger seemed perilously entwined. I had
no idea that music was capable of such expressive opulence or such
immediate, almost shocking impact. The orchestral sound, as it
glittered, swooned and shifted in infinite restlessness, struck me as
being, quite literally, beyond belief. I was mesmerized by the vocal
line, which dipped and soared, fractured into something that
resembled the terseness of human speech and then reconstituted itself
in rapture. I still believe Strauss to be the most subtle musical
psychologist since Mozart and, above all, the most expressive writer
for the human voice in history.

Awareness of the man, and of the issues surrounding his life and
work, came later. Of all twentieth-century composers, he is perhaps
the most controversial and paradoxical. The facts surrounding his
position seem clear enough. He died in 1949 at the age of eighty-five
after a prolific career spanning seventy-nine years. His output is
uneven and his reputation rests on a fraction of it, a group of works
first performed between 1889 and 1911 – the tone-poems *Don Juan*,
Tod und Verklärung ('Death and Transfiguration'), *Till Eulenspiegel*,
Also sprach Zarathustra ('Thus Spake Zarathustra'), *Don Quixote* and
Ein Heldenleben ('A Hero's Life'), the operas *Salome*, *Elektra* and *Der
Rosenkavalier* ('The Rose Bearer' or 'The Rose Cavalier'). Although
each was initially accompanied by sensation or scandal, they remain at
the core of the orchestral and operatic repertoires. With the exception
of the posthumous *Vier letzte Lieder* ('Four Last Songs'), his other

works met with a varied response and have remained subject to the vagaries of public and critical taste.

Two assumptions are commonly made about Strauss's music after *Rosenkavalier* (1911): that the succeeding works mark a decline in his creative powers which would not be fully recovered until his final opera *Capriccio* in 1942; and that *Rosenkavalier* itself represents a definite shift in his style, essentially equated with his abandonment of harmonic experimentation – he goes off the rails, develops a dependence on pastiche and parody, veers towards sentiment or nostalgia. Strauss, held up as a pivotal figure linking the chromatic experiments of Wagner's *Tristan und Isolde* (1865) with the breakdown of tonality after the turn of the century, suddenly seems conservative, reactionary, anachronistic.

These assumptions colour much Strauss criticism and have often led to an attack on the works he wrote after *Elektra* (1909). They are based, however, on a belief that musical modernism equates solely with tonal experimentation. The parody and pastiche of *Rosenkavalier* are, in fact, present in his work as early as the *Burleske* for piano and orchestra of 1886, and the comparatively simple harmonic structure of his first operatic comedy *Feuersnot* ('Fire Famine', 1901) anticipates *Rosenkavalier*'s supposed shift in style by ten years. Though *Elektra* contains Strauss's most sustained use of dissonance, there are individual passages in *Die Frau ohne Schatten* ('The Woman without a Shadow') of 1919 which surpass it in terms of density. And in *Rosenkavalier* itself, the fluid beauty of the music of the Marschallin, Octavian and Sophie disguises the fact that the third act opens with a prelude as dissonant as anything Strauss wrote.

To isolate harmony side-steps the question of the function of dissonance in Strauss's music, and narrows a discussion of his relationship with twentieth-century culture. Experiments in structure and form, the subject matter, world view and attitudes expressed in individual works are often overlooked. If the ideological stance of Strauss's output is taken into account, a rather different picture emerges. A shift in attitude is markedly discernible around the time of World War I, between *Ariadne auf Naxos* ('Ariadne on Naxos', 1912, revised 1916) and *Die Frau ohne Schatten*. The former, questioning whether desire can remain permanently focused on one object, celebrates the fluidity of human sexuality and, in the demand made by the character of Zerbinetta that a woman's pleasure should equal a man's, anticipates the radical feminism of the 1960s by nearly half a century. *Die Frau ohne Schatten*, on the other hand, states that human sexuality is valid only when contained within the framework of marriage and aligned with the capacity for reproduction. Delight in pleasure has been equated with immaturity, even lack of humanity; the family is elevated as a moral imperative and celebrated as the opera's ideological focus. The attitude has become illiberal, and Strauss's slide towards a conservative outlook is more effectively located here than in the apparent stylistic retrogression of *Der Rosenkavalier*.

The relationship between subject matter and expression is of paramount importance in evaluating Strauss's achievement. To play down the relevance of non-musical sources is perilous. His best-known orchestral works are programmatic and the impetus behind them is crucial to their understanding and interpretation. The argument that one need have no knowledge of Lenau or Nietzsche to appreciate *Don Juan* and *Also sprach Zarathustra* is, on one level, true, but we need to be aware of why both writers took such a hold on Strauss's imagination to understand why the tone-poems took the forms that they did.

Understanding Strauss's inspiration is also crucial in relating the music to the man. The apparent incongruity between Strauss and his work perplexed his contemporaries. The French novelist and musicologist Romain Rolland, a friend and admirer of Strauss, admitted that 'his music stirs me to my very depths,' but professed himself fazed by the man. 'One always wonders how *that*,' he wrote, on hearing Strauss conduct the *Sinfonia Domestica* in 1906, 'can have come out of this.' The emotional subtlety of Strauss's music, with its ability to portray a range of psychological experience from everyday reality to insanity, might lead one to suspect that its composer was either a man of unique and mature understanding, or the ultimate moody Romantic, prone to Dostoyevskyan fits of elation and despair. On the surface, however, the opposite is true. The creator of *Salome* is commonly described as a bourgeois type, a family man of extreme conventionality, happily married if henpecked, a rather flamboyant *bon viveur* with a passion for card playing and a permanently watchful eye on his bank balance.

There is no doubt that Strauss could be opportunistic, self-seeking and anxious to be in the public eye. During the period in which his reputation was established, he was effectively the equivalent of a modern rock star, followed everywhere by reporters. His fondness for money became the subject of hype and speculation (100,000 Marks for the score of *Elektra*, $1,500 for a concert in New York, the press surmised). The whiff of capitalist allure that surrounds Strauss squares uneasily with his genius. Fritz Busch, the conductor to whom he dedicated *Arabella*, famously remarked that Strauss wore his talent like a suit of clothes which he could put on or take off at will. Busch may have been fooled, for one important facet of Strauss's personality was his reticence to talk about his personal or emotional life, despite portraying it in the *Sinfonia Domestica* and his 1924 opera *Intermezzo* with an explicitness that continues to embarrass some.

Strauss spoke publicly on many occasions. He also wrote copiously – letters, journals, memoranda, memoirs – often in elegant prose that combines polish with wit. Yet he seldom spoke or wrote regarding the matters that we most want to know about. Only rarely, notably with Rolland, did the mask drop. He was mostly private and intensely secretive. His writings are not always a reliable witness to his life, and he occasionally rewrote the facts. His memoirs, dating from 1942 but not published until 1949, are significant both in what they say and in what they leave out. Strauss writes lovingly, for instance, of his admiration for the soprano Lotte Lehmann, recalling her in the role of the Composer in the revised version of his *Ariadne auf Naxos* conjuring her up as one of the ideal interpreters of his music. The passage is uncommonly vivid, and it takes a while for its full significance to sink in – namely that he was no longer able to hear her, for she was in exile in the United States while he was living in increasing isolation in Hitler's Germany.

The most troubling question raised by Strauss's life and career is his involvement with the Nazis. It is concerning this period that his reticence is most acute. He never made a statement openly condemning the regime, which he initially appeared to support and which he served as President of the Reichsmusikkammer (Reich's Music Chamber) for eighteen months. His actions during this period do, however, reveal much about him. He insisted on continuing his collaboration with his Jewish librettist, Stefan Zweig, even proposing a complex plot of secrecy, aliases and pseudonyms should the authorities try to prevent it. And his work as President of the Reichsmusikkammer shows him to be at odds with Nazi artistic policy almost from the beginning. He behaved like one who believed himself immune to the proscriptions of Nazism. Yet his dismissal led to compromise on his part, not protest and exile. What followed was a war of attrition for survival, during which some of Strauss's works betray a congruence with fascist ideology and aesthetics that raises questions about the relationship of art to politics and, above all, the moral responsibility of the composer in the face of the ultimate human obscenity. The persona of the apolitical artist, maintained by Strauss himself and many of his commentators, does not always hold up to scrutiny.

Strauss's conflicts with figures in authority, his assertion of belief in the self as being above and beyond prevailing cultural or moral trends, followed by collapse or apparent willingness to compromise – all constitute a predominant pattern both in his life and in his work. The heroes of many of his tone-poems and operas are rebels who kick against the moral and social order in acts of self-assertion, only to be brought down or to withdraw from the struggle.

Strauss's humour and the warmth of many of his letters should not blind us to the fact that many of his most important relationships consisted of battles of wills. His correspondence with his librettist Hugo von Hofmannsthal hides a struggle for control in their collaboration of many years; it was Strauss who, more often than not, gave in and let the poet have his way. Strauss was married to a woman whose tongue was famously vicious, who often derided his work and to whom he frequently appeared subservient. But there was never any question of his leaving her. However, the first, and most important, battle of wills was with his father who, until his death in 1905, was the composer's most remorseless critic. Many of the attitudes which inform Strauss's life and works evolved early, in his Bavarian childhood, which is where this study begins.

Its aim is to relate Strauss's career to the influences – personal, cultural and political – which shaped it, and in order to place him in context, I have divided his life according to the epochs of German history and culture in which he worked. It is not intended as an attack on Strauss (several have been published), nor as an unqualified defence that attempts to rescue him from the moral quagmire into which he unquestionably sank. Strauss's personality may be understandable, but there are times when neither his actions nor his attitudes are defensible. No short study can hope to do justice to the range and complexity of his output and there will inevitably be omissions. In discussing his music, I have restricted myself to those works which the listener will encounter with most frequency, along with lesser-known works which are of major importance in assessing the development of his music or personality.

There are many people whose help has been invaluable while I was working on this book and whom I would very much like to thank: David Allenby from Boosey & Hawkes, who arranged for the loan of scores; Stephen Bayard, who helped me track down most of Romain Rolland's relevant writings; Michael Kennedy, for his unstinting encouragement; Alison Latham, who asked me to write about Strauss for the Royal Opera House Programme in 1993, and whose advice about the manuscript at every stage of its development has been invaluable; Hubert Lehn, who has made Berlin my second home; Klaus Pokatzky for his advice on Wilhelmine Germany; Lizzie Vee, for suggesting how I might approach Strauss's family background. I am also grateful to Andrew Clements and Claire Armistead of the *Guardian*, Rodney Milnes and John Allison of *Opera*, Auberon Waugh and Nancy Sladek of *Literary Review*, Antony Peattie and Katie Tearle of the Glyndebourne Education Department and Margaret Stonborough of the Friends of Covent Garden, all of whom ensured that I worked on related material while I prepared this book. I would like to thank Norman Lebrecht for suggesting I should write a biography of Strauss in the first place; thanks also to Ingalo Thomson, Daniel Cunningham and Sophie Hartley at Phaidon Press for their help and support, and to Hans Dieter Reichert of hdr design.

Tim Ashley
London, 1999

I

Richard Strauss
photographed at
the age of two

The only purpose of life is to make art possible.

Strauss to Willi Schuh, 1947

Bavaria 1864–70

Ludwig II of Bavaria, painted by Gabriel Schachinger one year after the king's death in 1886

On 3 May 1864, a month before Richard Strauss was born, the eighteen-year-old Ludwig II of Bavaria summoned Richard Wagner to Munich, an action which changed the course of musical history. 'For you alone, whom I love so ardently, have I come into the world,' he later wrote to Wagner, in idolatrous tones. It was also a politically disastrous move, for Wagner was not above meddling in affairs of state.

That he could do so points to the uneasy relationship between music and politics in the conglomerate of independent states that formed pre-unification Germany. Music was dependent for its survival on a system of aristocratic patronage, dating back to the eighteenth century, and dangerously reliant on monarchical whim as well as public taste. It was a system which Wagner was prepared to exploit and in which Strauss would in time be conditioned to function. It was also, however, a system under threat. The French Revolution of 1789 had dealt the European aristocracy a blow from which it had never recovered and the subsequent Romantic movement brought with it a shift in emphasis in power from patron to musician.

Wagner arrived in Munich with his entourage, consisting of the brilliant pianist and conductor Hans von Bülow and his wife, Liszt's daughter, Cosima (who became Wagner's mistress within weeks of their arrival, and later his second wife). Their appearance was greeted with suspicion on both political and artistic fronts, and when Wagner started offering Ludwig political advice, pressure was put on the king to have the composer removed. Ludwig eventually gave way. In December 1865 Wagner was banished from Bavaria, and fled to Geneva, though he remained in contact with Ludwig.

In 1866, Bavaria became involved in a war between Austria and Prussia, the ostensible cause of which was a dispute over control of the northern duchies of Schleswig-Holstein. What was principally at stake, however, was the curbing of Prussia, which had grown formidably powerful under its imperialist prime minister, Otto von Bismarck. As the political situation worsened, Ludwig dithered, heftily backed by Wagner who encouraged him to steer an independent course between the two feuding states. When war finally broke out on June 16th, Bavaria, unable to maintain its neutral front any longer, had to come out in support of Austria. On July 3rd, however, the battle of Sadowa decided the outcome in Prussia's favour and the German states slid towards the empire of Bismarck's dreams.

While battles raged about Wagner's ministerial interference and the press gossiped about the Wagner–Cosima–Bülow ménage, resentment was growing among the employees of the Munich Court Theatre, where *Tristan und Isolde*, as yet unperformed, was in rehearsal. Wagner and Bülow were soon lording it over the orchestra. Chief among their opponents was the principal horn player, Franz Strauss, Richard's father, whose attitudes were inherently reactionary. Nothing of value, he maintained, had been composed since Beethoven. Haydn he adored, the greatest composer of all was Mozart, Mendelssohn and Schumann could be considered avant-garde – Wagner, however, was beyond the pale, a Mephistophelian figure whose music was nothing short of subversive. The loathing was not mutual, however, for Franz was widely regarded as the greatest horn player in Germany, thus earning Wagner's intense admiration. His professionalism was such that he played the horn solos in *Tristan, Die Meistersinger von*

A watercolour by Joseph Resch (1845) of the young Franz Strauss, who was then widely regarded as the finest horn player in Germany

Nürnberg, the *Ring* and *Parsifal* to perfection, though he was rarely
prepared to do so without fuss. Tensions flared during rehearsals. Franz
Strauss publicly derided Wagner's music and openly fought with Bülow.

'With his high forehead and his aquiline nose rather reminiscent of
a Circassian chieftain,' Richard Strauss wrote in his memoirs, 'my
father may well, in my opinion, have been of Bohemian stock. He was
what they call a character. He would have considered it dishonourable
ever to revise an artistic opinion and would never listen to me until
very late in his life.' This passage points to a dominant trait in Franz's
personality, an opinionated inflexibility of will which manifested itself
in rigidity and emotional remoteness. It also hints at an element of
secrecy concerning his origins.

Franz Strauss was born in Parkstein in north-east Bavaria, near the
Bohemian border, in 1822, one of two illegitimate children of a soldier
and a penurious local girl. Johann Urban Strauss gave his children his
name, but refused, possibly for financial reasons, to marry their
mother, Maria Walter, whom, after five years of cohabitation, he
abandoned. The Walter family consisted of musicians, both
professional and amateur. One of Franz's maternal uncles, anxious to
foster the boy's talent, taught him the horn, trumpet, violin and
dulcimer. And later, when two of the Walter brothers subsequently
went to Munich in search of musical employment, the fifteen-year-old
Franz accompanied them. The gifted adolescent, the star of his uncles'
chamber trio, was soon in demand and at twenty-five he joined the
Munich Court Orchestra.

When he was twenty-nine, Franz married Elise Sieff, a bandsman's
daughter. Their first child, a boy, succumbed to tuberculosis ten
months after he was born and, just three years after their marriage,
Elise and their two surviving children died in a cholera epidemic that
swept Munich. When he remarried, aged forty-two, he did so 'above
his station', as his son Richard would later be accused of doing, by his
own wife, among others.

Franz's bride, seventeen years his junior, was Josephine Pschorr, a
member of a clannish family of brewers, whose considerable
commercial empire flourished under the guidance of Josephine's father
Georg. His apparent *bonhomie* hid domestic tyranny, and Josephine's
upbringing, though materially comfortable, was overshadowed by
brutality. Every Saturday, Georg Pschorr flogged his sons on the

grounds that beating was good for them. Josephine grew up to be timorous, sensitive and shy, but when she married Franz there were no signs of the madness that later claimed her and took the form of delusions that her family was persecuting her.

Franz Strauss met Josephine when she was seventeen and it took him seven years to pluck up the courage to propose. An impecunious court musician did not seem to be the ideal husband for a Pschorr, but Josephine's family gave their consent. They were keen amateur musicians of varying talent and may have liked the idea of a professional in their midst. The couple were married in August 1863 and moved into an apartment that the Pschorrs provided over the brewery and beer hall at No. 2 Altheimer Eck. It was here that their first child, Richard Georg, was born on the morning of 11 June 1864. Two days before his third birthday, his sister Johanna was born and the family, needing a larger apartment, moved to the nearby Sonnenstrasse.

Strauss's childhood has frequently been described as extremely happy, though the tensions that simmered beneath the surface and flared as he moved into adolescence were already present. Both his father's capacity for rigid self-control and his mother's hypersensitivity left their imprint on his personality. From the beginning he was surrounded by music, the sounds of which were as familiar to him as speech. When he was born, Mozart's *Don Giovanni* was in rehearsal at

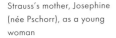

Strauss's mother, Josephine (née Pschorr), as a young woman

the Court Theatre, and it is possible that the first notes he heard consisted of the horn part played by Franz. Then there were the Pschorrs, who regularly assembled to play chamber music or to enjoy informal family singsongs round the piano. By the age of four Richard was taking piano lessons from August Tombo, a harpist from Franz's orchestra. Transcriptions of operatic melodies fascinated the boy, and at six years old, he was taken to the Munich Court Theatre where he heard two radically different works, Mozart's *Die Zauberflöte* ('The Magic Flute') with its mixture of fairy-tale symbolism, Enlightenment rationalism and Baroque theatricality, and Weber's *Der Freischütz* ('The Free-Shooter'), its emotional opposite, an irrationalistic Gothic thriller in which music of hitherto unattempted savagery combined with the folk elements of burgeoning nationalism.

Richard's first composition, produced when he was six, was a *Schneiderpolka* ('Tailor's Polka'), notated by Franz as his son played it on the piano. His first song, *Weihnachtslied* ('Christmas Carol'), swiftly followed and was dedicated to his aunt Johanna Pschorr and intended to be sung at one of the family gatherings. On this occasion Richard notated the music himself, though writing the words eluded him and Josephine had to add them to the manuscript's vocal line.

In sending Richard to Tombo, Franz set in motion a somewhat unorthodox musical education for his son – essentially informal and geared towards practicalities rather than theory – by means of his network of colleagues and contacts. Strauss never entered an academy and never, unlike Wagner or Schoenberg, became a theoretician or the proponent of an aesthetic creed. Franz was unstinting in his efforts to facilitate his son's progress. Doors and avenues opened at the mention of Franz's name, and Richard's scores and manuscripts were shown to colleagues and accepted for performance. Yet the benefits were not without price. Franz was rigid in his perfectionism and what passed for encouragement was often carping criticism, veiled insults or blatant put-downs. He demanded playing (and, later, conducting) of metronomic regularity. If Richard gathered speed, his father's comment, much repeated throughout his son's early career, was 'You hurry like a Jew.'

He was an inveterate anti-Semite. It was the one thing Franz Strauss had in common with Wagner and Bülow, both of whom were virulent in giving voice to their prejudice. Bülow wrote about 'the

The composer Richard
Wagner (1813 – 83),
photographed in 1877

general degradation – i.e. Judaization', and imagined 'the coming of
the opposite of a Messiah – namely one who would fasten his people
to the cross'. Wagner's racism had erupted in print as early as 1850
with the anonymous publication of the essay *Das Judenthum in der
Musik* ('Judaism in Music') in which the stereotype of the Jew as an
anti-cultural money-grabber leads to a disturbing demand that the
Jews renounce their Jewishness. In February 1869, Wagner reissued
Das Judenthum in der Musik under his own name, adding a paranoid
preface complaining that he himself was the victim of Jewish
persecution. It was a carefully timed gesture. Bismarck, now in control
of the North German Confederation, was working towards full
emancipation of the Jews and in July of the same year approved laws
abolishing discrimination.

The essay's reappearance similarly embarrassed Ludwig, whose
views were close to Bismarck's, and added further stress to the now
tense relationship between himself and Wagner. Wagner's plans for the
festival theatre which was to form his own shrine had been
temporarily abandoned. Ludwig, however, anxious to follow the
success of the première of *Meistersinger* in 1868, exercised his
prerogative as royal patron with a demand that the completed
instalments of the as yet unfinished *Ring* cycle be staged in Munich,
despite Wagner's insistence that performance conditions were

A children's fancy-dress
party during the 1870
Munich Carnival; Strauss
(back row, right), is dressed
as a troubadour, and
holds a conductor's baton.

inadequate. *Das Rheingold* accordingly received its première on 22 September 1869. Franz played in the orchestra. Wagner pointedly stayed away.

Prussian dominance, acquired through the repeated annexation of neighbouring territories, could no longer be ignored, and by 1869 anti-Prussian sentiment in Bavaria was rife. Faced with the emergence of the left-wing Social Democratic Party, Bismarck was ever more determined to achieve a united empire with the Prussian King Wilhelm as Kaiser. On 19 July 1870 France was provoked into declaring war. Many of the southern German states that had previously resisted unification, swept away by a rising tide of nationalist fervour, now supported Prussia. The Franco-German war – the first of the series of convulsive turning-points that characterize German history – had begun. With the German victory unification was now certain, though Bavaria held out until the end in its demand for equality with Prussia in the newly formed Empire. Finally, Ludwig, allowing himself to be bribed with the offer of a subsidy of 300,000 gulden a year (it would help build the castles he had set his mind on), gave in and signed a letter drafted by Bismarck, asking Wilhelm to accept the title of Kaiser. On 1 January 1871, the new German Reich came into being and Bismarck was appointed Chancellor. The individual German states were carefully allowed a certain measure of autonomy. Ludwig retained his title of King.

In Munich, where the Strausses had moved in 1869 to another apartment over the Pschorr brewery (this time with its front door on the Neuhauserstrasse), Franz and his family seemed impervious to events. The city, now deferring to the new capital Berlin, turned out to greet the returning troops. There is no indication that any of the family witnessed the event, nor that the political situation was even discussed. What, after all, did politics have to do with music, other than that one was essentially dependent on monarchs for one's job? The greatest music, surely, transcended temporal shifts in government. Richard's political attitudes – or lack of them – were fostered here, as was his curious need both to challenge and earn the approbation of people in authority. It was an attitude that would prove disastrous later in his life.

2

'Iron Chancellor'
Prince Otto von Bismarck,
the ideologue of German
unification and empire,
addressing the Reichstag
in 1886

*It is hard to imagine a more progressive
viewpoint than the one I now hold.*

Strauss to Dora Wihan, 9 April 1889

Bismarck 1871–90

Once he had achieved his dream of unification, Bismarck set about transforming Germany into a world power and centralizing its government. A façade of constitutional democracy was maintained. The elected Reichstag met regularly, though the Chancellor was not responsible to it. The Liberals were consequently wary and the left anxious. The Bundesrat (Federal Council) was frequently convened, its membership apportioned according to the prominence of the individual state: Prussia had seventeen of the fifty-eight seats, Bavaria six, the remainder one each. Capitalist expansion, rapidly and vigorously encouraged, was accompanied by a sustained attack on philosophies of altruism. Socialism and the church – particularly the Catholic church, following the declaration of papal infallibility in 1870 – were identified as the Empire's enemies within. In 1878 there was an attempt on the Kaiser's life and anti-socialist laws were passed through the Reichstag with an overwhelming majority. A half-hearted attempt at a welfare state was established which looked after the well-being of a handful of workers and kept the political left at bay for a while. Self-interest continued to flourish, however, and a new class, an industrial *grande bourgeoisie,* challenged the power of the prevailing aristocracy.

In 1874, when he was ten, Strauss was sent to the Ludwigs-gymnasium to continue the more formal aspects of his education, begun when he was seven at the local Cathedral School. He already had a number of compositions to his credit. The *Weihnachtslied* was followed by six more songs, some written for Aunt Johanna. The *Schneiderpolka* likewise had its sequel, the *Panzenburg Polka* ('Beer-Barrel Polka'). There was a *Fantasia* for solo piano, dedicated to 'his beloved Papa'. He had learnt to play the violin – Franz sent him, aged eight, to his cousin, Benno Walter, now the leader of the Court Orchestra. Another of Papa's friends, Friedrich Meyer, a court conductor, taught him theory. Richard had also made various attempts at orchestral composition but they remained unfinished. At twelve he finally completed his first full score, producing one of the pieces which, although now ignored, put him on the musical map.

Strauss aged twelve, with his sister Johanna, almost exactly three years his junior

This was the *Festmarsch* ('Festival March') in E flat, its principal theme clearly derived from the finale of Beethoven's Seventh Symphony. Five years later, Josephine's brother Georg decided he would defray the expenses of publication, and accordingly sent the score to the well-known firm of Breitkopf & Härtel, who eventually brought the piece out as Strauss's Opus 1. Uncle Georg's willingness to invest money in his beloved nephew's future would later prove useful.

The curriculum at the Ludwigsgymnasium, meanwhile, was classically orientated and organized on rigid lines. Many writers, notably Strauss's future librettist Stefan Zweig, and Heinrich Mann (elder brother of the novelist Thomas), have attested to the stultifying nature of the German Empire's educational system. Strauss, it would seem, did not share their antipathy, though he admitted preferring composing to studying. Apart from mathematics, which he hated (he sketched a Violin Concerto for cousin Benno in his maths exercise book), he seems to have embraced school life with unquestioning enthusiasm. A report, dating from when he was eleven, describes him as hard-working and something of a favourite with his teachers, his only fault being an inability to sit still.

'A good musician must also be educated,' he wrote to his friend
Ludwig Thuille in March 1878. 'Recently we had a Greek exam, a
Greek quiz, a Latin and a maths exam … We have geography and
history exams next, for which I have to study conscientiously.' Thuille
was the most important friend of Strauss's early years, an orphan three
years his senior, and something of a musical prodigy. He is best
remembered as a composer of chamber music, some of which has
great charm. His friendship with Strauss, which began in 1872, was
encouraged by Josephine who treated him as one of the family, while
Franz kept an eye on his musical education. The boys were forced to
separate in 1876, when Thuille was sent to the Gymnasium at
Innsbruck. The letters they exchanged until his return to Munich in
1879 remained unpublished until 1980. In later life, Strauss became
uncomfortable if any of them appeared in print. One does not have to
look far for the reason: they betray a number of attitudes and opinions
which Strauss would later reject, above all the mocking anti-
Wagnerian stance fostered by his father.

Strauss regularly attended performances at the Court Theatre and
in June 1878 first heard Wagner's *Siegfried*. 'I was quite frightfully
bored,' he wrote to Thuille, 'so horribly that I cannot even tell you …
Of coherent *melodies* not a trace … The dissonances were so horrible

that even rocks would have turned to puddles … the last act is so boring you could die … all this terrible howling and whining.' Wagner is the subject of continuous derision throughout. Strauss is snide about *Die Walküre* ('At a couple of points in the Third Act … one can still tell what key one is in') while *Lohengrin*, nicknamed 'Lohengreen' or 'Lohenyellow', is described as 'terribly sweet and sickly … the orchestration is rough, the whole opera has terribly much in common with *Euryanthe.*' Weber's opera *Euryanthe* had an undeniable influence on Wagner, and in time it would also influence Strauss: the melodic resemblance between the overture's lurching opening theme and the beginning of Strauss's *Don Juan* is unmistakable.

Though his anti-Wagnerian views did not last, his enthusiasm for Beethoven and Mozart, whether fostered by his father or not, was formed early and was genuine. Beethoven's Third Symphony, the 'Eroica', in particular seized his imagination – he loved it more each time he heard it, he told Thuille – while he revered Mozart as the greatest of all composers throughout his life. 'Beethoven is *never* greater than Mozart,' he told Thuille on one occasion when the latter had unfavourably compared the 'Jupiter' Symphony with Beethoven's Overture *Leonore No. 3.*

Ludwig Thuille, one of Strauss's earliest friends; they remained close until Thuille's death in 1907.

The competing demands of education and composition sometimes led to a life of frenetic activity, as the correspondence shows. 'I can't write you a longer letter just now,' he wrote in February 1878, 'since by next Tuesday I must finish three songs for the fortieth anniversary of a famous singer here, and I still haven't copied the third.' Only two of these songs have survived. The third was either lost, never finished or never written. The singer was Caroline von Mangstl, celebrating forty years as a chorister at the Court Opera. Strauss's work, hitherto kept within the family circle, was beginning to reach a wider local audience. In 1881 Sophocles' *Electra* first impinged upon his consciousness and Strauss's setting of one of the choruses was performed by his school choir. The same year, a flurried succession of premières finally flung him before the public, largely as a result of Franz's pervasive influence: on 14 March, cousin Benno's string quartet gave the first performance of Strauss's Quartet in A major, written in the winter of 1879–80; a semi-professional orchestra, the Wilde Gung'l, which Franz Strauss conducted, played the E flat *Festmarsch* a fortnight later; four days after that, the Court Orchestra gave the première of his first large-scale orchestral work, the Symphony in D minor.

The score reveals the dominance of Mozart's influence. The first movement – in the same key as *Don Giovanni*, and opening with an almost identical thundering chord – contains repeated melodic allusions to Mozart's portrait of the famous libertine before the rest of the symphony scampers off along lines reminiscent of Mendelssohn, in particular the incidental music for *A Midsummer Night's Dream*. The symphony's first conductor was Hermann Levi, Kapellmeister in Munich since 1872, to whom Franz had shown the score. There is unfortunately little indication as to how the piece was received, and it was later disowned by Strauss on the grounds that it was slight.

Public approbation of his son's talent was growing, but Franz's criticism remained relentless and Strauss began to look forward to music-making with his father with considerable apprehension. There were frequent rows in which Josephine, ever anxious to placate her irascible husband, had to intervene. 'How much suffering that may have caused my mother with her very sensitive nerves is impossible for me to judge,' Strauss later wrote.

Strauss was not to endure the constraints of formal education much longer, and after two terms at Munich University during the winter of 1882–3, where he read art history, philosophy and aesthetics, he left to devote himself entirely to music. His reputation was spreading. His Serenade for thirteen wind instruments, Mozartian in scale though not in its cyclic one-movement structure, was first performed by the Court Orchestra in Dresden on 27 November, with Franz Wüllner as conductor. The critic Eduard Hanslick, a fierce opponent of Wagner, noted, in the only favourable review he gave Strauss, that he had 'unusual talent'. A week later, Strauss and Benno Walter gave the première of the Violin Concerto in the Bösendorfersaal in Vienna. Strauss played a piano reduction of the orchestral score.

That summer, Franz took him to Bayreuth. The Wagnerian sanctuary had opened in 1876 with the first performances of the completed *Ring* cycle. Wilhelm I was in the audience. So were Bruckner, Grieg and a slightly incredulous Tchaikovsky. Though an artistic success, which saw the founding of a cult round which nationalist aspirations soon hovered, the first festival ran up colossal debts. Ludwig and the Intendant at the Munich Court Theatre, Karl Perfall, agreed to underwrite the debts in exchange for the rights to what was to be Wagner's last major work, *Parsifal*. Wagner's demand that *Parsifal* should remain the sole province of Bayreuth for thirty years after his death was respected, though Ludwig insisted that the festival honour a clause in its contract which stipulated that the première be given to the Munich forces. The conductor was to be Hermann Levi, much to Wagner's annoyance a Jew. When Franz arrived in Bayreuth for *Parsifal*'s première, protesting as usual, Richard was with him. On 13 February 1883, less than a year after the first performance, Wagner suffered a fatal heart attack in Venice. The following morning, Levi, whose devotion to Wagner was such that he was prepared to ignore his anti-Semitism, asked the Munich orchestra to stand in tribute. Franz remained obdurately seated.

The year of Wagner's death was also the year in which Strauss finally emerged as a composer of stature. It opened with the completion of his most ambitious and best work to date, the First Horn Concerto, intended not for 'his beloved Papa' but the virtuoso Oscar Franz. That did not stop Franz trying it out at home and declaring it unplayable. Strauss was now tentatively pulling away from his father's musical values. He began a second symphony, in F minor, and was uneasy about the paternal reaction. 'Papa will open his eyes wide when he hears how modern the Symphony sounds,' he wrote. Despite some protracted chromatic sequences, the symphony contains nothing that would nowadays be deemed outrageous. Papa, however, was alarmed, though this did not prevent him foisting the score on another old friend, this time Theodor Thomas, a former Munich colleague and now a conductor in New York, who had opportunely arrived in Munich to pay a visit. The première of the symphony duly took place in America on 13 December 1884.

Franz also decided that his son should now travel in order to broaden his horizons, particularly if he was not going to return to university. That autumn, Strauss was accordingly dispatched to Dresden, to visit Papa's old friend Ferdinand Böckmann. In the Saxon capital Strauss, already a haunter of art galleries, fell in love with Raphael's *Sistine Madonna* in the Gemäldegalerie which he likened to 'the pianissimo G major point in the beginning of [Beethoven's] *Consecration of the House*'. Just before Christmas he left Dresden for Berlin.

After unification, Berlin had rapidly transformed itself into a vast, cosmopolitan metropolis, expanding both outwards and upwards. The district of Berlin-West, the area round the Kurfürstendamm, acquired fashionable bourgeois status as the new plutocracy poured in, and thumbed its nose at the old, aristocratic neo-classical city of Frederick the Great that lay on the opposite side of the Tiergarten beyond the Brandenburg Gate. In the south-west, out towards the Wannsee, imposing villas sprang up. In the poorer districts, tenement blocks, built round a series of interlocking courtyards, heaved skywards in an attempt to house the growing working population. The back yards, the *Hinterhöfe* as they were called, slowly emerged, thanks to a generation of artists such as the writer Gerhart Hauptmann and the painter Heinrich Zille, as the symbol of human misery hidden behind the Empire's smiling face.

Strauss appears to have been unaffected by Berlin's lower depths, for on 26 December he wrote to his father that he was living 'in a beautiful room … in the liveliest and most beautiful part of a beautiful city'. Generous royal subsidies had turned the city into a cultural centre of unparalleled vibrancy that flaunted its nickname 'the Paris of the North'. Strauss enthusiastically reported his findings both to his father and to Thuille. He had a free pass to all the theatres. He heard the Joachim Quartet and began to listen to the music of Brahms, guardedly telling his father that he had heard the Third Symphony no less than three times and that, after initial disquiet, he had found it 'quite beautiful'. Even in Berlin, however, he was not free from parental criticism, for Franz's expressions of approval were mixed with barbs. 'I note with pleasure that you are moving in good social circles,' he wrote to Strauss on 10 January 1884. 'This is of great use to you in your worldly development ... Try not to give offence. You express yourself too impetuously: don't be too forward.'

Franz's name furnished him with numerous introductions – to the impresario Hermann Wolff, Philipp Spitta, the musicologist and biographer of Bach, Karl Klindworth, a pupil of Liszt who prepared the first vocal score of the *Ring*, and to the conductor Ernst von Schuh, who later moved to Dresden where he gave premières of many of Strauss's operas. He went to balls and parties, often stayed out all night and indulged in a very public flirtation with a certain Frau Begas, the wife of a sculptor.

Two encounters in the capital had important consequences. He met Hermann Klose, a Munich coffee merchant who taught him to play skat, the German national card game. It became a lifelong obsession. Strauss was never happier than when playing cards, and he was overjoyed to discover a card player in a fellow musician. He also met Hans von Bülow. Since his departure from Munich in 1869, Bülow's career had been subject to considerable fluctuations. Pilloried in the press as Cosima Liszt's cuckolded husband, he had spent most of his time travelling, notably in Switzerland, Italy and the United States. He was finally rescued by Duke George II of Saxe-Meiningen, who, anxious to have a star conductor in his employ, appointed him Kapellmeister in 1880. The Duke's principal passion was the theatre. There was no opera at the Meiningen court, and the orchestra, which was on the small side, was restricted to the symphonic repertoire. Bülow turned it into one of the finest ensembles in the country. 'Beethovenopolis', as Meiningen was nicknamed, had also become doubly famous thanks to Bülow's championship of Brahms, whose music, with its strong emphasis on classical structure, was now accepted as a radical alternative to what was considered Wagnerian sonic chaos. The orchestra toured regularly and in the winter of 1883–4 it was in Berlin.

Hans von Bülow (1830-94), the brilliant, temperamental conductor and pianist, who championed Strauss's works and eventually hailed him as Wagner's successor

Breitkopf & Härtel, apparently unsure about Strauss's talent, had turned down his scores after the appearance of the *Festmarsch*. His new publisher, under the aegis of the small firm of Joseph Aibl, was Bülow's friend Eugen Spitzweg. In 1881, Spitzweg had sent Bülow a number of Strauss's piano pieces which Bülow had dismissed as 'unripe and precocious'. Two years later, however, Bülow received the score of the *Serenade*. 'By far the most striking personality since Brahms,' he told Hermann Wolff and promptly decided to include the piece in the Meiningen orchestra's Berlin programme. 'Bülow will perform my serenade!!!' Strauss wrote to Franz in great excitement on 7 February 1884, struggling to overcome his terror at the thought of meeting the great man, though when it came to the actual concert, Bülow relinquished his task to his assistant Franz Mannstädt, and sat in the audience applauding enthusiastically.

A commission for another piece for similar forces promptly followed. Strauss worked feverishly on it over the summer, producing the more formal Suite for wind instruments. Bülow decided it would receive its première that autumn when the Meiningen orchestra was visiting Munich. As the day of the performance drew near, he asked Strauss to conduct it. Strauss had never held a baton in his life and his alarm increased when, on asking for the rehearsal schedule, he was curtly told that the Meiningen orchestra never had time to practise on tour. The première, and Strauss's début as a conductor, took place in the Odeonsaal (Munich's principal concert hall) on the afternoon of 18 November. He somehow got through it – 'in a state of slight coma', as he later described it – without making any mistakes, though any sense of achievement was quashed when Bülow picked a fight with Franz after the performance.

Bülow had been in the foulest of moods all day. Strauss found him in his hotel that morning railing against the city that had treated him shoddily and rejected Wagner. The tirades continued as they made their way to the concert. During the performance Bülow refused to listen and paced up and down in the green room, smoking. Afterwards, when he and Strauss were talking backstage, Franz arrived to thank him. 'Like a furious lion,' Strauss wrote in his memoirs, '[Bülow] pounced upon my father: "You have nothing to thank me for," he shouted, "I have not forgotten what you have done to me in this damned city of Munich. What I did today I did because your son has talent and not because of you." Without saying a word my father left … This scene had, of course, completely ruined my début for me. Only Bülow was in the best of spirits.'

This unpleasant incident did not affect Bülow's regard for Strauss, whom he nicknamed Richard III – Wagner was the first, there could be no second – and whom, six months later, he invited to be his assistant in Meiningen, Mannstädt having gone to Berlin. Bülow recommended Strauss to Duke George in Mannstädt's place, describing him as 'an uncommonly gifted young man (as well as the grandchild of the famous beer Pschorrs) whose only fault is his youth'. To clinch the matter, he also persuaded Strauss to pay a courtesy call on the Duke's daughter Marie, who was suitably impressed. Strauss duly moved to Meiningen in September 1885 to take up his appointment on 1 October. It was one of the most important events in what proved a remarkable, if at times unhappy, year.

First of all, it marked his emergence as a lieder composer of considerable stature, with the composition of the nine songs to poems by Hermann von Gilm, an Austrian whose work Thuille had discovered in Innsbruck. They count as his first genuine masterpieces and, in their passionate yet restrained Romanticism, they leap ahead of his contemporary works to mark the emergence of his own individual voice. *Die Nacht* ('Night') melodically foreshadows the sensuality of *Don Juan. Zueignung* ('Dedication'), which remains one of his most popular songs, reiterates the words 'Habe Dank' (thank you) with a restless intensity over an urgently arpeggiated accompaniment. The finest, however, is *Allerseelen* ('All Souls' Day'), in which the singer, on the day of the dead (2 November, in the church calendar), fondly remembers the spring when he and his lover were together.

It was written on 3 October, three days after Strauss had begun work in Meiningen, and its inspiration was acutely personal. That summer he had embarked on his first, and probably only, serious affair with Dora Wihan, a friend of his sister Johanna and the wife of Hans Wihan, a Czech-born cellist in the Munich orchestra for whom Strauss had written a Cello Sonata in 1883. The exact circumstances of their relationship remain shadowy. Dora gave instructions that Strauss's letters be destroyed after her death (only three survive, dating from 1889 to 1890) and Strauss similarly destroyed most of Dora's

letters before he married. The emotional density of the Gilm songs
do, however, bear witness to the depth of his feelings and the heart-
rending nostalgia of *Allerseelen* reflects his sadness at what may well
have been their first enforced separation.

Strauss also essayed his first major work for chorus and orchestra,
the cantata *Wandrers Sturmlied* ('Wanderer's Storm Song'), a setting of
a poem by the young Goethe which the poet rejected later in life as
'half senseless'. Yet the text is an important example of the
Hellenization of German literature, the love affair with ancient Greece
that served as a model for the humanistic cultural ethos that Goethe
was anxious to propagate. Strauss's setting echoes Brahms's
Parzengesang ('The Song of the Fates'), the text of which is from
Iphigenie auf Tauris ('Iphigenia in Tauris'), the greatest of Goethe's
attempts to rework Greek tragedy in German.

In the Strauss family, tension was mounting. Franz's criticism
continued relentlessly. 'Dear Richard,' he wrote to his son in one of
his typical verbal assaults, 'you have to get over this habit of
conducting with snake-like arm movements. It looks ugly, particularly
when one is as tall as you are. It is not even pleasing when Bülow does
it, and he is small and graceful … When conducting, the left hand
should do nothing except turn the pages of the score, and if there is
no score, it should remain at rest … I ask you, dear Richard, to follow
my counsel and not to "carry on".' Strauss turned increasingly to his
mother for support. 'How,' he wrote to her, 'does Papa know that I
"carry on" when conducting? I am no clown.' (How much Richard
took Franz's criticism to heart can only be a matter of conjecture,
though it is perhaps significant that when Strauss made his American
conducting début in 1904, Richard Aldrich, the music critic of the
New York Times, noticed that he hardly ever used his left hand.)

In 1885, in the first of a number of similar episodes that persisted
until her death, Josephine's mental health gave way. There was no
option other than to summon medical help, but an adverse reaction to
opiates provoked complete derangement and she had to be taken to a
sanatorium. One of her psychiatrists, Dr Gudden, coincidentally, was
also treating King Ludwig, whose own sanity was now becoming
questionable. Strauss believed he had to provide emotional support for
his destructive father. 'I pull myself together as best I can and comfort
Papa,' he wrote to his sister Johanna, who was away at the time of

Studio photographs, dating from his Weimar days, of Strauss conducting. Much criticized at the beginning of his career for using ostentatious gestures, Strauss later became famous for his comparative stillness on the podium.

their mother's attack. 'It's a waste of time trying to distract him – that's the sad thing … I do the best I can to work off part of the immense debt I owe him in these circumstances, and I hope my resolution will hold out until you come home.' Father and son would remain locked in an ambivalent dependency.

Strauss's experiences in Meiningen, meanwhile, proved formative but they, too, were soon fraught with trauma. To begin with, all went well. He attended Bülow's morning rehearsals, assiduously following every piece with the score, ready to answer the searching questions which Bülow repeatedly asked. He impressed Princess Marie, who swept into his rehearsal of the Brahms Serenade, and asked to hear the overture from Wagner's *Der fliegende Holländer* there and then. When his initial expression of protest met with a frown of royal disapproval, he conducted the piece at sight. In private, he and Bülow played through Johann Strauss's waltzes at the piano, which was the start of Strauss's lifelong interest in his unrelated namesake.

His début, on 15 October 1885, provoked mixed reactions. He played Mozart's C minor Piano Concerto with Bülow conducting, before taking over on the podium for his own F minor Symphony. Bülow, who had capriciously derided Strauss's keyboard skills, now told him he could make a career as a pianist. Brahms, who was in the audience, was politely disparaging about the symphony – 'quite pretty, young man' – and he advised Strauss to study Schubert's dances. They would, Brahms said, teach him how to construct a simple eight-bar melody and end his reliance on 'thematic irrelevances … this piling up of many themes which are only contrasted rhythmically on a single triad'.

Brahms was in Meiningen to oversee rehearsals of his Fourth Symphony, the first performance of which he had entrusted to Bülow and which took place on 25 October. 'An enrichment for our art,' Strauss wrote to his father the day before the première. Bülow's triumph did not last long. Four days later, Brahms announced that he himself would conduct the second performance in Frankfurt. Bülow threw one of his tantrums and resigned, though it is possible he used the episode as an excuse. Many of his carefully trained players were being lured elsewhere by the prospect of higher salaries. Duke George, though protective of his Kapellmeister, had never increased the orchestra's strength. The Duke made every effort to persuade Bülow to return, but to no avail. By the time Bülow left the city on 1 December, Strauss, aged twenty-one and with little experience, had been Kapellmeister for a month.

At this time, Strauss was working on a Scherzo for piano and orchestra, written with Bülow's credentials as a Liszt pianist in mind, though Bülow sourly dismissed it as unplayable. Strauss promptly shelved it and only returned to it five years later, when the virtuoso pianist and composer Eugen D'Albert asked him to reconsider. The première of the renamed *Burleske* for piano and orchestra took place in 1890. Chronologically, however, it belongs to Strauss's Meiningen years and it marks the emergence of a number of important features.

Experimentalism is masked as humour and the sense of brazen mischievousness that later characterized *Till Eulenspiegel* is very much to the fore. Essentially the piece is a colossal joke, turning the grandiloquence of the nineteenth-century concerto on its head. Brahms is affectionately parodied throughout. The Lisztian forces join in a waltz – Strauss's first – of penetrating sweetness. The cadenza is approached not from the usual dominant chord, but from a series of explosive discords from which the soloist has to struggle free. The ending is unconventional: the piano's final squeak is followed by a pizzicato string chord and a solitary timpani thud.

The *Burleske*'s ambiguous attitude to late Romantic music indicates that the Classical edifice built up by Franz Strauss was finally crumbling. Bülow had been influential in drawing Strauss towards Brahms. Wagner, and *Tristan* in particular, had exerted a strange fascination for some time. On one occasion, in 1880, Franz returned home from the theatre earlier than expected to find his son secretly playing through the score. A furious row ensued, Strauss stood his ground and his father stormed out of the room.

Some critics have seen an ambiguous parody of the 'love theme' from *Tristan* in the *Burleske*, in the form of a snatch of chromatic melody, first heard on the flute, then subjected to *scherzando* repetitions. It was while Strauss was in Meiningen that his antipathy towards Wagner finally collapsed, and his change of heart was due to the man who replaced Bülow in the role of mentor. His name was Alexander Ritter, and Strauss later described his influence as being 'in the nature of a storm wind'. A school friend of Bülow's, Ritter had gravitated early towards the avant garde. From 1851 to 1859, his mother, Julie Ritter, had subsidized Wagner with the sum of 800 thalers a year. Ritter subsequently mixed with Liszt's circle in Weimar, where he eventually married Wagner's niece, Franziska. In addition to being a violinist of considerable skill, Ritter was a conductor and a composer of minor talent. He was in Meiningen thanks to Bülow, who had given him a position among the Meiningen violins after he had fallen on hard times.

Wagner's 'music of the future' was Ritter's obsession, and his heroes also included Liszt and Berlioz, on whom contemporary musical circles looked askance. Ritter was well-read and had absorbed Schopenhauer's philosophy which, with its quasi-Buddhist doctrines of an irrational Will dominating the universe and the need of humankind to renounce its strivings, Wagner had nominally but not ethically espoused. A staunch Catholic, Ritter had also absorbed the anti-Semitism which Wagner, in the last years of his life, had turned into a doctrine of pure racism.

Intrigued by Strauss's comparatively conservative background and anxious to proselytize, Ritter pressed invitations upon the younger man. Strauss soon became a regular visitor in Ritter's house, where his conversion was achieved. 'I owe to Ritter alone,' he wrote, 'the fact that I came to understand Liszt and Wagner; it is he who showed me the importance in the history of art of the writings and the works of those two composers. It is he who … made of me a musician of the future and put me on the path along which I can now tread independently and alone.'

Ritter also convinced him that Beethoven had pushed the sonata form to its utmost limits and that Brahms was consequently 'an empty shell'. 'New ideas,' Strauss went on, 'must search for new forms – the basic principle of Liszt's symphonic works, in which the poetic idea was really the formative element, became henceforth the guiding principle for my own symphonic works.' Liszt held that absolute music, with its reliance on conventional symphonic form, was now outmoded and should be replaced with a more fluid structure which followed the contours of an extra-musical idea or programme. The concept owed much to Berlioz, who had already transformed conventional symphonic structures by welding them to a programmatic or literary model. Liszt's 'symphonic poems', in a free-flowing form often leading to music of an episodic nature, decisively influenced a subsequent generation of composers (Tchaikovsky and Smetana, for example) who found in them the means of liberation from the shackles of standard structure as well as the potential for expressing poetic or nationalistic ideals. Some composers, notably Tchaikovsky, were equally successful in both genres, producing symphonic poems as well as four-movement symphonies. As far as Strauss was concerned, a vestige of classical form remained and his symphonic works are often staggering as a result of their structural logic.

Ritter's impact can be gauged by Strauss's next major work, *Aus Italien* ('From Italy'), begun in the summer of 1886. He had by then left Meiningen. Dissatisfaction had rapidly set in after Bülow's departure. Duke George offered to renew Strauss's contract, though in virtually the same breath announced his intention to cut subsidy and reduce orchestral forces. Munich's Intendant, Perfall, meanwhile, anxious to have Strauss back in Munich, had offered him the post of Third Conductor at the Court Opera. 'Delay,' Bülow advised him when pressed on the matter. 'Do not run the risk … of becoming a Philistine, a lout or a snob on the banks of the Isar [the river that runs through Munich].' Strauss, who was capable of rebelling against his mentors, just as he resisted parental pressure, ignored his advice and signed a three-year contract with Munich starting on 1 August 1886. On 3 April, he conducted his last Meiningen concert and a few days later he left for Italy, on a trip funded by Uncle Georg.

He visited Mantua, Bologna, Florence, Rome, Naples, Sorrento and Capri, saw every tourist attraction, ruin, gallery and artwork, and fell in love with everything. In Bologna, Raphael's *Saint Cecilia* altarpiece moved him to tears. He went to a performance of Verdi's Requiem and heard his *Aida*. Italian music failed to make much of an impression, but he would later change his mind; Verdi's *Falstaff* would become one of his favourite operas. In Rome, he was so astounded by the Forum that he missed his lunch. He complained of being overcharged wherever he went, and at one point had his luggage and

Strauss visited Naples in 1886, as part of the holiday which inspired his symphonic fantasy *Aus Italien*

laundry stolen. 'Such a bumbling German as I,' he wrote to Bülow, 'not knowing a word of Italian and very little French, alone and for the first time in Italy, quite overwhelmed by the magnificent landscape and art – such a fellow is an easy prey for the Italians, who could compete with any Jew.' On the way back, he stopped in Bayreuth to hear *Tristan* and *Parsifal*. When he arrived back in Munich, the sketches for *Aus Italien* were in his case. He completed the score the following winter.

A 'Symphonic Fantasy' in four movements, *Aus Italien* is an uneven and occasionally derivative piece, though marked with prophetic moments of greatness. Schumann's influence is discernible in the second movement, 'In the Ruins of Rome', a rhythmically monotonous Allegro, relieved only by splashes of orchestral brilliance. The finale, 'Neapolitan Folk Life', a vibrant tarantella, has unfairly provoked derision for its inclusion of Luigi Denza's popular song, *Funiculì, Funiculà*, written to celebrate the opening of the funicular railway on Mount Vesuvius. Wagnerian elements are, for the first time in his music, openly present. The opening movement, 'On the Campagna', the finest of the four, begins with undulating chordal progressions that immediately suggest the *Ring*, though the shimmering orchestration is now uniquely Strauss's own. Wagnerian density has been replaced by a transparency which brings with it an immediate whiff of hedonism. Sensual pleasure and an erotic sensibility, essential elements in Strauss's music, are now very much in evidence. In the third movement, 'On the Beach at Sorrento', divided strings and fluttering woodwind convey an impression of glistening heat that will later recur in the torrid atmosphere of *Salome*.

The première, in Munich on 2 March 1887 with Strauss conducting, divided the audience into two camps, who alternately hissed and applauded. The city's concert-going public, still wary of Wagner, had pigeonholed Strauss as a Brahmsian. *Aus Italien* was a rude awakening. Ritter, who had followed Strauss to Munich and now played in the Court Orchestra, was enthusiastic, and so was Hermann Levi. Franz Strauss, however, was bewildered both by what he had heard and by the audience's reaction to it. In the green room he sought out his son, and found him clearly delighted in the sensation that his music had caused – thus further infuriating Franz. 'I was incredibly proud,' Strauss later wrote to his friend Lotte Speyer. 'This is the first work of mine to have met with opposition from the mob, so it can't be insignificant.'

Munich swiftly became as dissatisfactory as Meiningen. Strauss's return to Bavaria in the summer of 1886 coincided with a political crisis that further weakened the state's standing in Germany. Ludwig, his mental stability in tatters, had become a crazed aesthete unfit for government. In June, he was finally deposed and taken, along with his psychiatrist, Dr Gudden, to the castle at Starnberg. The following morning, Ludwig and Gudden were found drowned in the nearby lake. Foul play has always been suspected though never established. On 19 June, watched from a window by the Strausses, Pschorrs and various family friends, Ludwig was interred in the Michaelskirche across the road from the Strausses' flat.

The Munich Opera had been very much Ludwig's plaything, and with his death the House lost its prestige. Strauss also fell victim to its internal politics. Levi, ill much of the time, increasingly withdrew from the limelight. His assistant, Franz Fischer, had little time for his new third conductor and zealously kept the most important items in the repertory for himself. Strauss was consequently given little to do and in the course of his three-year tenure, he conducted only forty-three performances, mostly of works that were considered unimportant. He found himself performing Boieldieu, Cherubini, Marschner and Lortzing. There were, however, compensations. Verdi's *Un ballo in maschera* was one, and his acquaintance with it did much to lessen his antipathy towards Italian music. Bizet's *Carmen*, which he considered a masterpiece of orchestration, was another. But most important was his first encounter with Mozart's *Così fan tutte*, which the early nineteenth century had condemned as pornographic and which was still looked upon as trivial. The opera would remain among Strauss's favourite works, and the ambiguities and hints of tragedy that lurk beneath the surface froth of his *Rosenkavalier*, *Intermezzo* and *Arabella* owe much to it.

If the obstreperous Fischer was one source of grief, then the conservative, dilettantish Perfall soon proved to be another. A failed writer and a sometime composer, he loathed Strauss's music and resented the fact that he was beginning to be in demand elsewhere. In 1887 Strauss appeared as guest conductor in Frankfurt, Hamburg, Cologne and Leipzig, where he met Gustav Mahler, four years his

senior. 'A new and very attractive acquaintance,' he described him to
Bülow, 'who seemed to me a highly intelligent musician.' The
admiration was, and remained, mutual, despite differences in outlook.
Mahler's questing, uncertain spirituality contrasted sharply with
Strauss's worldliness which found expression in a growing exploration
of psychology and sexuality. The two men held for each other the
fascination of alter-egos. Each became a regular interpreter of the
other's music and there were inevitable overlaps in both subject matter
and influence between the two. They both essayed major works based
on Nietzsche (*Also sprach Zarathustra* and the Third Symphony). The
sumptuousness of Strauss's orchestration with its translucent handling
of Wagnerian forces clearly intrigued Mahler, while the latter's
determination to push conventional symphonic structures to their
absolute limits left an indelible impression on Strauss's orchestral
works after the turn of the century – the *Sinfonia Domestica* and the
Alpensinfonie, the two works most Mahlerian in tone, were the last of
Strauss's works to be designated 'symphonies'. They were both in their
twenties when they met. They went on to become the two greatest
composer-conductors of their age, and it is possible that in later life
there was an element of professional rivalry between the two. (It has
been suggested that Strauss's decision to concentrate on music for the
stage was partly prompted by his envy of Mahler's pre-eminence in the
orchestral repertoire, though this is not borne out by the evidence of
Strauss's letters or diaries.)

In August 1887, Strauss went on holiday to Feldafing, a popular
resort, an hour or so by train from Munich, on Lake Starnberg, where
Uncle Georg and Aunt Johanna had a villa. During his stay, the young
composer was received, with some alacrity, by the family of General
Adolf de Ahna, a local luminary and an amateur singer of considerable
talent, well known in Feldafing musical circles for his rendition of
'O Star of Eve' from Wagner's *Tannhäuser*. The General had two
daughters, the elder of whom, Pauline, a strikingly elegant brunette,
had studied singing at Munich University and drama with Franziska
Ritter. Despite an impressive examination-recital in the Odeonsaal,
during which she was egged on through Agathe's arias from *Freischütz*
by a coterie of military admirers, Pauline had made little progress in
her career. Strauss had been suggested as a potential teacher for her by
Max Steinitzer, who was one of her tutors and an old friend from

Strauss's Ludwigsgymnasium days. Pauline possessed exemplary breath control and the ability to sustain the long, high-lying phrases above the stave that soon became a feature of Strauss's own vocal writing. She also had a dreadful temper and was very much a prima donna in the making, off-stage as well as on it.

Strauss, immediately intrigued, agreed to give her lessons and eventually formed her career. They later married. It was not, however, love at first sight. He continued – much to his parents' consternation – to pursue his affair with Dora Wihan, who lies behind the Op. 17 group of songs to texts by Adolf Friedrich von Schack, completed the previous spring and including *Ständchen* ('Serenade'), one of his most popular songs, depicting the excitement of the lovers' secret meeting before they consummate their passion in a garden where the roses, unfolding in the morning, bear witness to the 'shuddering showers of ecstasy' of the night. The accompaniment ripples in tremulous, erotic anticipation before sweeping the vocal line to a brief, furtive yet powerful climax.

In 1887 Strauss also began work on *Macbeth*, one of his most ground-breaking works. He completed the first version in 1888 and dispatched the score to Bülow, who was less than impressed. He found its level of dissonance offensive, and thought the ending – a march depicting Macduff's arrival at Macbeth's castle – both musically and dramatically implausible. Strauss stuck to his defence of the work. 'The precise expression of my artistic ideas and feelings and stylistically the most self-reliant of all my works to date is *Macbeth*,' he wrote to Bülow the following August, though he was by then working on *Don Juan* and had temporarily shelved the *Macbeth* manuscript. Bülow's criticism, however, sank in, for when Strauss revised the score in 1889, the offending march was replaced by a brief, distant fanfare. Despite a successful première in Weimar in 1890, Strauss was still dissatisfied. The score was yet again withdrawn and reworked, the final version not being complete until the winter of 1891. By then, Bülow had backed down.

Macbeth remains one of Strauss's most underrated works, rarely receiving the public or critical attention it deserves. He dubbed the score a *Tondichtung*, a 'sound' or 'tone-poem'. The word was his own creation, and in using it he was staking a radical claim to the creation of a new genre, departing from the symphonic poems of Liszt and his successors. The new name mirrors a shift of emphasis in Strauss's handling of the subject matter. The symphonic poem was essentially illustrative, whether conveying the beauty of the Czech countryside in Smetana's *Ma Vlast* ('My Country') or the hellish whirlwind that lashes Tchaikovsky's *Francesca da Rimini*. Strauss turned away from pictorialism to psychology, to the delineation of character, the exploration of emotional states and even, in *Also sprach Zarathustra*, the nature of philosophical aspiration. The term 'tone-poem' applies to all his major orchestral works, up to and including the *Alpensinfonie* ('Alpine Symphony') of 1915, though he occasionally slipped back into describing his works as 'symphonic poems' in his correspondence.

Macbeth is a stark, uncompromising portrait of the murderous Thane and his Lady, both of whom have a cluster of themes which are presented as the first and second subjects of a sonata before undergoing a rigorous and complex development that characterizes their dark colloquies. The vainglorious opening fanfare that acclaims the successful militarist is followed by churning chromatics that peer through Macbeth's ambition to reveal the obsession with power beneath. Lady Macbeth manipulates him with a mixture of wheedling and contemptuous stridency, her seductive, aristocratic woodwind theme rapidly giving way to shifting string harmonies and sudden violent syncopations. The mental instability that manifests itself in terrifying insomnia is present from the start; one wonders just how much Strauss's experience of Josephine's first breakdown informed it. The metaphysics of the play have been stripped away. There are no witches, ghosts or apparitions. Only Duncan's arrival, the unmistakable pounding on the castle doors and the final appearance of Macduff intrude as self-contained musical episodes woven into the development and recapitulation. The work's dramatic and emotional trajectory is one that Strauss was to repeat – a slow assertion of identity, followed by a rapid disintegration. Macbeth's gradual assumption of power takes up the bulk of the score. His defeat and his wife's psychological collapse occur with catastrophic suddenness minutes before the end as their respective themes crumble into nothing.

At the Munich Opera House, meanwhile, the tension between Strauss, Perfall and Fischer was reaching breaking-point. In the winter of 1888, when Strauss's contract had only a few months left to run, he was assigned a revival of Wagner's first completed opera *Die Feen* ('The Fairies'). Shortly before the dress rehearsal, Perfall announced that such an important revival could not be entrusted to a third conductor and that Fischer would take Strauss's place. Strauss, already heartily sick of the 'beery swamp', as he called Munich, was bailed by Bülow, who recommended him to the Intendant at Weimar, Hans von Bronsart, and the chief conductor, Liszt's successor, Eduard Lassen. Strauss was appointed assistant conductor from 1 October 1889. Bülow also managed to obtain for him a post as repetiteur at Bayreuth to commence that spring.

On 9 April, Strauss sent an enthusiastic letter to Dora Wihan. It overflows with his artistic self-confidence as well as some less admirable sentiments. 'Where am I going? … to the city of the future, Weimar, to the post where Liszt worked for so long! I have great hopes … With the help of Ritter, I have now acquired a stronger viewpoint of art and life. I can now dare to begin the fight against the Jews and the Philistines.' The letter also indicates that his relationship with Dora was beginning to cool. Circumstances were forcing them apart and their unhappiness was clearly mutual. 'The fact is that your letter, my dear sweet Dora, has moved and saddened me, since it has postponed to an unforeseen future the prospect of my seeing you again … You really must not leave me alone for so long.' The letter ends, 'Farewell! Continue to love me. And this time don't let me wait so long for an answer.'

He had already begun work at Bayreuth and the letter makes no mention of the fact that Pauline de Ahna was with him. Whether Pauline and Strauss were already lovers at this time is not known, but there is little doubt that his relationship with Dora was effectively over by the following year. Their last meeting would take place in 1911 in Dresden, during the first run of *Der Rosenkavalier*. Dora was working as co-repetiteur at the opera house. Strauss's sister Johanna tactlessly invited Dora to a family dinner, which provoked a jealous scene on Pauline's part. Strauss took his wife's side and rebuked Johanna in no uncertain terms. He never saw Dora again, though she and Johanna remained friends until Dora's death in 1938.

In Bayreuth, where Cosima tended her husband's shrine with near-fanatical zeal, Strauss sat through performances in a state of rapt absorption, conducted the off-stage choruses in *Parsifal* and worked

Cosima Wagner
(1837–1930), walking
through the streets of
Bayreuth in 1927

on rehearsals for *Tristan*, a work which would become something of an enduring obsession. During a second Italian trip in the summer of 1888, he had heard the score again and had decided it was 'a most beautiful *bel canto opera*', an unexpected but not totally inappropriate description given the beauty of Wagner's vocal writing. His devotion to the Wagnerian cause impressed Cosima and it was not long before he and Pauline were regular guests at Bayreuth's inner sanctum, the Villa Wahnfried, the Wagner family home. They stayed on after the Festival was over so that Cosima could advise them on their interpretations of *Lohengrin* and *Tannhäuser*. Her interest in Strauss was, however, not entirely altruistic. Anxious to preserve her artistic dynasty, she hoped the recent convert to the Wagner faith would marry her second daughter, Eva. Strauss was uninterested and Eva eventually married Houston Stewart Chamberlain, the racial theorist later responsible for bringing Hitler into the Bayreuth circle.

Strauss's years in Weimar were the turning-point in his career. Home to the poet Goethe from 1775 until his death in 1832, during which time writers such as Schiller and Wieland gravitated towards it, the city is one of the most important in the history of European culture. Germany now produced, for the first time in its history, a literature of world stature, an achievement comparable only with Elizabethan England, seventeenth-century France and nineteenth-century Russia. Weimar became synonymous with progress, enlightenment and humanism. In the mid nineteenth century it housed the avant garde. Liszt made it his home from 1844 to 1860. *Lohengrin* had its première at the Court Opera in 1850. In the city's liberal atmosphere, away from the conservatism of Munich, Strauss flourished.

He was immediately put in charge of the Opera's German repertory and Pauline was soon a member of the ensemble, singing roles such as Pamina in *Die Zauberflöte* and Elisabeth in *Tannhäuser*. Strauss lost little time in playing *Don Juan* on the piano for Bronsart and Lassen; both Intendant and conductor urged him to include it in his concert programme. The tone-poem was duly put into rehearsal.

The exact genesis of *Don Juan* remains something of a mystery. For a long time it was assumed that the piece was begun in the autumn of 1887, shortly after Strauss's first meeting with Pauline, and consequently expresses the unleashing of the desire he immediately

Strauss's future wife,
the soprano Pauline de
Ahna, as Elisabeth in
Wagner's *Tannhäuser* at
Bayreuth, 1891

felt for her. Since the main object of his passion was still Dora Wihan,
however, this seems questionable. In later life he claimed he made the
initial sketches in the monastery of St Anthony in Padua, during his
Italian trip in the spring of 1888, which is more plausible, given
Strauss's adaptation of his literary source in which the blasphemous
desecration of a monastery forms a significant episode, though not
one which found its way into the finished tone-poem.

Don Juan is based not on the most obvious versions of the legend
(the literary treatments by Molière, Pushkin and Byron; Mozart and
Da Ponte's *Don Giovanni*) but on an unfinished 'dramatic poem' by
Nikolaus Lenau, published in 1851, a year after the poet's death.
Hungarian-born, German-speaking, Lenau saw himself as Goethe's
successor, though his work cultivates elements of emotional extremism
which Goethe shunned. His version of the *Don Juan* legend has a
number of curious features. The Don flings himself from one sexual
encounter to another in a quest for a single, overwhelming erotic
experience which will validate his existence, only to be confronted at
every turn by the disastrous consequences of his actions which leave a
train of chaos in their wake. In the end, he is forced to accept that his
quest is futile and he allows himself to be killed by the son of a man
he has murdered.

Lenau's stance is nihilistic, prefiguring the ideas of the philosopher
Nietzsche in his presentation of a world view in which conventional
metaphysical structures no longer have any meaning. The
supernatural elements of the original legend are essentially subverted;

his Don, like Pushkin's, Mozart's and Molière's, does indeed invite the statue of one of his victims to supper, but in place of the expected ghost, the Don is confronted by his own all too human son, accompanied by a procession of wronged women clutching his illegitimate progeny. Lenau's conscious avoidance of the fantastic may well have appealed to Strauss, who had already cut the witches and prophecies from *Macbeth*.

Equally importantly, Lenau's Don functions in an atmosphere where he is by turns permanently rebelling against, and endlessly harried by, a series of paternal figures. The poem opens with the arrival of his brother, Diego, sent as his father's ambassador to try to turn him away from his life of sensuality and draw him back into the family fold. The Don's seduction of Maria is attempted as a challenge to her father's stern moralizing – once the father's power over his daughter is broken, the Don has no further use for her. And it is the appearance of the final paternal emissary that leads to his death. Strauss's initial inspiration may well have been his own desire for Dora and perhaps, already, for Pauline too, but the element of rebellion against parental authority is too dominant a feature of Lenau's text to be overlooked. The Don's rebuke to Diego is printed in the score.

In this 1863 lithograph by Herbert König, the poet Nikolaus Lenau (1802–50), author of *Don Juan*, is depicted surrounded by romanticized images of the Hungarian and German landscapes where he spent most of his life.

When the piece was put into rehearsal, the horn players, significantly, were up in arms. 'The orchestra huffed and puffed but did its job famously,' Strauss wrote gleefully to his father. 'One of the horn players sat there out of breath, sweat pouring from his brow, asking "Good God, in what way have we sinned that you should have sent us this scourge!"' The brass writing may have been considered infamous, but the score changed musical history.

Don Juan closely follows *Macbeth* in its use of a single extended sonata movement containing a number of interpolated episodes which represent the Don's sexual encounters. What gives the piece its phenomenal impact is its melodic originality, heady eroticism and remarkable orchestration. The Don's opening theme lurches upwards with restless, resolute abandon. His first encounter (swooning, descending strings) is rapid in its consummation and voluptuous in its sensuality. The second is more tender, a slow yielding, which makes the Don's erotic ascendancy complete. Immediately afterwards, under a high string tremolo, four horns blare out an unforgettable, virile melody which transforms him from sensualist to hero. The theme returns ecstatically on the strings as his career reaches its apogee. The ending, as in *Macbeth*, is brief and chilling. A single trumpet stab, portraying the fatal sword thrust, is followed by shuddering trills as the music rapidly sinks to silence. The trumpet and trills would reappear when Strauss turned to Salome, whose career forms the operatic counterpart of the Don's.

Before *Don Juan*, explicit musical portrayals of sexual pleasure were rare. *Don Juan*'s hedonism, bursting into the atmosphere of seriousness that characterized the debate as to whether the future of music lay with Wagner or Brahms, broke new ground. Nor had anyone used such a colossal orchestra with such thrilling transparency. The transmutation of Wagnerian forces into textures of unbridled sensuality, first heard in the opening movement of *Aus Italien*, finally found its fulfilment. The première, on 11 November 1889, was an overwhelming success and Strauss was acclaimed as the greatest German composer since Wagner. The Second Reich had found its star.

There were, of course, those who disagreed. Franz Strauss was one. His criticism, significantly, did not touch on the work's emotional content. He admitted that the piece was 'brilliantly orchestrated', but added that it suffered from 'too much cogitation'. 'In all your compositions,' he went on, 'I find too much reflection … The work is terribly difficult and only good orchestras will be able to play it. I think without harming the work it could be much less difficult.' The private, parental voice continued to nag, though public dissent was soon swallowed by adulation.

With fame, however, came pride. Strauss began to rebel against Bülow's influence. *Don Juan* marked the start of a rift between Strauss and his former mentor, which never quite healed. Bülow conducted the Berlin première on 30 January 1890. It was a resounding success, but Strauss professed himself unimpressed with the performance. 'Bülow no longer understands poetic music,' he wrote to his father. What Bülow had put before the Berlin public was 'merely an interesting piece of music, but not my *Don Juan*'. Strauss blamed the Jews. Bülow, he claimed, was now in with 'an ugly Jewish circle'. The anti-Semitism of Ritter and Cosima was becoming shrill in its influence and expression, though Ritter and Cosima would also eventually be dismissed by Strauss in their turn.

Strauss's breach with Bülow coincided with the dawn of a new era in Germany. January 1890 finally saw the collapse of Bismarck's power. When the 29-year-old Crown Prince Wilhelm, known simply to history as 'the Kaiser', ascended the throne, Bismarck felt at ease in the fond belief that he could manipulate the young man. Wilhelm, however, was a product of Bismarck's policies and grew up to be an autocrat with a fixed belief in empire, his head stuffed with ideas of rapid capitalist expansion, colonies and militarism. Despite public expressions of mutual support, Kaiser and Chancellor were soon at odds and finally quarrelled on 15 March 1890. Bismarck, the Kaiser railed, was consorting with Jews and Jesuits. The following day brought an accusation of the mismanagement of foreign policy. Two days later Bismarck resigned, and the balance of power swung in the direction of the monarchy. The Kaiser's personal rule had effectively commenced.

3

'We were born for one another': a silhouette of Strauss and Hugo von Hofmannsthal by Willi Bithorn (1914); their collaborative partnership is widely regarded as one of the greatest in operatic history.

His conversation shows me how right I was to see in him the typical artist of the new German empire, the powerful reflection of that heroic pride, which is on the verge of becoming delirious, of that contemptuous Nietzscheism, of that egotistical and practical idealism, which makes a cult of power and disdains weakness. In addition to this he has certain dispositions which I had not seen clearly before, and which strictly speaking belong to the people of Munich, the south Germans: an element of clownish humour, paradoxical and satirical, of a spoilt child or of Till Eulenspiegel. — In order not to consider some of his ideas odious, one must bear this in mind.

Romain Rolland in his diary,
1 March 1900

The Kaiser 1890-1914

Wilhelm's first move following Bismarck's departure was to appoint
General Leo von Caprivi as Chancellor, thus giving the army a central
place in government. Very much the Kaiser's 'yes man', Caprivi was
bent on a unified Reichstag and a show of national unity. Within
months, Bismarck's anti-socialist laws had been repealed and the
socialists, hitherto a strong anti-establishment front, were now fully
integrated into the empire's shaky democratic process. (They proved
tragically malleable, and in 1914 would sacrifice principles for
nationalistic values.) By the turn of the century, the atmosphere in
Germany was one of hope. Steel and coal output had doubled,
business was booming and the bourgeoisie was earning substantial
sums of money. The sinister elements that gradually began to emerge
in the political sphere – the Kaiser's autocracy, a rhetoric based on
violence, a powerful army and an increasingly anti-Semitic right wing
– were largely ignored as Germany enjoyed its prosperity.

Strauss, the empire's musical hero, flourished. His third tone-poem,
Tod und Verklärung, begun in the autumn of 1888, had its première,
along with the newly titled *Burleske*, in Eisenach on 21 June 1890. On
this occasion, the scenario was his own. 'It was six years ago,' he wrote
in 1894, 'that it occurred to me to present in the form of a tone-poem
the dying hours of a man who had striven towards the highest
idealistic aims, maybe indeed those of an artist.' Ritter's and Wagner's
Schopenhauerianism lurks behind the piece: the artist's ideal, briefly
glimpsed through the transient phenomena of life and memory, is
only fully attainable after death. Musically, *Tod und Verklärung* was
something of a retrogression on Strauss's part. In its free-flowing form
it comes close to the Lisztian 'symphonic poem' while the
orchestration gravitates back towards Wagnerian density.

Although Strauss denied that his artist-hero was a self-portrait, the
music does have personal associations – childhood is ushered in by
harp arpeggios, which hint at Strauss's own first music lessons with the
harpist, Tombo. The young adult first makes his appearance to

dashing fanfares in the 'Eroica' key of E flat. There is a short, but passionate, erotic interlude that echoes *Don Juan*. When death occurs, it is shockingly brief. The stabbing rhythm, which depicts the dying man's heartbeat, judders to a standstill as the strings lurch upwards to an inconclusive silence. What follows, the Transfiguration (*Verklärung*) of the title, is impressive, though it points to a flaw. Strauss pushes for the first time into spiritual territory as a theme associated with artistic idealism, characterized by a distinctive upward octave leap, is developed into a massive peroration which fades away to an echo of the close of *Tristan und Isolde*. In the concert hall the decibel count is frequently overwhelming, though it is hard to escape the impression that the passage is the product of technique rather than conviction. Nevertheless, audiences continued to be impressed. Romain Rolland considered *Tod und Verklärung* to be one of the most disturbing works of its time. 'So modern,' was Cosima Wagner's comment when she heard it, 'yet he knows how to conduct *Tannhäuser*.'

At Weimar, Strauss flung himself into conducting, tackling a colossal repertoire and frequently training singers himself. He conducted works by Bellini, Weber, Marschner, Lortzing, the major operas of Mozart and most of Wagner (including the early *Rienzi*, denied sanctification in the Bayreuth canon). He championed his contemporaries, notably Ritter. Many of the new operas he conducted have vanished into obscurity, although one of them, Humperdinck's *Hänsel und Gretel*, remains a popular favourite. He was determined to follow Wagner in his resurrection of the works of Christoph Willibald Gluck, and in 1890 undertook a performing edition of the latter's *Iphigénie en Tauride* ('Iphigenia in Tauris'); Wagner had prepared a version of its prequel, *Iphigénie en Aulide* ('Iphigenia in Aulis'). The cultural climate of Weimar also hung over Strauss's choice. The classical humanism which the city so assiduously fostered reached its ultimate expression in Goethe's adaptation of the original play by Euripides; Strauss grafted sections of Goethe's *Iphigenie auf Tauris* onto Gluck's score. His version was published in 1895, though Weimar was not to hear it until 1900, six years after he had left.

His heavy workload eventually took its toll. In May 1891 he developed pneumonia and spent the following summer convalescing, first at the Pschorr villa in Feldafing, then at Bayreuth as a guest of

The opera house in Weimar, where Strauss enjoyed some of the greatest triumphs of his career; the photograph dates from 1920.

Cosima. 'Dying may not be so bad,' he wrote to the critic Arthur Seidl, 'but I should first like to conduct *Tristan*.' Bronsart and Lassen offered him the opera for the 1891–2 season and he spent the following Christmas at Bayreuth going through the score with Cosima. Franz was testy about the whole business. '*Tristan* will cause you much work and worry,' he wrote to Strauss. 'Quite a few orchestra members are elderly and cannot stand such extraordinary exertions. Be sensible, dear Richard.' Strauss ignored him and insisted on conducting the score uncut. The first performance took place in January 1892. While he was working on the opera, he tried to mend his rift with Bülow. 'Nothing in this world could extinguish or even diminish my boundless love, admiration or deep gratitude to you,' he wrote to his former mentor on New Year's Day 1892. Even so, the two were never as close as they had previously been.

It was also not long before there was tension between himself and Bronsart, who was becoming increasingly worried that Cosima's influence would turn Weimar into a Bayreuth satellite. Bronsart was also concerned that Strauss was advancing the modern repertoire at the expense of the classics. Even worse, the young composer-conductor was giving himself airs. 'You must learn to respect individualities in your dealings with *your* artists,' Bronsart wrote. 'You must not call it style-less every time somebody feels different from yourself about a matter.' By June 1892 Strauss was writing to Bülow accusing Bronsart of blocking his career prospects and announcing that he wanted to leave.

His schedule during the 1891–2 season was particularly punishing. Stress once again took its toll and by June he was critically ill with pleurisy and bronchitis. His family insisted he spend the winter abroad. Uncle Georg produced 5,000 Marks, and in November Strauss left for Egypt via Greece. He spent Christmas in Cairo, visited Alexandria, Luxor and Aswan, then travelled back via Italy, where he stayed with Bülow's daughter, Blondine. When he returned, the manuscript of his first opera was in his suitcase. The short score, completed in Cairo on Christmas Eve 1892, was inscribed 'by the grace of God and Saint Wagner'. The first two acts were fully orchestrated by the time he reached home. The opera, named *Guntram*, was an inauspicious beginning to one of the greatest of all operatic careers. It also marked the start of the cooling of Strauss's relationships with Ritter and Bayreuth.

Ritter had come up with the idea for the work as early as 1887. He had given Strauss a copy of an article published in the *Wiener Neue Presse* about medieval Austrian secret societies, which functioned as a

Strauss, photographed in Egypt with a local boy, winter 1892

sacred counterpart to the cult of the *Minnesänger* (usually translated as 'troubadours', though the word literally means 'singers of desire'). The links with *Tannhäuser* (in which sacred and erotic love do battle at one of the singing contests of the *Minnesänger*) and *Parsifal* (which focuses on an elevated, redemptory, male religious community) were obvious. Strauss decided to approach the subject as a Wagnerian music-drama and began work on the libretto himself. The central emotional situation derives from the triadic relationship of Siegmund, Sieglinde and Hunding in *Die Walküre*, the second opera of the *Ring* cycle. Guntram, a member of the awkwardly named *Streiter der Liebe* (Champions of Love, *Liebe* meaning emotional and spiritual love, as opposed to the desire of the troubadours), is gradually drawn to Freihild, who is trapped in a sexually violent marriage with the autocratic Duke Robert.

Progress on the text was slow. Strauss showed it to Franz, who denounced it as having 'too many words', which occasioned a drastic rewrite. Bülow, too, was uneasy about it. Strauss was still redrafting his text in January 1891 and did not begin work on the score until April 1892, and took the libretto and his sketches with him on his Greek and Egyptian travels that winter. By the time he returned, however, the project had undergone a radical change. While he was away, Strauss read Nietzsche for the first time. The philosopher's impact on the young composer was colossal.

Friedrich Nietzsche (1844–1900) is one of the most important philosophers to have influenced twentieth-century thought, as well as the most controversial. He first came to prominence in 1872 with *Die Geburt der Tragödie aus dem Geiste der Musik* ('The Birth of Tragedy from the Spirit of Music'), a major work of aesthetic theory, written while he was heavily under the spell of Wagner's music. Greek tragedy, Nietzsche argued, was the product of two contrasting and conflicting forces – the Dionysiac (emotion and instinct) and the Apollonian (reason) – resulting in an art form which consequently contained the irrationalism of music within the formal serenity of words; in the works of Aeschylus and Sophocles the two elements were held in perfect balance, but with Euripides' introduction of irony and sentimentality the equilibrium was fatally destroyed, until Wagner's operas appeared to restore it (Wagner was more influenced by Greek drama than might first appear – the *Oresteia*, Aeschylus' cycle of plays

A heavily idealized lithograph of Friedrich Nietzsche by Karl Bauer, based on a portrait painted in the 1880s

about the legend of Orestes, was the structural model for the *Ring*). Nietzsche first met Wagner in 1866. For a while, the two were close and it may be that Nietzsche's growing distrust of organized religion influenced the final shape of the *Ring*. But they quarrelled violently in 1876 over the libretto of *Parsifal* which Nietzsche believed to be a retrogression towards Christianity on Wagner's part. Thereafter Wagner's music, the sanctity of Bayreuth and the nationalism which the festival gradually came to represent became the target of Nietzsche's obsessive polemics.

The *Ring*'s influence, nevertheless, endured; indeed, the kernel of Nietzsche's philosophy derives from his application to Christianity of the closing scenes of the cycle's final opera, *Götterdämmerung*. At the very end, the Valkyrie Brünnhilde, stripped of her divinity for disobeying divine will, sends the home of the gods, Valhalla, up in flames, so releasing the rest of humanity from its need for subservience to metaphysical ideals. It was in Nietzsche's *Die fröhliche Wissenschaft* ('The Gay Science'), published in 1882, that his key concept was thundered out with full force. 'God,' he announces, 'is dead.' Our sense of the divine, he means, is redundant and mankind consequently is alone in a universe which exists independently of moral imperatives. In Nietzsche's *Also sprach Zarathustra*, not published complete until 1892 (by which time he had had a complete mental breakdown), the implications of this shattering dictum are dealt with. The Persian poet Zarathustra (or Zoroaster) is resurrected

to undo the damage done in antiquity by his pronouncement of
absolutes of good and evil. If 'God is dead,' he argues, then all
conventional moral values are redundant and consequently must be
superseded or 'transvaluated'. Nietzsche propounded the notion that
individuals, motivated by their own 'Will to Power', have the ability to
form their own moral code, unhampered by dogma. By this, he was not
advocating a quest for political brutality, as many (including the Nazis)
were later to assume. Humanity, free from the constraints of religion
and morality, must pass 'beyond good and evil'. In place of man, the
human being (*Mensch*), Nietzsche posits the idea of 'superman' or
'overman', the *Übermensch*, the individual of the future, who is
dependent solely on self-created morality for his ethical standards.

One of the fundamental problems in assessing Nietzsche's
achievement lies in his terminology. He employs an aggressive
language that derives its images from power structures; he uses the
term 'slave morality', for example, to signify the morality of
convention, defining its opposite, the moral code of the *Übermensch*,
as 'master morality'. Deeply anti-nationalistic, Nietzsche detested the
hypocrisy of the Second Reich. His terminology, however, was rapidly
appropriated by the political right. When Nietzsche's philosophy first
appeared in the 1890s, his attacks on conventional morality and
organized authority appealed to the progressive avant garde. Strauss
was attracted to his attacks on Christianity. 'Reading him,' Strauss
wrote, 'strengthened and corroborated the antipathy which I had
unconsciously felt since my fifteenth year for this religion which frees
its believers of responsibility for their own actions.' Under his
influence, he hastily rewrote the text of the last act of *Guntram*.

In both versions, the eponymous hero, horrified by Freihild's plight
and by Duke Robert's brutal treatment of the poor, arrives at the
latter's court to sing his message of peace. The incipient conversion of
his men to pacifism so inflames the Duke that he violently attacks
Guntram who kills him in self-defence. Guntram is imprisoned by
Robert's father, but Freihild, in love with her husband's killer, attempts
to set him free. At this point the two texts diverge. Strauss initially
intended to end the opera with a long duet in which Guntram rejects
Freihild's love and returns to the *Streiter der Liebe* in order to submit
to their judgement. The renunciation of love for the sake of salvation
was a powerful Wagnerian motto, the sentiment of which Nietzsche

loathed. In the revised version, Guntram and Freihild are now confronted by the mysterious figure of Friedhold, the representative of the *Streiter*, who appears to demand Guntram's willing submission to the brotherhood's law. Guntram, however, rejects him with the demand that he be allowed to work out his moral salvation purely in his own terms. 'The laws of my mind determine my life,' he states. 'My God speaks to me through myself alone.'

Ritter was appalled by the new text, and implored Strauss to read the gospels, re-read Schopenhauer, re-read Wagner's *Religion und Kunst* ('Religion and Art') and then re-draft the final act. Strauss refused to budge and sent Ritter a long reply attempting to win him over. His efforts were in vain and Ritter never quite forgave him. When Wagner's son Siegfried heard the opera, he was similarly alarmed and saw the revised final act as a betrayal of his father's beliefs. This is somewhat ironic since the score of *Guntram* has frequently been dismissed as a derivative Wagnerian farrago. Even though musically as well as dramatically there are important points of departure, the accusation is not entirely unjustified, as its sonic world is closer to Wagner than anything Strauss had written before. The orchestration is dense. The Prelude, with its high, shimmering strings, is modelled on the opening of *Lohengrin*. Guntram's massive narration in Act II, the so-called *Friedenserzählung* (Peace Narrative), brings in its wake memories of Siegmund's rapturous apostrophe to Spring from *Die Walküre*. The Wagnerian structure of symphonically developed leitmotifs (leading motifs, short phrases associated with people, objects or ideas) is firmly in place, and handled with considerable assurance. It was a structural procedure Strauss never abandoned in his operas.

Yet there are also differences. One important feature of *Guntram* is its brevity. While Wagner aspires to spaciousness, Strauss introduces an element of compression – there are fewer than two and a half hours of music. Strauss also pushes beyond Wagnerian harmonies and is anxious to expand the expressive potential of the singing voice. Musically, the soprano dominates; Freihild is the most interesting character. When she first appears, fleeing from her husband and bent on suicide, strange, squealing woodwind and unresolved harmonies hint at incipient madness. The vocal line sometimes tends towards the rhythmic patterns of human speech. The characteristics of Strauss's

The opening scene of
Strauss's first opera *Guntram*
at the Weimar première in
1894, with Heinrich Zeller
(second from right) in the
title role

soprano writing, veering from fragmentary recitative to strenuous, rapturous, high-lying phrases, is already in evidence. The role was written for Pauline, with whom he was now falling in love.

On 12 February 1894, Bülow died in Cairo. He had for some time been plagued by violent headaches and the underlying cause, a brain tumour, had remained undetected. Strauss was shattered, though his attitude towards his former mentor remained ambivalent. Asked to conduct a memorial concert in Hamburg, he stipulated that 'only serious music, therefore no Brahms' should be performed and chose Liszt's symphonic poem *Héroïde funèbre* as the main work. It was a controversial decision; Bülow had detested the piece. Attempts to make Strauss change his mind failed. He withdrew from the concert and Mahler conducted a programme of Schubert and Beethoven in his place.

Guntram soon ran into difficulties. The opera house at Karlsruhe, which had asked for the première, abandoned the piece on the grounds that the title role was unsingable. Mahler's attempts to stage the work in Hamburg were similarly fruitless. Strauss finally scheduled it for Weimar in May 1894. Heinrich Zeller, cast as Guntram, protesting that his music was too strenuous, needed constant attention during rehearsals. Pauline, who felt Strauss was ignoring her, threw an attention-seeking tantrum during one rehearsal, in which she hurled her score at him and stormed off-stage with Strauss in pursuit. A deputation from the orchestra followed them to Pauline's dressing room, where raised voices could be heard. The leader finally knocked on the door. When Strauss answered, he was told that the orchestra were so appalled by Pauline's behaviour that they were no longer prepared to play in any performance in which she sang. 'That pains me very much,' Strauss replied,' for I have just become engaged to Fräulein de Ahna.'

They had, in fact, been engaged since March, though Pauline, worried that marriage would force her to relinquish her career, had temporarily got cold feet, and had to be persuaded by her father and her sister to put aside her doubts. Two days after the première of *Guntram* – a *succès d'estime*, no more, on 10 May – the couple made an official announcement. They were married in Marquarstein the following September. As a wedding present, Strauss gave Pauline four songs, which rank among his greatest, *Ruhe, meine Seele* ('Rest, My Soul'), *Cäcilie, Heimliche Aufforderung* ('A Clandestine Invitation'), and *Morgen!* ('Tomorrow!'). As with all the music he wrote for Pauline, the depth of his affection is never in doubt, and her voice remained the model for much of his vocal writing long after she had retired from the stage. The public storminess of their marriage became the stuff of mythology, though their devotion to each other, marked occasionally by genuine vicissitudes, remained touchingly constant to the last. Later there were rumours, even accusations, of extramarital affairs on Strauss's part, though there is no concrete evidence that he ever strayed.

Three weeks after their marriage, he took up a new post as associate conductor in Munich. Remembering his first experiences there, he was initially wary. The proposed salary, however, was double his earnings at Weimar, and he would be allowed to conduct the most important pieces in the repertoire as opposed to third-rate works. He might be able to revive *Guntram*. Hermann Levi's health, he well knew, was precarious and there was consequently the potential for promotion. He turned to Cosima for advice, and she persuaded him to accept.

Right, the title-page of the four Opus 27 songs which Strauss gave to Pauline as a wedding present. Many of his lieder were written with her voice in mind, even after she retired from professional singing in 1908.

Below, Strauss's wedding photograph: Pauline's father, General de Ahna, is on her left in the front row. Strauss's sister Johanna and her military husband Otto Rauchenberger are to the bridegroom's right.

His second period in Munich was not much happier than the first, even though Levi's retirement in 1896 eventually left him in charge. Fischer was obstructive. Perfall remained hostile, and when he too retired, handing over the reins to his assistant, an actor-producer named Ernest von Possart, the latter proved tetchily manipulative and kept Strauss dangling on a string by alternately inserting *Guntram* into the schedules then withdrawing it, while Pauline was offered guest contracts which were never ratified. 'A second Perfall. Munich, good night!' Strauss noted in 1895, though the two men, after a struggle, eventually arrived at a satisfactory working relationship.

Just over a year after his arrival in Munich, he finally managed to secure *Guntram* a place in the schedules. It was a disaster from the start. The orchestra, never more than indifferent, turned hostile. Cousin Benno was forced to lead a deputation to the Intendant's office imploring that the players be released from this 'scourge of God'. Strauss was openly mocked in rehearsals. 'We never get this passage right in *Tristan* either,' one cellist protested when Strauss was attempting to correct mistakes. The tenor, Max Mikorey, grandly announced that the vocal writing was ruinous to his health and refused to sing unless his pension rights were substantially increased.

The première, on 15 November 1895 with Pauline as Freihild, was a fiasco, and the opera was withdrawn after a single performance. Its failure rankled with Strauss throughout his life. Later, when he was established as Germany's most successful opera composer, he erected a memorial plaque in the garden of his Garmisch villa. 'Here lies the honourable, virtuous, young Guntram,' it reads, 'who was horribly slain by the symphony orchestra of his own father. May he rest in peace.'

Yet he knew from the beginning that *Guntram* was weak, and its disappointing reception in Weimar was partly responsible for Strauss's decision to turn his next planned opera into a tone-poem. Its central character was also a Nietzschean figure, rebellious, amoral, contemptuous of the demands of authority, society and religion, though on this occasion his origins were folkloric and *Guntram*'s lofty gloom was replaced by farce. Till Eulenspiegel, the great practical joker of German legend, who lives purely by his wits and is permanently on the run from the law, made his first appearance in an anonymous collection of tales published in 1515. Strauss's original plan, drafted during his homeward journey from Egypt, was to let Till run amok among the stuffily self-satisfied bourgeoisie in the legendary town of Schilda, whose inhabitants were proverbially imbecilic. Strauss finally came to the conclusion that the libretto was 'too superficial' and never began work on an operatic score (though the idea of a rebel outsider challenging a stuffy group of burghers would form the basis of his next completed opera, *Feuersnot*).

Till Eulenspiegel, now a tone-poem, occupied him for most of the winter of 1894 and was finally completed in May the following year. The first performance took place in Cologne that November, eleven days before the *Guntram* catastrophe in Munich. The conductor was Franz Wüllner, who had given the première of the Wind Serenade fourteen years previously. Despite the odd critical squawk, notably from Eduard Hanslick, who denounced the piece as 'a veritable world's fair of sound effects', it was another triumph.

Till Eulenspiegel represents a return to classical structure after the comparatively discursive shape of *Tod und Verklärung*. The tone-poem is cast as an enormous rondo, in which the varied repetitions of Till's own theme are intercut with a series of episodes representing his escapades: Till careers on horseback through a market, wrecking the traders' stalls in the process; he dresses as a priest in order to preach an unctuous mock sermon, preens before a young woman who promptly sees through his macho games and dumps him; finally he passes himself off as a student and throws a group of pedagogues into confusion with his questions. The ambiguous ending, however, marks a departure from the original sources. The Till of legend got away with everything he did, lived to a ripe old age and died in his bed. Strauss, however, repeats the pattern of *Don Juan*. Assertion is followed by collapse. Till is captured, handed over to the law and hanged. Only his spirit, in a last statement of his main theme, lives on after him. Temporal authority ultimately triumphs, despite individual assertion to the contrary.

The manuscript was annotated by Pauline with caustic comments. 'Mad' and 'awful' are among the phrases scribbled on the score. They were probably intended in jest, though what began as a joke on her part hardened with time into a habit of openly deriding her husband's work and putting him down in public, usually with the comment that she, a general's daughter, had married beneath her into a family of brewers. Strauss's acceptance of her criticism often mystified his friends.

When the couple moved to Munich, there was soon friction between Pauline and Strauss's parents. Franz, who had disapproved of Strauss's relationship with Dora Wihan, was equally vociferous in his condemnation of 'the actress' his son had married. As so often in times of family stress, Strauss turned to his mother, sending her a forceful letter, which reveals his acceptance of Pauline: 'I haven't the slightest

intention of continuing to explain … the character of my wife while
you don't take the least trouble to get to know her,' he wrote. 'Both
Pauline and I want dearly to see you … peaceful and happy. I
conclude with much pain that that cannot be the case, so long as the
woman whom … I have chosen as my wife, and whom, in spite of her
faults I love and admire, irritates you and embitters your life … If, as I
fear, you really want it, she will submit to voluntary banishment from
your family circle and remain by the side of her husband.'

By the end of 1896, the relationship between Strauss and his
parents was more amicable. Franz managed to treat Pauline with a
modicum of politeness though he remained wary of her. A decisive
factor in the reconciliation may well have been Pauline's pregnancy.
Strauss's only child, a son, was born on 12 April 1897 after a long and
difficult labour. Strauss was away at the time of the birth, in Stuttgart,
on a concert tour with Possart for whom he had written a Melodrama
(a work for speaker and piano), setting Tennyson's *Enoch Arden*. On
hearing the news, he was beside himself with joy, and proud of
Pauline for having gone through her ordeal 'heroically'. The boy, on
whom both Strauss and Pauline possessively doted, was christened
Franz (after Strauss's father) Alexander (after Ritter, who had died the
year before), though he was swiftly given the nickname 'Bubi'. The
appellation stuck, even when Franz Alexander had grown to
adulthood.

Though Strauss was discontented in Munich, there were
compensations. He added *Meistersinger* to his list of Wagner
interpretations. Possart instigated a Mozart season at the
Residenztheater and Strauss conducted *Don Giovanni, Die Entführung
aus dem Serail* ('The Elopement from the Harem') and *Così fan tutte*.
He was now in demand on the international circuit and made his
conducting débuts in Switzerland, Hungary, Moscow, Antwerp,
Amsterdam, Paris and London. In Barcelona, he was lionized. 'This
kind of applause is new to me,' he wrote to his father. 'The people
must be used to this from the bullfights.'

Till Eulenspiegel was barely completed before its successor was
begun. This was *Also sprach Zarathustra*, based on Nietzsche's magnum
opus, the most familiar of Strauss's tone-poems, though not
necessarily the best. It is a work around which controversy continues
to rage, its detractors claiming that music is incapable of expressing

philosophical constructs. Strauss was well aware of this. 'I did not intend,' he wrote, 'to … portray Nietzsche's great work musically. I meant rather to convey in music an idea of the evolution of the human race from its origin, through the various phases of development, religious as well as scientific, up to Nietzsche's idea of the *Übermensch*.'

Nonetheless, the piece is rooted in the philosophy. In an interview with an American newspaper in 1921, Strauss was explicit both about *Zarathustra*'s programme – 'The relationship of Nature and the Human Will' – and his working method – 'C major is Nature, Man as a being; B minor (at the end of the work B major) his metaphysical aspiration.' The conflict of keys is the essence of *Zarathustra*, which, in its form, replaces classical structures with a free-flowing narrative fantasia. The imposing and familiar C major opening for three trumpets depicts Zarathustra's contemplation of the sun before he descends from the mountains to take his message to man. 'The sun rises,' Strauss wrote in the short score. 'The individual enters the world or the world enters the individual.' The symbolism of the sun is ambiguous. In *Die fröhliche Wissenchaft*, which contains in embryo many of the main concepts of *Zarathustra*, the 'Death of God' has led to the 'unchaining of this earth from its sun'. Man is consequently 'wandering through an endless nothing'. The crashing chords are followed by a murky, irresolute rumbling, during which the music slips down a semitone into B minor. In the new key, and prefaced by a brief, grotesque parody of plainchant, the theme of man's strivings staggers tentatively upwards.

Thereafter the two keys remain in warring opposition as man struggles to 'overcome' himself. The comforts of the 'afterworldly', those dependent on conventional religion and consequently on the idea of an afterlife, are brief and illusory, if gorgeous. Man's 'Great Longing' brings him into conflict with both nature and dogma. Strauss plunges into bitonality as C major and B minor are garishly jammed against each other. Thereafter, the comforts of religion are replaced by the equally illusory values of science. A fugue, the most academic of musical forms, slowly unfolds from the depths of strings, its principal theme taking in all twelve notes of the chromatic scale as science coldly tries to understand all phenomena. Both passages possess great ingenuity and daring, and are widely cited as prefiguring the subsequent breakdown of tonality in the work of Schoenberg and the Second Viennese School. Harmonic structure in Strauss's music, however, is always allied with the search for expressive means to portray his given subject and not with any specific need for experimentation. There is another irony here. Though Schoenberg was less overtly influenced by Nietzsche than Strauss, he is in some respects closer to him in spirit. Nietzsche's demand for the 'transvaluation of all values' finds its greatest musical expression in Schoenberg's corresponding 'transvaluation' of musical structure, his twelve-note system of composing, in which tonality, dependent upon major and minor keys, is replaced by a prearranged note row, consisting of all twelve notes of the chromatic scale.

The most controversial section of *Zarathustra* is its ending. Man's strivings pass beyond the arid values of pure science and he is ready for Zarathustra's pronouncement of the *Übermensch*. Yet the prophet, his mental powers taxed by his search for new ideals, collapses in temporary exhaustion before his key concept can be given voice. Gradually, in a section called 'The Convalescent', his idea bubbles out to gurgling orchestral laughter and overwhelming joy. 'Lift up your hearts, brothers, high, higher,' Nietzsche reads. 'I have canonized laughter; overmen, learn to laugh.' When the concept of the *Übermensch* finally comes into being, it does so to a luscious Viennese waltz that has been derided ever since, though Strauss's choice of the waltz form is by no means unsuitable for Nietzsche's ebullient, dancing prose at the thought of this notorious figure.

At this point Strauss departs from Nietzsche in tone. The jubilation is interrupted by the clanging of an enormous bell. Midnight has struck. In the book, this is Zarathustra's cue for an

The closing bars of the short score of *Also sprach Zarathustra*, annotated with the words 'When? Never! When? Never! When? Never! Never! Never! will there be decent weather.'

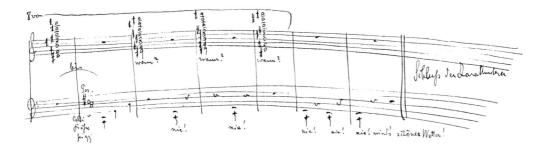

imposing eleven-line poem intoned between the bell's strokes which leads in turn to a lengthy exposition of the key concept of the *Jasager*, the 'Yes-sayer', the individual whose acceptance of a world free of dogma prefigures the *Übermensch*'s arrival. The book closes, as it begins, with a sunrise while Zarathustra triumphantly intones: 'This is my morning, *my* day is breaking: *rise now, rise, thou great noon!*' In Strauss, however, it remains night and the tone-poem ends with a gigantic question mark. The clanging bell finally gives way to a slow, exquisite nocturne which moves towards its eventual resolution in the striving key of B major. Its calm, however, is undercut by thudding pizzicato Cs, low in the orchestra. Nature, not metaphysical aspiration, has the final word. The *Übermensch* remains an unfulfilled idea.

The original subtitle, 'Symphonic optimism in *fin de siècle* form, dedicated to the twentieth century', was removed. The title-page of the finished score simply reads '*Also sprach Zarathustra*, tone-poem freely after Nietzsche'. The première, in Frankfurt on 27 November 1896, predictably, caused a stir. There were mutterings in the critical ranks, though the tone-poem proved an inspiration to many. The young Bartók, struggling with creative block, first heard it in 1902. 'At last I saw a way that would lead me to something new,' he wrote, and he buried himself in a study of Strauss's scores and began to compose again.

With *Zarathustra*'s sequel, Strauss descended from abstraction and structural experimentation to humanity and classical form, though the new tone-poem was actually conceived as part of a diptych. 'Symphonic poem *Held und Welt* begins to take shape,' he wrote in his diary in April 1897. 'As satyr-play to accompany it – *Don Quichote*.' *Held und Welt* ('Hero and World') was temporarily put aside and its companion piece came first. *Don Quixote*, completed in December 1897, is characterized by an emotional ambiguity and a psychological subtlety worthy of Mozart. For the first time since his portrait of Lady Macbeth, Strauss tackles the theme of insanity in his portrayal of Cervantes' tragi-comic Don, who is under the romantic delusion that he is a chivalric knight and sets forth in search of adventures. 'Whether he was a fool or wise is not clear,' Cervantes wrote of his hero. Strauss forces an astonishing double perspective on his listener; deranged Don Quixote may be, yet his mind possesses an inner logic of its own and his fantastic visions have an emotional reality that those around him can neither conceive nor comprehend.

The subtitle 'fantastic variations on a theme of knightly character' indicates the work's structure. A prologue, depicting the Don's descent into madness, is followed by a theme and ten variations portraying his adventures and an epilogue describing his death. The 'theme' is in fact a compound of several snatches of melodic material, some of which are first heard in the prologue. A *concertante* group of solo instrumentalists within the body of the orchestra delineates the Don and his squire. A whiff of a fanfare and an imperious, mournfully rising theme for the solo cello characterize 'The Knight of the Doleful Countenance' as he calls himself. A hint of a folk tune on bass clarinet and tuba indicates the squire's peasant origins, while a swirling viola reveals his loquaciousness. The Don sees himself as a lover, albeit a chastely virtuous one, and Strauss gives his asexual passion for his imaginary Dulcinea a hesitant oboe theme of tenuous beauty. The theme gradually becomes associated with the Don's chivalrous ideals: as he sets out on his adventures it wafts before him in the

'The Knight of the Doleful Countenance' and his squire Sancho Panza; the illustration for Cervantes' *Don Quixote* (an edition of 1863) is by Gustave Doré.

stratospheres of the strings as his own cello theme leaps upwards in an attempt to reach it.

As in *Zarathustra*, Strauss plunges into extremes of dissonance for the sake of dramatic or psychological effect. The onset of the Don's insanity is catastrophic in its suddenness, his love duet with Dulcinea fragmenting into polyphonic chaos as both their themes are deliriously wedged against each other. The flock of sheep he attacks in the mistaken belief that they are an army bleat with a surreal garishness as muted brass and woodwind play flutter-tongued seconds. In contrast to Quixote's fevered yet noble imagination, the world through which he moves is depicted with onomatopoeic literalness; we hear the breeze slowly move the arms of the tilted windmills; a massive pedal-point anchors the horse on which he believes he is flying firmly to the ground. His illusions are finally shattered to the sounds of a funeral march and he dies to the most touching of all Strauss's orchestral finales. Yet his death is not quite the end. His little fanfare reappears once more after he has gone. Like Till Eulenspiegel, he has passed into legend and the realm of human imagination.

Arguably the greatest and certainly the most subtle of the tone-poems, *Don Quixote* is also the most difficult to perform. Strauss envisioned the *concertante* solos as being played by the leaders of the relevant orchestral sections, though the cello part, in particular, is so difficult that the work is often treated as a concerto. At the première, in Cologne on 8 March 1898, there were many mutterings and the episode with the sheep sent a number of critics into a tailspin. 'The complete negation of everything that I understand music to be,' was how one described it. 'It's always the same. You get used to it,' was Strauss's response.

Don Quixote was also the last of his major works completed in Munich. *Guntram*'s failure was neither forgotten nor forgiven, and Strauss's dissatisfaction had now become acute. As early as 1896, he began looking for employment elsewhere, and even went so far as to apply for the music directorship at Mannheim at a far lower salary than the one he was receiving. In 1897, Mahler left the Hamburg Opera for Vienna. The Intendant, Bernhardt Pollini, was anxious that Strauss should replace him but he was adamant that he would not engage Pauline. Strauss flatly turned down his offer, even though

Pauline, placing his career before her own, begged him to reconsider. Munich held on to him briefly by substantially raising his salary, but by 1898 it was time to move on. Offers came in from both Berlin and New York. The Metropolitan Opera tried to lure him with a lucrative short-term contract. The offer from Bolko von Hochberg, the Intendant in Berlin, was less extravagant but more secure – a ten-year tenure, a life pension and a widow's pension, and generous summer and winter breaks during which he could compose. There was little choice in the matter. The year Bismarck died, Germany's musical star decided to make his mark in Germany's capital. Strauss, Pauline and the eighteen-month-old Bubi moved to fashionable Berlin-West, to an apartment at No. 30 Knesebeckstrasse. On 1 November 1898, Strauss became Imperial Kapellmeister in Berlin, and made his début conducting *Tristan*. He was now the Kaiser's employee.

Held und Welt, its title now changed to *Ein Heldenleben* ('A Hero's Life'), occupied him during his summer break. The score was completed after his arrival in Berlin and the première took place in Frankfurt the following March. 'Beethoven's 'Eroica' is so little beloved of our conductors,' he wrote, 'that to fulfil this need I am composing a largish tone-poem entitled *Heldenleben*, admittedly without a funeral march, yet in E flat, with lots of horns, which are the yardstick of heroism.' In addition to writing his own 'Eroica', he made himself the hero of the work, a decision which opened him up to accusations of questionable taste and self-propaganda. There is an element of truth in this, though the real problem of *Heldenleben* derives from an apparent discrepancy between the conventionality of the man and the enormity of the music. Far from aspiring to an iconoclastic life-style, Strauss was becoming bourgeois, a happily married family man, the professional composer extremely successful at his job. His Nietzschean stance was increasingly a public persona, often abandoned in private.

Two further aspects of *Heldenleben* deserve consideration. Firstly, although it was conceived as a companion piece to *Don Quixote*, it actually belongs with the two major works that immediately follow it, the opera *Feuersnot* and the *Sinfonia Domestica*, in each of which Strauss is identified with a central figure. Secondly, the tone-poem echoes *Zarathustra* in that it does not follow the logical progression one might expect. Just as the former ends with a question mark as

The subject of media gossip, Strauss was frequently caricatured in the press: here he is depicted as the hero of his own *Ein Heldenleben*, loftily ignoring his 'enemies', the music critics who try to attack him.

opposed to the book's culminative blaze of glory, *Heldenleben* in the end depicts stalemate rather than battles won. The Hero (Strauss) faces his opponents (a gang of music critics), meets his companion (Pauline), wages a war on his enemies which ends in only temporary victory, proudly presents his 'Works of Peace' (which fall on deaf ears), then gives up the struggle and retires from the world into domestic contentment. The heroic quest, despite being presented as valid, is ultimately abandoned.

The vaunting, over-confident theme with which the piece begins is effectively undercut by its subsequent developments. Heroism only exists when the cause is worthy and the Hero's enemies, though biliously depicted in a series of lightning character sketches for solo brass and woodwind, are nonentities. Pauline is portrayed, tantrums and all, by a solo violin cadenza which leads to a surge of desire on the hero's part. The battle, described simply as 'an atrocity' by one contemporary critic, is a ferocious piece of musical militarism, imperial in scale, so extreme that its bombast seems ironic. The hero's 'Works of Peace' are a series of self-quotations, taking in the main themes from all the tone-poems from *Macbeth* onwards, plus sections of *Guntram* and two of Strauss's songs, the liltingly sexy *Traum durch die Dämmerung* ('A Dream at Twilight') written in 1895, and the rapturous *Befreit* ('Freed'), written contemporaneously with the tone-poem and a heartfelt declaration of his love for Pauline. The ending is an E flat nocturne of exquisite beauty as the heroic vision becomes one of quiet domesticity, prefiguring Strauss's own withdrawal to his Garmisch villa. 'I am not a hero,' he told Romain Rolland, when the two of them were discussing *Heldenleben*. 'I haven't the necessary strength. I prefer to withdraw.' The statement was made when Strauss's guard was down, as it occasionally was with Rolland.

　　Their relationship, though only intermittently close, remains one of the most important of Strauss's friendships for posterity, largely because the French writer's letters and journals provide us with the most detailed portrait of Strauss left by any of his contemporaries. An undervalued writer, Rolland, who was born in Clamency, Burgundy, in 1866, was from the beginning a man alienated from his culture and his times. His critique of French culture was regarded by many with

'The great poet and highly esteemed friend'; Strauss highly regarded the French writer and pacifist Romain Rolland, photographed here in 1928.

suspicion, for his inspiration came from Germany, not France. His greatest novel, *Jean Christophe*, portrays a German composer taking the jaded Parisian musical scene by storm. German music, Rolland maintained, possessed a boldness and a vitality that French music lacked. It also – and this was crucial to his ideology – possessed the ability to transcend politics and knock down the barriers of nationalism and imperialism that he detested. In France he was frequently written off with contempt as a 'Germanophile'. He was outspoken and not above telling Strauss exactly what he thought of his music. Strauss respected him for it.

They first met at Bayreuth in 1891, at a lunch party given by Cosima Wagner, though their friendship did not begin until Strauss was in Berlin. In the intervening period Rolland, in his role as a roving music journalist, had familiarized himself with Strauss's work, heard him conduct and studied his scores. In April 1899, he visited Strauss at his Knesebeckstrasse apartment and found him fuming about the Kaiser's interference. Strauss's position at the Royal Court Opera was prestigious, but subject to considerable restraints. He had no say in the choice of repertoire, which fell to Hochberg, who was clearly under the Kaiser's thumb. Strauss had just been pressurized into conducting an opera by the Belgian Fernand Le Borne which the Kaiser, whose artistic judgements were appalling, insisted be performed to show evidence of Francophile sympathy. Thereafter Rolland became Strauss's confidant on imperial matters. It was not long before the Kaiser and 'the serpent I harboured in my bosom', as Wilhelm described Strauss, met face to face, as an entry in Rolland's diary from March 1900 reveals:–

His first interview, – The Emperor summons him, frowns as he looks at him: 'You're yet another of these modern musicians?' He bows. 'I have heard [Max von] Schilling's Ingwelde; *it is execrable; there's no melody.' – 'Forgive me, your Majesty; there is melody, but it is hidden beneath the polyphony.' – He looks at him with a stern eye: 'You are one of the worst.' Another bow. – 'The whole of modern music is worth nothing; there's no melody.' Same game. 'I like* Freischütz *better.' 'Your Majesty, I too like* Freischütz *better.' – 'Verdi's* Falstaff *is a detestable thing.' – 'Your Majesty, one must bear in mind that Verdi is eighty years old, and that it is a splendid thing, after having created* Il trovatore *and* Aida, *to renew oneself again at the age of eighty.' 'I hope that when you're eighty you'll write better music.'*

Even allowing for a certain element of exaggeration in Strauss's telling of the story to Rolland, it is clear that an element of impish humour *à la Eulenspiegel* characterized his dealings with Wilhelm, though Strauss's subservience remained. The Kaiser's authority, while questioned in private and mocked with double entendres, was never flouted. Berlin's conservatives regarded Strauss with suspicion, but when Wilhelm demanded he write military marches and brass band music, he did so. A pompous setting of Klopstock's *Bardengesang* ('The Song of the Bards') was also written as an offering for Wilhelm in 1906. Strauss may have challenged authority, but he also wrote to order.

Yet if Strauss was playing with fire as far as the Kaiser was concerned, he was also now involved with politics in a more serious fashion. In 1898, along with two Munich friends, the lawyer Friedrich Rösch and the physicist-turned-composer Hans Sommer, he founded the Genossenschaft Deutscher Tonsetzer (The Fellowship of German

Kaiser Wilhelm II in 1898, the year of Strauss's appointment as Imperial Kapellmeister

Composers), the aim of which was to lobby for the protection of composers' rights and to ensure the passing of adequate copyright laws through the Reichstag. The Fellowship wanted an imposition of minimum fees, an increase in royalty percentages and the establishment of an agency to supervise the collection of payments. Almost immediately there was an outcry. Many composers were suspicious and distrustful, though D'Albert, Humperdinck and Mahler were among Strauss's supporters. Most politicians protested that unionization would be detrimental to composition and performance. It took seven years before the Fellowship was finally recognized and even then Strauss remained unsatisfied. His later willingness to collaborate with the Nazis was partly motivated by his continuing desire to advance German copyright laws in the composer's favour.

Strauss has been accused of founding the Fellowship with a view to personal financial gain. It seems unlikely that this was his prime motivation: while he could undoubtedly drive a hard bargain, he seems to have acted fairly when it came to the question of remuneration, out of a genuine belief that an adequate financial reward was an expression of respect and that no one should struggle for a pittance. Strauss's fondness for money later became the stuff of legend and many critics have portrayed him as coldly venal. There is no question that Strauss enjoyed material comfort, but he was also remarkably careless with money, frequently invested unwisely, was certainly financially wiped out in 1914 (and, it was rumoured, also in 1929), and at the end of his life he was struggling to survive by copying and selling manuscripts of his works.

'I am an apolitical composer,' he remarked on one occasion after the Nazi acquisition of power, a statement which many have taken at face value. His willingness to write to order for the Kaiser, however, together with his role in founding the Fellowship, contradicts his words. His actions may not have directly involved him in party politics (from which he often attempted to remain aloof), but they do testify to a level of political involvement which cannot be ignored.

After his arrival in Berlin, Strauss returned to writing for the stage. Though the failure of *Guntram* had pained him, he had contemplated various subjects before leaving Munich. A brief association with the playwright Frank Wedekind, a controversial eroticist, came to nothing. Wedekind, best known for his plays *Erdgeist* ('Earth Spirit') and *Die Büchse der Pandora* ('Pandora's Box'), which eventually formed the basis of Alban Berg's opera *Lulu*, supplied Strauss with the scenario for a ballet-pantomime about a flea's voyage through the underwear of a lady. A comic subject – erotic, provocative and scabrous – was clearly what Strauss was looking for. In 1900, he began work on a ballet, *Das Insel Kythere* ('The Isle of Cythera'), named after the legendary pleasure-island of Venus, and inspired by Watteau's painting *L'Embarquement pour Cythère* ('The Embarkation for Cythera'). The project was to be abandoned (most of the material appearing in later works), though the choice of subject marks the start of Strauss's fascination with Baroque theatricality in which the world of classical antiquity is seen through a double layer of anachronism. A *commedia dell'arte* troupe rubs shoulders with gods, goddesses, nymphs and shepherds, prefiguring his later opera *Ariadne auf Naxos*. The music from *Kythere* that is incorporated elsewhere (mostly in *Ariadne* itself and the ballet *Josephslegende*) reveals a move away from Wagner towards Mozartian elegance and harmonic simplicity.

While Strauss was working on the score, he was approached by Hugo von Hofmannsthal, the Austrian writer who would become his most famous librettist, with a scenario for a ballet entitled *Der Triumph der Zeit* ('The Triumph of Time'). Strauss gently but firmly rejected it, and it was not until 1905 that the collaboration began in earnest. Hofmannsthal has frequently been held responsible for leading Strauss away from the post-Wagnerian ethos towards a self-conscious Baroque stylization, but the *Kythere* project indicates that Strauss was toying with such a move years before it was attempted.

The ballet might well have been finished, had not another idea captured his imagination. During his last months in Munich, Strauss had met the writer Ernst von Wolzogen whose main literary mode, having discovered Nietzsche, was scabrous iconoclastic satire. Distantly associated with Bayreuth through his brother Hans, who had gravitated towards the Wagner shrine and founded the journal *Bayreuther Blätter*, Wolzogen deeply distrusted the artistic conservatism of Munich which chimed with Strauss's bitterness at the rejection of *Guntram*. When Strauss asked him to work on an opera that would satirize the Philistinism of his native city, which had scorned Wagner as well as himself, Wolzogen declared himself more than willing. The libretto, full of allusions and puns, was in Strauss's hands by October 1900 and he finished the score on 22 May 1901, Wagner's birthday. The opera was *Feuersnot*, an 'intermezzo against the theatre', as Strauss later called it, born of grudges and resentment.

The source material, Strauss's discovery, was a medieval legend with Flemish origins known as *The Extinguished Fires of Audenaarde*. A young man, publicly humiliated by his girlfriend, seeks the aid of a sorcerer in order to wreak revenge. The latter kills all the fires in the city and demands that the girl be paraded naked before the citizens. When this is done, a jet of flame shoots out of her rectum, from which the fires in the city are relit one by one. Wolzogen's handling of this grotesque fable tones down its scatological emphasis. The scene shifts to medieval Munich on Midsummer's Eve (shades of *Meistersinger*), when solstice fires burn and lovers leap ritualistically together through the flames. Fire and desire are equated throughout. 'Feuersnot! Minnegebot!' ('Fire famine! The decree of desire!') sings the hero, Kunrad. A conflation of the young man and the wizard, Kunrad is himself the apprentice of a benevolent sorcerer called Reichart der Wagner whom the citizens have previously driven out. The girl, Diemut, is spared her public ordeal and the rekindling of the fire coincides with the loss of her virginity.

The text piles up with Wagnerian allusions and the puns flow fast and thick, but the allusory sections of *Feuersnot* are the least interesting passages of the score. In a letter to his father, Strauss described the opera as 'pure Lortzing' and, for all its allusions, there are elements of a drastic melodic and harmonic simplification that leap back over Wagner to the early Romantics and anticipate much of Strauss's later music. The waltz anachronistically dominates, prefiguring *Rosenkavalier* and *Intermezzo*. The one-act form was a structure to which Strauss would repeatedly return. *Feuersnot* also contains the first of his many depictions of sex (consummation has hitherto been hinted at and anticipated, rather than portrayed). Kunrad's taking of Diemut's virginity is graphically enacted in music, with erectile horn calls and yielding, swooning strings. The prelude to *Rosenkavalier*, which repeats the pattern, is not far away.

Strauss was hesitant about staging the opera's première in Berlin, well aware that to do so would provoke a moralistic imperial backlash. Mahler, in Vienna, and Strauss's old friend Ernst von Schuh in

Dresden both requested the first performance. Schuh was a conductor whom Strauss intensely admired. The première was accordingly given to Dresden, and took place on 21 November 1901, with some textual alterations. It was a notorious success. Mahler managed to get the opera past the puritanical Viennese censors and the Austrian première followed two months later. Pauline alarmed everyone in rehearsals by denouncing the work in Strauss's presence as being shoddily unoriginal. 'My wife is dreadfully rude sometimes,' Strauss told Mahler. 'But it's good for me, you know.' Strauss's fears about the work's reception in Berlin were well founded. Wilhelm's wife, the Kaiserin Victoria Augusta, considered the piece obscene and after seven performances it was withdrawn by imperial edict until Hochberg threatened resignation unless given the right of free

Leo Pasetti's set design for the 1930 Munich production of *Feuersnot*; the vast perspective and distorted proportions of the buildings suggest the influence of German Expressionism.

presentation. The court backed down and *Feuersnot* was restored to the Berlin repertoire.

The erotic explicitness of *Feuersnot* surfaced again in the *Sinfonia Domestica*, begun in April the following year, in which Strauss attempted a further self-portrait, this time of himself, Pauline and Bubi in the privacy of their home. The symphony is widely regarded as being the joker in the pack, as far as Strauss's major orchestral works are concerned, a genuine curio, its subject matter for the most part in appalling bad taste. This view is unjustified; although uneven, the work contains some of his finest music. Its composition coincided with a period of unrest in the Strauss marriage. He had barely begun work on the sketches when Pauline filed for divorce.

While Strauss was away, staying briefly on the Isle of Wight, a letter had arrived at his apartment which Pauline opened. 'Dear Herr Strauss,' it began, 'I expected to see you yesterday in the Union Bar, but in vain, alas. I am writing therefore to ask if you will be so kind as to let me have a few tickets for Monday and Wednesday of this week. With my best thanks in anticipation, yours sincerely, Mieze Mücke. Lunebürgerstrasse 5, ground floor right.' Having brooded for a week on the letter's contents, Pauline decided that Strauss, in addition to frequenting bars behind her back, was having an affair with the aforementioned Fräulein Mücke. She contacted the family lawyer, telegraphed Strauss to inform him of her intentions, demanded an authorization to draw a large sum from the bank and prepared to close the apartment in the Joachimstalerstrasse where the family now lived.

Strauss's response on 26 May was characteristic. Alarm and anger were mixed with – and half hidden by – humour and affection.

My dear Pauxerl, this business with the Mücke woman is so stupid ... you get the precious document on Whit Monday, and spend a week harbouring fearful resentment against your adulterous spouse, while I sail off to England in blissful ignorance of the thunderstorm brewing at my back ... the first act of your revenge is to draw my beautiful money out of the bank. I wish I knew what you intend to do with the full 2,000 marks ... I have never been to the Union Bar, I don't even know where it is, any more than I know who Mücke is ... You could have thought that out for yourself instead of demanding great statements from me and

*simultaneously sending back my letters … as you still do not know what
you have in me, and* never will know*, I must ask you to seek out the
proof and the explanation you want yourself in Berlin, as I am not in a
good position to do it on Wight … I am asking Rösch to check the address
of the said Mücke … he can ask her who the letter was intended for …
Loving greetings and kisses from the adulterer to yourself and Bubi, who
can have no knowledge of this horrendous business.*

The lawyer duly obtained the necessary explanation. Fräulein
Mücke had met up in the Union Bar with a Czech conductor called
Josef Stransky, on tour in Berlin with an Italian opera company, and a
tenor by the name of De Marchi, who, unable to pronounce German
correctly, had repeatedly called Stransky 'Strausky'. Fräulein Mücke
had extracted a promise from Stransky to send her two tickets for one
of his performances. When they failed to arrive, she looked up
'Strausky' in the Berlin city directory, and not finding his name,
assumed she should contact Herr Strauss in the Joachimstalerstrasse.
The story sounds far-fetched, but is widely accepted as accurate. The
Strauss marriage was patched up, and the whole episode eventually
formed the basis of his opera *Intermezzo* (1917–23). Pauline, however,
continued to have her doubts. 'Who knows whether there wasn't
something in that Mieze story or not,' she was later reported to
have said.

How deeply the *Sinfonia Domestica* was affected by this episode is
hard to judge. Work on it went slowly. During the course of the
composition, Franz Strauss was dismissive and told his son that the
title would imply to the public that this was a work about servants.
Strauss interrupted it to compose a vast choral hymn, *Taillefer*, in
honour of Heidelberg University, which had bestowed on him an
honorary degree. The *Domestica* was not finished until December 1903.

It is an oddly ambiguous work, at once subversive and
conservative. A vast Wagnerian sonic panoply is pressed into service to
portray a day in the life of the Strauss family, a picture of bourgeois
conventionality far removed, despite the erotic explicitness of one
episode, from Wagnerian subject matter. Though it runs continuously
and is usually classified as a tone-poem, it falls into four clearly
differentiated sections. The Romantic symphonic convention of
linking movements by thematic material (Berlioz's *Symphonie*

Fantastique and Tchaikovsky's Fourth are prime examples) is pushed to extremes, as all four sections present comparative developments of the opening material. There are three, not the usual two, symphonic subjects, each composed of a cluster of motifs and associated with 'Papa', 'Mama' and 'Bubi' respectively.

Although the *Domestica* portrays the Strauss marriage as solid, 'Mama' does not always come out of the symphony particularly well. In contrast to *Heldenleben*, where Pauline makes her first appearance with a seductively descending solo violin phrase, she now enters throwing an almighty tantrum, working herself up to a frenzy, which the music of 'Papa' dismisses with charitable cheerfulness. The erotic sequence is the centrepiece of the adagio in which Strauss's compositional labours, depicted by grandiloquent, Brucknerian soaring phrases, are interrupted by Pauline's appearance, leading to the most graphic of Strauss's sex scenes in which the couple reach simultaneous orgasm in two separate keys, bitonally juxtaposed.

'Bubi', meanwhile, has, it would seem, the lungs of the century, and his cherubic *cor anglais* phrase is constantly interrupted by powerful sonic caterwauls. He seems remarkably quiet when a chain of relatives make admiring noises over him in the Mahlerian *Ländler* that forms

This photograph of Strauss was taken around the time of the *Sinfonia Domestica*. The composition of this work depicting his own domestic life coincided, ironically, with a period of strain in his marriage to Pauline.

the symphony's scherzo, though he vocally erupts once more when his parents prepare him for bed. 'All the cataclysms of the downfall of the gods in burning Valhalla,' the Wagner conductor Hans Richter remarked, 'do not make a quarter of the noise of one Bavarian baby in his bath.' Only the finale, a jovial fugue, is weak, as climax follows climax in forced profusion.

The work's première was to be the most important event of Strauss's first American tour. As a conductor he was frenetically active, conducting an average of eighty performances a season in Berlin. He was also permanently in demand elsewhere. In 1898 he had been in Amsterdam with the Concertgebouw. The orchestra had so impressed him on his first visit the preceding year that he dedicated *Heldenleben* to them and their conductor, Willem Mengelberg. He regularly visited Britain, appearing in London, Birmingham, Manchester and Glasgow. From 1901 until 1903, he had been conductor of the Berlin Tonkünstler Orchestra, its repertoire made up exclusively of contemporary music. It was not long before America beckoned. His music was already causing a stir on the other side of the Atlantic. Hans Hermann Wetzler, a German émigré musician who had founded his own orchestra in New York, finally lured Strauss to the States with an offer of substantial fees, hoping that Strauss's reputation would help boost his orchestra's fading status.

Strauss and Pauline arrived in New York in February 1904. The reporters were waiting, and his every move and statement was held up to public scrutiny. There was constant speculation as to the size of his fees. 'Earning money for his wife and child is no disgrace, even for an artist!' was Strauss's comment when pressed on the matter. At his Carnegie Hall début on 27 February he conducted *Heldenleben*. 'One hell of a Leben,' the press jeered. The *Domestica* caused a furore at its première on 21 March and was described as 'a cataclysm of domestic plumbing'. Rolland, who blew hot and cold about the piece, later told Strauss he should play down its programmatic nature.

He caused an even greater stir by accepting an offer from Wanamaker's Department Store to conduct two matinée concerts in the store itself for a fee of $1,000 a throw. This time the German press went on the rampage and accused him of 'the prostitution of art'. 'True art ennobles any hall,' was his response. The tour took the Strausses to Chicago, Philadelphia, Cleveland, Washington,

Minneapolis and Boston. Though the critics remained hostile, the public flocked in. In Morgantown, West Virginia, a German colony gave him the keys of the city. In Washington he met President Theodore Roosevelt. The high point, as far as Strauss was concerned, was a charity concert he gave with the Boston Symphony, which he described as 'the most marvellous orchestra in the world'. The Strausses left America at the end of April, still the subject of media gossip. During the tour, Strauss was tinkering with the manuscript of his next opera, a work which would make him notorious.

Early in 1902, Strauss had been approached by the Austrian poet Anton Lindner with an offer of a libretto based on Oscar Wilde's *Salomé*, which had received its German première, in a translation by Hedwig Lachmann, in Breslau the year before. Lindner, clearly hoping for a collaboration (Strauss had set one of his poems in 1898), sent a copy of the play to Strauss with a draft version of the opening scene. Strauss, disliking his versification, turned it down, though the opening line of Lachmann's translation, 'Wie schön ist die Prinzessin Salome, heute Nacht' ('How beautiful is the Princess Salome tonight'), struck him as full of musical potential. Later that year, the play opened at the Kleines Theater in Berlin, directed by Max Reinhardt, and with Gertrud Eysoldt in the title role. Strauss saw it that November. After the performance he met an old friend, Heinrich Grünfeld, who remarked, perhaps in jest, that the play would make excellent material for an opera. 'I am already composing it,' Strauss replied. The libretto, consisting of the German version of Wilde's text cut roughly by a third, is his own. Strauss's copy of the play, complete with the famous illustrations by Aubrey Beardsley, functioned as his first sketchbook.

Wilde, who was virtually bilingual, wrote *Salomé* in French in 1891–2 for the actress Sarah Bernhardt, filling his text with the lurid tropes of the then fashionable Decadent movement. The erotic extremism of his treatment draws heavily on the imagery of writers such as Flaubert, Baudelaire and Mallarmé. The teenage, virginal Salome experiences a sexual awakening when she first sets eyes on Jochanaan (to give John the Baptist his Hebrew name, which Wilde and Strauss use throughout). His rejection leads to her fearsome demand for his severed head, whose lips she kisses in necrophiliac ecstasy. Her actions so revolt her stepfather Herod that he has her killed.

In many respects, Strauss's opera is very different from Wilde's play, with its halting dialogue and florid soliloquies. Strauss's characters, by contrast, inhabit a world of febrile tension audible at the beginning in the opening clarinet swirl that leads to heat-drenched strings and a statement of Salome's own twitchy motif. Nerves are already at breaking-point. The opera proceeds at almost catastrophic speed, as if it had been composed in a single, unbroken, unremitting span (which it was not). The leitmotif structure is closely and intensely wrought, so much so that Gabriel Fauré, one of the work's early commentators, dubbed it 'a symphonic poem with voices added', a criticism which has stuck, though in some respects it is inappropriate. The opposite view – that the tone-poems are voiceless operas – has rarely surfaced and is equally valid.

Sonically, *Salome* is a tour de force, a masterpiece of orchestration, glittering, opalescent, teeming with sex and violence, restless throughout. The vocal lines, breaking new expressive grounds in their angularity, frequently inhabit a middle ground between song and speech. Herod, a tenor, faced with Salome's demands for Jochanaan's head, gabbles incoherently while the orchestra flails beneath him. Herodias, Herod's wife and Salome's mother, mocks him, cackling dementedly, her laughter jubilantly echoed by the rearing horns. As Salome kisses Jochanaan's dead lips, the orchestra shudders with the most grinding dissonance imaginable as C sharp major is momentarily wedged against a chord a semitone apart. The music peers back though the bitonal orgasm of the *Domestica* to the key structure of *Zarathustra*. Salome herself has progressed into territory 'beyond good and evil'. Like Don Juan, she is an amoralist who has sought consummation in a moment of intensely powerful experience. The stabbing trumpet and trills that send the Don to his death reappear. Kissing the Prophet's lips, she notices a bitter taste. His blood, perhaps – or, maybe, love. The taste of love, she has been told, is bitter.

That she uses the word 'love' while fondling a bloody lump of flesh is horrifying, yet the scene points to the secret of *Salome's* overwhelming power. Salome is the only character in the opera to use the word. She dares to speak its name in a world in which all mention of its existence is repressed. The remaining characters reject the desires that drive them. Herodias nags Herod not to gawp at his stepdaughter. Hearing Salome's declaration to Jochanaan, Narraboth, the captain of the guard who is fascinated by her, begs her not to utter such words. Jochanaan's prurient invective – he has Herodias's sex life permanently on his mind – is only broken by his series of injunctions to Salome not to touch him.

Strauss, however, takes Salome at her word. Her final monologue, in which an awareness of Jochanaan's now destroyed beauty intrudes on her desire, is the most remarkable love scene in opera, forging a curious empathy between heroine and listener. At this moment of utter horror, she voices the universal emotions of love and loss, both of which are audible in the flood of Strauss's score. Her emotional reality, conveyed in the music, is completely adrift from her external actions, embodied in the tearing dissonances that accompany her rapturous song. In so portraying her, Strauss is drawing a portrait of someone who is, in psychoanalytic terms, neurotic, whose inner and outer realities have been separated. It is no coincidence that in the year of *Salome*'s première the psychoanalytic movement gained ground with the publication of one of its most seminal texts, Sigmund Freud's *Three Essays on the Theory of Sexuality*, which examines the legacy of repression and posits a theory of desire as a universal motivation.

Salome is not without flaws. Strauss's cutting of Wilde's text leads to occasional awkwardnesses. The grotesque family history – Herod had murdered his own brother in order to have Herodias, originally his brother's wife, for himself – is not always clear. There is a hiatus in the build-up to the dance, where it feels that Strauss has snipped too much away. More worrying is the whiff of anti-Semitism which characterizes the Jews who squabble, to a strenuous fugue, about theology. The dance, a seditious waltz that draws into itself all the opera's main themes, is problematic, with a hardness of timbre that sets it apart from the rest of the score. The exact order of the composition of *Salome* remains a mystery, though we do know that the dance was written last. The rest of the score was complete, with the exception of some of the orchestration, by the spring of 1905. The orchestration was completed on 30 June, and the dance added in August.

Strauss played the opera through to his father. 'God, what nervous music!' was his comment. 'It's like having an enormous beetle in your pants.' The cruel remark, which Strauss in his memoirs treated almost as a joke, proved to be Franz Strauss's final rejection of his son's music.

He died on 31 May 1905 at the age of eighty-three. Strauss buried himself in work.

Salome caused ructions even before a note of it had been heard in public. Mahler was initially uneasy, fearing censorship problems (though he changed his mind when he heard the music). Rolland, who worked with Strauss on a French edition of the score, thought the subject beneath its composer's dignity. Strauss had been impressed with Schuh's handling of *Feuersnot* and offered the première to Dresden, thus setting up a tradition of giving his operatic premières to the city which continued until 1938 (*Ariadne* and *Frau ohne Schatten* were exceptions).

Chaos broke out almost from the moment the music of *Salome* arrived at the theatre. At the first piano rehearsal, the cast, with one exception, handed their scores back on the grounds that the piece was unsingable. The exception was the Herod, a Czech tenor called Karel Burian, who announced that he knew the role by heart. The others, rather shamefacedly, backtracked and struggled to learn it. The Salome, a sizeable lady by the name of Marie Wittich, went on strike and refused to continue. 'I won't do it,' she protested. 'I'm a respectable married woman.' Strauss threatened to withdraw the score and give it to Mahler in Vienna instead. This was a bluff, but it worked. Wittich agreed to proceed, though not without further

The Dance of the Seven Veils at the première of *Salome* (Dresden, 1905), with Marie Wittich in the title role. Strauss had grave doubts about her suitability for the dance on account of her ample size.

protests that nearly led to the postponement of the première yet again. Offended members of the bourgeoisie cut Schuh dead in the street and prophesied disaster. The orchestra protested that the piece was unplayable. The première, on 9 December, was a *succès de scandale*, though the critics fumed and accused Strauss of sensationalism. Almost at once, every opera house in Europe was vying for the piece, not always successfully. To Mahler's fury, it was banned in Vienna – a ban which remained in force until 1918. The rest of the country proved more tolerant. The Austrian première took place in Graz on 16 May 1906. Mahler and his wife Alma were in the audience. So was the seventeen-year-old Adolf Hitler.

In Berlin, the Kaiser – whom Strauss had pacified by saying he was working on a biblical opera – was not amused and two years passed before *Salome* was performed in the capital. Even then imperial permission was only granted on condition that the Star of Bethlehem twinkle on the backcloth. In New York the media went on the war-path and ensured that a riot broke out at the first performance at the Metropolitan. The remainder of the opening run was cancelled, and *Salome* was not heard again in New York until 1934.

The London première, at Covent Garden in 1910, was conducted by Sir Thomas Beecham, to the end of his days an ardent champion of Strauss. The Lord Chamberlain insisted on textual changes, demanded that the head should not appear and sat stonily through the first night. Salome addressed her final apostrophe to an empty plate, and yet the cast, whether by accident or design, reverted to the original libretto halfway through the performance without the Lord Chamberlain being remotely aware of the fact. The country that had destroyed Wilde on the grounds of his homosexuality received *Salome* with comparative equanimity, and its success did much to restore his posthumous reputation.

Salome turned Strauss into the most successful opera composer of his day, though it also made him enemies. The Wagner contingent were appalled. Cosima described the opera as 'an inane farrago, wedded to indecency', and thereafter Strauss's relationship with Bayreuth was strained. Thomas Mann, another early admirer, turned away in fastidious disgust. The Kaiser remarked that *Salome* could only do Strauss damage. 'The damage enabled me to build the villa in Garmisch,' Strauss noted in his memoirs. The royalties from the opera

The Bulgarian soprano Ljuba Welitsch as Salome, a role of which she was considered the definitive interpreter, at Covent Garden in 1949. Peter Brook's production, designed by Salvador Dalí, caused as great a scandal as the 1905 première.

made him rich. He had finally become someone in the plutocratic world of the Second Reich, and a villa – the ultimate emblem of status – was now his by right. The building, which still houses his archive, was completed in the summer of 1908. His next opera, *Elektra*, was finished there that September.

Elektra and *Salome* are frequently bracketed together as a pair of not-so-heavenly operatic twins. In 1903, Max Reinhardt, anxious to follow his success with *Salome*, decided on a second vehicle for Gertrud Eysoldt and commissioned an adaptation of Sophocles' *Electra* from the 29-year-old Hugo von Hofmannsthal. Strauss saw the production that winter and was, yet again, struck by the play's operatic possibilities. Within months of *Salome*'s première he had approached Hofmannsthal with a view to adapting the play as a libretto. Hofmannsthal was more than willing. Yet the collaboration, one of the greatest creative partnerships in operatic history, got off to a strange start, in which elements of the creative dependency that kept them together were mixed with the seeds of the conflicts that could, and occasionally did, pull them apart.

Having decided on *Elektra*, Strauss hesitated, and sent Hofmannsthal a letter, rather half-heartedly explaining his reasons. 'I have not finally decided whether I wouldn't do better to wait a few years before approaching *Elektra*,' he wrote, 'until I have myself moved much further away from the *Salome* style … I should be glad to know if you have got anything else in stock for me.' What he would really like, he explained, was 'an entertaining Renaissance subject – a really wild Cesare Borgia or Savonarola would be the answer to my prayers.' The letter ends with an astonishing, and uncharacteristically effusive, declaration of attachment: 'I would ask you urgently to give me first refusal of anything composable that you write. Your manner has so much in common with mine; we were born for one another and are certain to do fine things together if you remain faithful to me.'

The charm and affection conceal an element of emotional confusion on Strauss's part. His father's death the previous year had led to the most serious of Josephine's mental breakdowns. Early in 1906, she was confined in a clinic at Eglfing near Munich, released too soon and later in the year had to be admitted again. The subject matter of *Elektra*, in which the matriarch Klytemnestra struggles to maintain her sanity in the face of her daughter's obsessive attempts to undermine it, may have been too close for comfort. Strauss mentioned nothing of this to Hofmannsthal.

The latter's reply is similarly significant. He assuaged Strauss's fears by pointing out that *Salome* and *Elektra* had little in common beyond Reinhardt, Eysoldt, a one-act structure and a dominant female central role. He was curtly dismissive, however, of Strauss's interest in a Renaissance subject, which he deemed outmoded. 'I should be very glad,' he added 'if you could manage to stick to *Elektra* for a start.'

In his enthusiasm, Strauss overlooked – or chose to ignore – the high-handedness of Hofmannsthal's remark and proposed other subjects – Sardou's *Ninth Termidor*, about the French Revolution, Friedrich Rückert's *Saul and David*, Pedro Calderón's *Semiramis, Daughter of the Air*. The last of these, with its steamy eroticism, came, if anything, even closer to *Salome* than the libretto Hofmannsthal was pressing on him. 'I should like … to explain to you,' Hofmannstahl wrote, imperiously, 'my notions (fairly liberal as they are) of what I consider possible opera subjects and what, on the other hand, I consider out of the question nowadays.' *Termidor, Saul and David* and *Semiramis* were, like the 'entertaining Renaissance subject,' quite definitely 'out'. Strauss, nevertheless, continued to hanker after *Semiramis* for many years. Hofmannstahl's assumption that he was an absolute arbiter of taste was to have an important – some would say detrimental – effect on their future relationship.

Hofmannsthal was an aristocrat, it should be remembered, and Strauss, despite the rebellious element in his nature, had been brought up to believe himself the musical servant of the aristocracy. In June, he capitulated. Hofmannsthal was given a contract stipulating he receive twenty-five per cent of their joint royalties, and the score of *Elektra* was begun. Work progressed slowly and not always smoothly. Klytemnestra's music gave Strauss trouble, and he found the ending of the play too perfunctory, asking Hofmannsthal to expand the final scene between Elektra and her gentler sister Chrysothemis. He also wanted an additional eight lines for the Recognition Scene in which Elektra finally encounters her long-lost brother Orest. 'You are the

A caricature of Strauss, escorting Salome and Elektra to a performance of *Der Rosenkavalier* in 1911. 'If my two girlfriends aren't invited, then I shan't go either,' the original caption read.

born librettist,' he told Hofmannsthal when the text arrived. His statement was true. There was an element of the vicarious in Hofmannsthal, a need to collaborate, to adapt and to express himself partly through the work of others.

Ten years Strauss's junior, he was born in Vienna in 1874 to an old patrician family. His father, a successful banker, was half-Austrian, half-Italian. His mother's family was Jewish. He was sensitive, erudite, cultured, prone to moments of self-doubt and melancholy. A poetic talent of almost incongruous maturity, he showed an early gift for languages and an almost encyclopaedic memory. By the time he left school he spoke French and Italian, knew classical literature backwards, had published his first poems and his first play, *Gestern* ('Yesterday'), under pseudonyms. At Vienna University he studied Romance languages, all the while continuing to write poetry and plays.

In 1899 self-doubt overcame him and his trust in the power of language as an adequate means of expression began to fail. The resulting crisis produced one of the prophetic works of the twentieth century, the *Chandos Brief* ('Chandos Letter'), a fictitious letter from Lord Chandos to Francis Bacon, towards the end of which Hofmannsthal voices his search for 'a language of which I am familiar with not a single word, in which dumb things speak to me, and in which I shall answer, when I am in my grave, to an unknown judge'. Hofmannsthal's obsession with the incommunicability of language later found its greatest expression in the works of Franz Kafka and Samuel Beckett. His own search for a language beyond words led to his gravitation towards music and towards Strauss.

As an adapter, Hofmannsthal was frequently radical, as *Elektra* proves. The outline of Sophocles' play is preserved, though many of the details are subtly changed. An exhaustive list of instructions written for Reinhardt's designer gives some indication of his method. The set must eschew the 'antiquating banalities' of pseudo-Greek pillars and columns, and should resemble 'the populated courtyard of a town house on a summer's afternoon'. The actress playing Elektra should 'wear a wretchedly vile dress that is too short for her'. Klytemnestra is described as wearing 'a magnificent, bright red dress. It looks as if all the blood from her sallow face is in her dress. Her throat, neck and arms are covered with jewels. She is hung with talismans and precious stones.'

Sophocles is pulled into the present. Elektra herself has been relegated to the *Hinterhof* of an urban tenement, hidden away from public view, her existence nonetheless a permanent reminder of what lies behind the tottering façade of respectability. Her 'wretchedly vile dress' hints at the trappings of naturalist drama, embodied in the works of Hofmannsthal's great contemporary Gerhart Hauptmann, with his depiction of the grinding squalor of tenement life. Naturalism, both literary and philosophical, sees man primarily as an animal, motivated solely by instinct. Elektra is in constant motion, 'rearing like a beast' and 'springing like an animal'. Klytemnestra's jewellery, on the other hand, together with her scarlet dress, suggests *Jugendstil* opulence. Hofmannsthal's description so closely resembles Klimt's painting *Hygeia*, hung in Vienna University (it was destroyed during World War II), that the coincidence cannot be overlooked.

Harry Kupfer's 1989 Vienna production of *Elektra*; the colossal statue represents Agamemnon, whose murder dominates the characters' minds and whose leitmotif is rarely absent from the score.

Equally important is Hofmannsthal's rejection of much of the plot's surrounding mythology. In Sophocles the characters are fatalistically driven by a curse in an endless chain of revenge and

retribution. No specific motivation is shown to have guided Klytemnestra's hands as she murdered her husband Agamemnon. Both play and opera end with a question mark. The classical Orestes was hounded by the Furies for his crime of vengeful matricide. Hofmannsthal's Chrysothemis bangs in vain on the palace doors, shrieking to her brother for help. Fate, in the sense of an impersonal, externally imposed destiny, does not drive the characters of *Elektra*, who are motivated solely by their own emotions.

Hofmannsthal was a native of Freud's Vienna, and while he worked on the play, a copy of the *Studies on Hysteria* was at his side; Freud was contemporaneously working on his major study of obsessional neurosis. Elektra, an obsessive, enacts her daily ritual howl for her father in the palace courtyard, but she is unable to carry out the slaughter that fills her fantasies. Finally confronted with its possibility, she even forgets to give Orest the axe she has been keeping for him. Freud's *The Interpretation of Dreams* had been published in 1900 and Klytemnestra, like a psychoanalytic patient, wants her dreams analysed. The remedy she seeks is tauntingly withheld by her daughter who tells her that only when she dies will her nightmares cease.

Listening to Strauss's score, there is no evidence that he found its composition a struggle. Using the largest forces ever required in opera, it is music of titanic grandeur and Dionysiac violence, soaked in blood, terror, grief and compassion. Strauss later claimed that the opera 'penetrated to the uttermost limits of harmony, psychological polyphony and of the receptivity of human ears'. Taken complete, the statement is untrue: the operatic output of Schoenberg, Berg and Zimmermann pushed the acceptable limits of harmony much further than *Elektra*. The phrase 'psychological polyphony', however, indicating the subordination of harmonic and orchestral structure to dramatic psychology, holds true. Harmony is welded to character. Elektra feeds her obsession musically by alternately drifting from tonal centres and returning to them as her father's image resurfaces in her mind. Chrysothemis's music is rooted in conventional E flat major, the key of the 'Eroica' and of the domestic heroism of *Heldenleben*. Klytemnestra's formless consciousness is unable to focus on any tonal centre at all. Her Nightmare Scene veers towards complete atonality, and is frequently cited, incorrectly, as the first major example of such. Tonality had finally collapsed, with no help

Leonie Rysanek, one of the finest post-war Strauss interpreters, as the self-degrading Elektra in Götz Friedrich's 1982 film

from Strauss, with the publication of Schoenberg's song-cycle *Das Buch der hängenden Gärten* ('The Book of the Hanging Gardens') in the year of *Elektra*'s première.

Once again, the première went to Dresden. Strauss told Schuh that for the title role he had better hire the loudest, most dramatic soprano he could find. His remark was perspicacious – even with the cuts that have now become a feature of many performances, *Elektra* is still the most gruelling challenge a dramatic soprano can face, and great interpreters of the part are rare. The unenviable responsibility for its creation fell to Annie Krull. Strauss reportedly sat through rehearsals screaming 'Louder! Louder! I can still hear the singers!' at the orchestra. The première, on 25 January 1909, was yet again surrounded by controversies, though nothing like the scandal which surrounded *Salome*. The public was initially perplexed and the critics, for the most part, snidely virulent in their condemnation. Contemporary cartoons showed Strauss and Hofmannsthal dismembering Sophocles, and a terrified audience penned in the orchestra pit while the musicians play eruptively round the auditorium.

Nevertheless, as with *Salome*, other houses were soon clamouring for the piece. Mahler's decision to stage the opera in Vienna led to a sudden attack of nerves on Hofmannsthal's part for fear the conservative Viennese would reject it. They did not and, later in 1909, Strauss made his conducting début at the Court Opera with it. Beecham gave the British première at Covent Garden in 1910.

Strauss was ambivalent about the work for the rest of his life. He frequently referred to it as his 'green horror' and in 1909 he made a press statement claiming that *Elektra* did not represent a break with tonality, the principles of which he firmly maintained. In old age, however, faced with accusations of being a 'renegade' for backtracking on the opera's harmonic extremism, he was anxious to state the opposite. Critics remain similarly divided over the nature and influence of the score's radicalism. The issue was permanently confused by his next move. He wanted to do something different. 'Next time,' he said, 'I'll write a Mozart opera.'

Hofmannsthal took him at his word. He went to Weimar for a few days to stay with his friend, the diplomat, pacifist and diarist Count Harry Kessler. Together they worked on an idea for an eighteenth-century comedy, its plot an amalgam of two plays by Molière, *Monsieur de Pourceaugnac* and *Les Fourberies de Scapin* ('Scapin's Impostures'), and a novel by the obscure Louis de Couvray, *Les Amours du Chevalier de Faublas* ('The Loves of the Chevalier de Faublas'). By 11 February 1909, the scenario was complete. 'It contains two big parts,' Hofmannsthal wrote to Strauss, 'one for a baritone and another for a graceful girl dressed up as a man, *à la* Farrar or Mary Garden. Period: the old Vienna of Maria Theresa.' Geraldine Farrar and Mary Garden were two American sopranos whose vocal allure was matched by their sexy presence on stage and who frequently performed in men's clothes.

Strauss was enthusiastic. 'Send Act I to me as soon as you can,' he wrote. He had time on his hands. The Berlin Opera had granted him a year's leave of absence for the 1908–9 season. Whereas the composition of *Elektra* had dragged on, he now couldn't get his hands fast enough on the material of *Ochs auf Lerchenau* (as the opera was originally called). 'The opening scene is delightful,' he wrote to Hofmannsthal on 23 April. 'It'll set itself to music like oil and melted butter; I'm hatching it already.' The poet was obliging and their collaboration on the piece was free from the arguments that marred their later efforts. In July, Strauss became dissatisfied with the shape of Act II and deemed it to be lacking in humour. Hofmannsthal refashioned it following Strauss's instructions. Strauss, similarly, took to heart Hofmannsthal's views on style. 'Do try and think of an old-fashioned Viennese waltz,' he wrote to Strauss, 'sweet and yet saucy, which must pervade the last act.'

Hofmannsthal also revealed another habit which was to have serious consequences for Strauss later on, namely that of withholding sections of the text. The ending of Act III was put on hold during the winter of 1909–10, in order to allow it to 'enrich and mature' inside his head. By the following spring, the first two acts were with the printers and Strauss was getting impatient. Dresden had already been chosen for the première, as usual. Alfred Roller, the great designer whom Mahler had championed in Vienna, had been hired to provide the sets and costumes. Georg Toller, who had directed the first production of *Elektra*, was to be in charge of the staging.

On 6 June, Hofmannsthal wrote to Strauss that the text was complete but, he admitted, the emphasis of the work had begun to shift. Both he and Strauss originally saw Ochs as the central character. The Marschallin, however, was beginning almost to develop a life of her own and had grown to predominance in the minds of both men. 'The Marschallin,' Hofmannsthal wrote, 'is the central figure for the public, for the women above all, the figure with whom they feel and *move*.' In some respects he was putting into words what already subconsciously existed in Strauss's mind as well. The emotional depth of the Marschallin's music was already apparent in the completed first act.

The working title *Ochs auf Lerchenau* could not remain. By the time Strauss returned from a conducting tour at the beginning of July, the opera was called *Der Rosenkavalier*. The score, finished in September 1910, was dedicated to the Pschorr family. Josephine Strauss had died on 16 May. Strauss, mentioning her death in his correspondence with Hofmannsthal, gives little indication of his feelings but he grieved and was depressed for some time. To the end Josephine's mental illness was a secret shared between the family and her doctors. (Although the Pschorr family, individually and collectively, were the dedicatees of many of Strauss's works, none was formally dedicated to Josephine alone.)

The composition of *Der Rosenkavalier* had gone smoothly, but getting the piece staged was a different matter. There were problems during the rehearsal period. The presence in Dresden of Dora Wihan, Strauss's former lover, caused Strauss and Pauline embarrassment and stress. Both Strauss and Hofmannsthal decided that Georg Toller's direction was provincial. To the fury of the Intendant Seebach, they drafted in Max Reinhardt to help. He was not allowed to intervene on set, however, and was forced to whisper instructions to the singers when they came off-stage into the stalls. Seebach, seeing the results, finally allowed Reinhardt on stage, though his name was kept off the official posters in order to pacify the offended Toller. Seebach also found the piece obscene, objected to the Marschallin being shown in bed and forced Hofmannsthal to provide him with a number of alternative phrases to cover up anything which might provoke public disquietude.

The première, on 26 January 1911, was such a success that fifty performances followed that year in Dresden alone, every one of them sold out. Within weeks the opera was similarly playing to packed houses in Nuremberg, Vienna, Munich and Hamburg. Berlin was predictably squeamish and the first performance in the capital was delayed until 14 November, by which time demand for the work had become phenomenal. So many people were prepared to travel to Dresden that special trains had to be laid on. 'This is no music for me,' the Kaiser stormed when he finally heard it. He was in the minority. It remains Strauss's most popular work.

Though it has its longueurs, *Der Rosenkavalier* is possibly the richest and most subtle of Strauss's scores. Significantly, sufficient time had elapsed after his father's death for the opera to contain a perfect stylistic balance between Franz Strauss's (and his son's) beloved Mozart and some of the Wagnerian elements that formed the focus of Strauss's rebellion against his father's influence. The structure is yet again based on leitmotifs, and the orchestral forces (though not as great as those required for *Elektra*) remain colossal. The Wagnerian apparatus, however, has finally become domesticated and is put at the service of a bittersweet comedy equalled only in the operatic repertoire by *Così fan tutte*, *Le nozze di Figaro* and Verdi's *Falstaff*. Verdi's fat knight, boorish, coarse, yet full of vitality, was uppermost in the creating minds of both composer and librettist when creating Ochs.

Hofmannsthal paved the way for this amalgam with his text. In a sequel to the original Beaumarchais play which inspired *Figaro*, the Countess had an affair with the pageboy Cherubino which formed the model for the relationship between Octavian and the married Marschallin, who is older, and wiser, than he. Yet Hofmannsthal also brings in allusions to *Meistersinger* and *Tristan*. Like Hans Sachs, the Marschallin must watch a younger beloved turn to someone else, then actively work to obtain his happiness. Like Tristan, Octavian is a proxy wooer who eventually makes off with the proposed bride. In love with the Marschallin, as he thinks, he babbles Wagnerian language about 'You and I' as an indivisible unit of souls, before the light of day that threatens Wagner's lovers as well as Strauss's intrudes to stop him.

The passage from dawn to full daylight at the beginning of the opera is the first hint of its central theme, the nature and effect of time. The ambiguity and profundity of *Rosenkavalier* depend for their existence on the audience's consciousness of time's remorseless passing, though only the Marschallin is aware of its implications. She seeks to halt its progress by stopping the clocks at night. Her wish is foolish, as a quiet ticking in the orchestra reminds us. She is aware, however, that nothing lasts and that 'today, tomorrow or the day after' her young lover will leave her 'for someone who is younger and more beautiful than I'. When she dispatches her servants to take the silver rose to Octavian, so that the latter might present it on Ochs's behalf to Sophie, Strauss's music tells us that she is half aware of the consequences of her actions. Face to face with Sophie, she realizes that time has played its last trick. 'Today, tomorrow or the day after' has arrived sooner than she expected and she gives Octavian up. To Faninal's remark that 'that's how young people are', she replies simply 'Ja, ja' ('Yes, yes') and sweeps from the stage. The word has Nietzschean associations, though here it expresses the antithesis of his philosophy. Nietzsche believed that saying 'yes' to a single moment validated the existence of his overman. The Marschallin knows the validity of a single moment is illusory. After she has gone, Octavian and Sophie contemplate the prospect of being together 'for all time

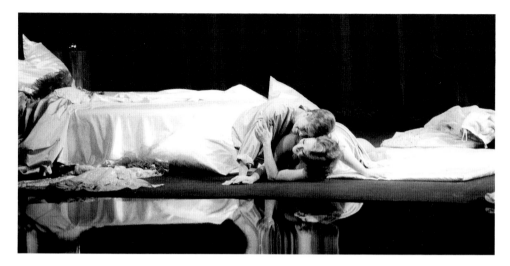

The lovers, Octavian (Yvonne Wiedstruck) and the Marschallin (Karan Armstrong), in the opening scene of *Der Rosenkavalier* in Götz Friedrich's 1993 Berlin production which updated the opera to the years preceding World War I

and eternity'. They do so to a melody of almost Schubertian delicacy, under which can be heard the chromatics of the theme associated with the silver rose that brought them together. Its tinkling sonorities peer back beyond their first meeting to the sound of the clocks the Marschallin initially dreads. Time, of which they remain unaware, lies in wait for them too.

Strauss lets himself view the world through the Marschallin's eyes and his score glides between three time schemes. The eighteenth century is everywhere apparent in the continuous Baroque flourishes in the orchestra. The nineteenth-century Vienna of Johann Strauss is also audible in the swirling waltzes which permeate the score, even when they are not immediately obvious. The great, unforgettable Trio, with its astonishing vocal writing for three female voices, derives from a rather coarse waltz heard earlier in the act when Octavian, dressed in women's clothes, is trying to fend off Ochs's attentions. Finally there are the moments of harmonic violence that pull us into the modern world, such as in the prelude to Act III during which the final discomfiture of Ochs is plotted by Octavian and a gang of louche intriguers from the city's underworld.

The dissonance of the prelude is worth bearing in mind, for *Rosenkavalier* is constantly held up as a harmonic retrogression after *Elektra*, and is consequently seen as the start of Strauss's slide into musical conservatism after an early period of harmonic experimentation. Strauss and musical modernism, we are told, effectively part company at this point. His refusal to plunge into atonality leads to accusations that he has suddenly become stylistically old-fashioned. The argument sidesteps the crucial issue of the function of dissonance in his music. Savage harmonies are used in *Rosenkavalier* (as in *Till Eulenspiegel*) for comic effect and the underpinning of farce, rather than the portrayal of mental or physical violence. This should blind no one to either the presence of dissonance or its level in the score.

As soon as it was finished, Strauss was anxious to begin work again. 'The time has now almost come to think of *Semiramis*,' he wrote to Hofmannsthal. Calderón's play was once more uppermost in his mind and he had been sounding Hofmannsthal out for some time on the subject. Hofmannsthal had quietly ignored his requests. Now, however, his answer was firmly in the negative. 'No intellectual or material inducements,' he wrote, 'could extract from me a play on this subject, not even a most determined effort of will.' Once again, Strauss chose to ignore his high-handedness, though in so doing he allowed the balance of control in the collaboration to pass into Hofmannsthal's hands. The writer proved to be singularly manipulative from that point on.

He mentioned Wilhelm Hauff's *Das kalte Herz* ('The Cold Heart') as a possible subject. Hauff, a writer of supernatural fairy tales, was a contemporary of Weber. *Das steinere Herz* ('The Stone Heart') was mooted as a working title for the project. Strauss was immediately enthusiastic. A 'Weber opera' was what was wanted after the 'Mozart opera' of *Rosenkavalier*. 'Cheers for *Das steinere Herz*,' he wrote in January 1911. 'Plenty of nature atmosphere, please: German forest. Thunderstorm as Holländermichel fells his trees: this is how the thing might start.' Hofmannsthal promptly put a dampener on the whole proceedings. 'What a confounded fool I was,' he wrote, 'to tell you the title and the subject and so direct your imagination to Hauff's fairy tale which, except for the central germ, has nothing in common with what exists in my imagination.' The imagery of Hauff's *Das kalte Herz*, however, in which a young charcoal burner's heart is turned to stone in the pursuit of earthly desire, remained in Hofmannsthal's eclectic mind and was soon interwoven with a number of other ideas; petrifaction was to be a key motif in the new work. Yet when he came to present his scheme to Strauss, his letter contained the basis of not one opera, but two.

Hofmannsthal had, for a while, been contemplating a project not unlike Strauss's abandoned ballet *Kythere*. He dreamt up the idea of an opera company and a *commedia dell'arte* troupe visiting a Bohemian castle to perform simultaneously for its wealthy owner. As with *Kythere*, the gods of classical antiquity and the characters of a frivolous Harlequinade were to mingle. It was during a visit to Paris that the final idea took shape. He went to a performance of Molière's *Le Bourgeois Gentilhomme*, and realized that his project could replace the balletic interlude (included by Molière), in an abbreviated translation of the original play, *Der Bürger als Edelmann*. The two troupes could be hired to perform at the same time for the wealthy bourgeois Philistine Jourdain as part of his scheme to woo the aristocratic Marquise Dorimène. The opera company would present a Baroque

A rare photograph of Strauss and Hofmannsthal together, taken at Rodaun, Hofmannsthal's house near Vienna, in 1912

opera seria dealing with the figure of Adriadne, who mourns the collapse of her relationship with her lover Theseus, who has abandoned her on the island of Naxos. The leader of the *commedia dell'arte* troupe was to be her antithesis, the gleefully promiscuous Zerbinetta. Reinhardt was in Hofmannsthal's mind as director from the beginning, and the piece was effectively a 'thank-you' present for his uncredited work on *Rosenkavalier*. On 20 March 1911, he accordingly presented Strauss with his ideas for both the play-cum-opera and the supernatural tale, which had already evolved into something infinitely more complex than Hauff's original story.

'If,' he wrote, 'we were to work together once more on something (and by this I mean something important, not the thirty-minute opera … called *Ariadne auf Naxos* … made up of harlequins and scaramouches representing the buffo element which is woven throughout with the heroic) … it would have to possess colourful and clear-cut action. I have something definite in mind … It is a magic fairy tale with two men confronting two women, and for one of the women your wife might well, in all discretion, be taken as the model – that, of course, is wholly *entre nous* and not of any great importance. Anyway she is a *bizarre* woman with a very beautiful soul, *au fond*, strange, moody, domineering yet at the same time likeable.'

Strauss was intrigued by both these proposals. Unknown to Hofmannsthal, he had already been thinking of setting Molière. In Paris, in 1907, he had discussed the possibility of a version of *Tartuffe* with Rolland and Albert Carré, director of the Opéra Comique. 'You should do no such thing,' was Carré's response. 'There's nothing less musical than Molière.' The idea was then dropped. Now, however, Strauss was fascinated by Hofmannsthal's 'little Molière thing', as he called *Ariadne*, the composite play and opera, as well as by the prospect of a 'magic fairy tale'. The latter, however, needed to 'enrich and mature' inside Hofmannsthal's head. It was *Ariadne auf Naxos* that was to be their next project. They were soon at loggerheads over it.

Strauss received the first draft of the text in May. His response was less than enthusiastic. He thought the first part 'very nice', described the second as 'thin' and added that 'For the dances … one could write some pleasant salon music.' He was distracted, however. The news of Mahler's death, two days previously, had depressed and shocked him and it was a while before he warmed to the piece, though when he did

it was not in the way Hofmannsthal had hoped. He was much struck
by the character of Zerbinetta and promptly decided that he would
create the role as a star vehicle for a great coloratura soprano such as
the immensely popular Luisa Tetrazzini or Selma Kurz. Hofmannsthal
was outraged – this was after all, intended to be a theatrical vehicle for
Reinhardt. Someone like Tetrazzini, whose rotundity was as great as
her vocal talent, smacked too much of 'grand opera'. That was all very
well, Strauss retorted, but what about other theatres that could not
call on a Reinhardt? 'The plot as such holds no interest and interesting
costumes won't turn the scale either,' he added.

A slanging match, described by Hofmannsthal as 'this frank
exchange of views', ensued. He wrote Strauss a very long letter
explaining 'the underlying meaning' of the opera: 'What it is about is
one of the straightforward and stupendous problems of life, fidelity;
whether to hold fast to that which is lost, to cling to it even unto
death ... Ariadne could only be the wife or mistress of one man, just
as she can be only one man's widow ... One thing is left for her: the
miracle, the God. To him she gives herself for she believes him to be
Death ... he it is who reveals to her the immeasurable depths of her
own nature ... But what to divine souls is a real miracle, is to the
earthbound nature of Zerbinetta just an everyday love affair. She sees
in Ariadne's experience the only thing she *can* see; the exchange of an
old lover for a new one. And so these two spiritual worlds are ...
brought together in the only way in which they can be brought
together; in non-comprehension.'

Strauss's response was barbed. 'Your letter ... is so beautiful and
explains the meaning of the action so wonderfully that a superficial
musician like myself could not, of course, have tumbled to it ... If
even I couldn't see it, just think of the audiences and – the critics.'
Even so, he was anxious to pacify his librettist and the letter tumbles
into a series of apologies. Hofmannsthal took Strauss's hint and
inserted into the text of *Der Bürger als Edelmann* a scene in which the
Composer of the opera explains its significance to Zerbinetta.
Meanwhile, he assured Strauss in February 1912, *Die Frau ohne
Schatten*, the magic fairy tale, was coming along nicely.

Ariadne was getting out of proportion, however. By the time
Strauss finished the score in April, the opera alone ran for nearly an
hour and a half. Attempts to have the piece staged caused further

problems. Even before the score was finished, it was apparent that *Ariadne* was going to be problematic for the theatre for which it was intended, Reinhardt's Deutsches Theater in Berlin. When Strauss began to look elsewhere Hofmannsthal, racked with doubt about the piece and terrified of losing Reinhardt, became nearly hysterical. 'That in this case you should find it possible to disregard everything that matters to me,' he wrote to Strauss, 'to disregard all that the realization of this work of my imagination means to me, to force me into a theatre where I could not appear without a sense of debasement, this *does* touch me … I beg of you … do not injure our relationship! If you now estrange me from yourself you can find, in Germany and abroad, men of talent and rank who could write your opera libretti for you, but it won't be the same.'

Another compromise was struck. Strauss coaxed Reinhardt and the Berlin company to the smaller of two theatres at Stuttgart, where rehearsals began in June 1912. This gave rise to problems, too. The plan was that the resident company should take over the work after an initial run with the Berlin performers. They were less than pleased, however, when they realized they would have to take part in the bulk of rehearsals before the Berlin principals arrived. The theatre management were indifferent, and when the resident producer queried a technical point Strauss antagonized him by saying, 'Reinhardt will settle that.' At the dress rehearsal half the technical crew walked out of the theatre to work on a production of Lortzing's *Undine* in the city's larger theatre.

Casting the piece proved equally difficult. For Ariadne, Strauss wanted the great Czech soprano Emmy Destinn, a notable Salome and a singer idolized by Puccini, the only living operatic composer to rival him in popularity. She was not open to persuasion, however, even when Strauss grovelled, and in the end he decided upon her younger compatriot, Maria Jeritza, whom he had heard singing Offenbach's *La Belle Hélène* in Munich. A great actress and a staggering beauty, she was the first of a number of sopranos whose individual voices became a source of inspiration. Casting Zerbinetta – for whom Strauss had indeed written a great coloratura aria of extreme difficulty – proved equally problematic. The role eventually fell, astonishingly, to Margarethe Siems, who had created both Chrysothemis and the Marschallin. No singer has tackled all three roles since.

The première, on 25 October, was a damp squib. The audience was composed of a mixture of play- and opera-goers, each group restively uninterested in the other genre. The King of Württemberg decided to hold a fifty-minute reception in each of the two intervals and the evening lasted for six hours. The critics were savage in their judgement. Though performances in Munich and Berlin swiftly followed, the initial failure of the work marked a turning-point in Strauss's fortunes. He was widely perceived as having gone off the rails. From then on, automatic success proved to be elusive.

The most damning of the original criticisms came from the Berlin-based journalist Alfred Kerr. 'Just what this manifestation of Hofmannsthal's weaknesses amounts to,' he fumed, 'I am unable to decide … The mixture of serious matter which is not serious with comic matter which is not comic … Meanwhile in another part of the wood, a score by Richard Strauss goes its own way, whispering, rattling, skipping, whistling, cajoling, humming, shrieking and wailing like – like something by a Mozart who has studied the warp and woof of *Meistersinger*.' What Kerr failed to realize, along with many of his contemporaries, is that it is the deliberate jumble of elements that gives the original *Ariadne* its stamp of greatness. The

A scene from the 1912 Stuttgart première of *Ariadne auf Naxos*, with Maria Jeritza, one of Strauss's favourite sopranos, as the faithful Ariadne and Margarethe Siems as her antithesis, the promiscuous Zerbinetta

play-cum-opera is a piece of iconoclasm worthy of Till Eulenspiegel in which nothing is either sacred or safe. Every musical *monstre sacré* – Strauss includes himself in the list – is pulled off his plinth and relentlessly subverted, and the sense of anachronism present in *Rosenkavalier* becomes almost giddy with allusion. Musical history turns gastronomic and is transformed into background entertainment for dinner as Jourdain entertains his guests. The Coronation March from Meyerbeer's *Le Prophète* leads the assembled company to table. They eat the sheep from *Don Quixote* and gorge on salmon to Wagner's Rhinemaidens trio, while a dish of song thrushes is accompanied by the Duke's jaunty aria from Verdi's *Rigoletto*. Jourdain's demand that the evening's entertainment shall consist of both the Composer's *opera seria* and the *commedia dell'arte* productions played simultaneously, leads to Mozart being rewritten as Wagner and Wagner as Mozart.

Accompanied by an eighteenth-century orchestra of thirty-seven players, Ariadne herself inverts the Wagnerian dramaturgy. In the *Ring*, the god Wotan abandons Brünnhilde to sleep on a rock from which she will be awakened by a hero (Siegfried). Ariadne, a similarly dramatic soprano, has been dumped by the less than heroic Theseus on her desert island – from which she will be rescued by the god Bacchus, or Dionysus to give him his Greek name. This character brings to mind the irrational god of Nietzsche's aesthetic theories. A group of Nietzsche's poems, originally entitled the *Dionysus Dithyrambs* and supposedly addressed by the mythical Ariadne to the god who claims her, were inserted into *Also sprach Zarathustra*, where they are put into the mouth of a character called 'The Magician' (Wagner in disguise). When Strauss's Bacchus arrives, he is a Wagnerian Heldentenor, whose glorious vocalism hides sleazy double entendres. He will transform the cave of her sorrows to one of pleasure, he tells her. She ignores him, for she believes to the end that he will lead her to the kingdom of the dead. (The 'non-comprehension' which Hofmannsthal perceived as existing between Ariadne and Zerbinetta ironically governs Bacchus and Ariadne's relationship as well.) Strauss's music whips up an imposing frenzy, which rings hollow, and Zerbinetta's final intrusion – the later revision of the opera is radically different at this point – pricks its growing pomposity like a bubble. The Wagnerian apparatus may be glorious, but it is also fraudulent. Jourdain, heading the 'on-stage' audience watching the entertainment, facetiously intervenes at one point to say Ariadne is a bore. The play reveals that these mythic creatures are in fact only a prima donna and a tenor prone to backstage tantrums.

Zerbinetta, on the other hand, is exactly the same off-stage as she is on it. She possesses the coloratura voice of Mozart's demonic Queen of the Night from *Die Zauberflöte* or Donizetti's deranged heroine of *Lucia di Lammermoor*. Strauss told Hofmannsthal to listen to both works while he was working on the text. Another operatic tradition is here subverted, for Zerbinetta uses coloratura to express sexual delight rather than vengeful fury or insanity. Her argument, accompanied by shuddering trills and gleefully ascending swoops up to a top F sharp, is essentially feminist, advocating equality in sexual pleasure between men and women, demanding that women play men at their own deceitful game. Significantly, her massive aria is cast in the rondo form that Strauss used to characterize that other comic iconoclast, Till Eulenspiegel. Though Hofmannsthal professed to dislike Zerbinetta, he and Strauss allow her to close the opera-within-the-play before giving the last word to Jourdain, who remains irrepressibly self-assured, despite the fact that his plans to seduce Dorimène have failed and his world is now crumbling round him.

Allowing song to collide with and be debased by speech has often been held against the original version of *Ariadne auf Naxos*, which is usually referred to as an unwieldy hybrid. Yet Strauss was not the only composer exploring the relationship between speech and song at the time. Schoenberg's *Pierrot Lunaire*, in which a cabaret singer speaks the text at specifically notated pitches, had its première in the same year. *Pierrot* is widely regarded as a modernist experiment, while *Ariadne* is held up as an example of Strauss's slide towards musical reaction. But the argument is specious. Schoenberg was experimenting with tonality as well as vocal style, and *Ariadne* comparably experiments with operatic and theatrical form. The resulting amalgam is in fact as radical as anything written by Schoenberg.

If critical and public incomprehension was one of the initial stumbling blocks to *Ariadne*'s success, the practicalities of mounting the work proved to be another; they still hamper its widespread acceptance. Hiring both theatre and opera companies for a single work remains a financially risky undertaking. The critic Richard

Specht gently suggested that the opera might be separated from the play, and Strauss and Hofmannsthal were soon contemplating revisions. In January 1913, the scene interpolated into the play at Strauss's insistence was being turned by Hofmannsthal into a fully-sung, operatic Prologue in which the initially shadowy figure of the Composer was expanded and developed. When the text finally arrived the following June, however, Strauss was not happy. 'I now cling so obstinately to the original work,' he wrote back. 'The second is no more than makeshift.' A year later, Hofmannsthal saw the original again in Munich and came to the same conclusion. The Prologue to *Ariadne* remained, as yet, unset.

That Hofmannsthal did not continue to press the revision on Strauss may well have been due to his awareness of the strain in their relationship. After completing *Ariadne*, Strauss had half-heartedly begun a tone-poem, *Eine Alpensinfonie* ('An Alpine Symphony'), written for the largest post-Wagnerian forces imaginable, with which he was to tinker for the next four years. Though Hofmannsthal had partly succeeded in pulling him away from Wagner's influence in *Rosenkavalier* and *Ariadne*, as well as subverting Nietzschean philosophy in the Marschallin's submission to the nature of time, influences of both Wagner and Nietzsche remained. At one point the *Alpensinfonie*, inspired by Strauss's love of the Bavarian Alps near Garmisch and by the adolescent experience of being caught in a storm while mountain climbing, nearly mutated into *Zarathustra*'s sequel. Mahler's death had turned Strauss's thoughts back to Nietzsche. 'The death of this aspiring, idealistic, energetic artist is a heavy loss,' he wrote in his diary, in 1911. 'The Jew Mahler could still be uplifted by Christianity. The hero Richard Wagner descended to it again as an old man, under the influence of Schopenhauer. It is absolutely clear to me that the German nation will only find new strength through liberation from Christianity … I will call my Alpine Symphony *The Antichrist*, because in it there is moral purification by means of one's own strength.' *Der Antichrist*, written in 1888, was Nietzsche's most bitter fulmination against Christianity which he perceived as corrupting both Jewish and non-Jewish ideology alike. Strauss's own anti-Semitism, though it occasionally flared, was on the wane thanks largely to the influence of Hofmannsthal, Mahler and a number of other close friends who were Jews, such as the conductor Leo Blech

and the Prague industrialist Emmanuel von Grab (to whom Strauss
had been introduced by Blech while overseeing the Prague première of
Salome in 1907).

Hofmannsthal, however, had grown genuinely alarmed when
Strauss began negotiating for a possible libretto with the right-wing
Italian Decadent Gabriele D'Annunzio, a writer of luridly violent and
at times misogynistic erotica. Their plans came to nothing, but
Hofmannsthal was well aware that there were aspects to Strauss's
genius for which he was not catering. 'The other element in which
you are equally at home, that mastery over the dark side of life –
which I deliberately refuse to nourish – remains nonetheless one of
your most precious gifts,' he wrote in February 1912. He was still
stalling on *Die Frau ohne Schatten.* Diaghilev's Ballets Russes,
meanwhile, were taking Europe by storm. Strauss had shown
sufficient interest in ballet with *Kythere*, and Hofmannsthal, thinking
of the composer of *Elektra*, proposed a 'tragic symphony' on the
subject of Orestes and the Furies as a vehicle for Nijinsky. Strauss was
not interested. But Hofmannsthal persisted with the idea of a ballet,
and together with Kessler began work on another scenario, this time
on the biblical subject of Joseph and Potiphar's wife. The image of the
attempted seduction of a chaste and saintly man by a predatory
woman carried inevitable echoes of *Salome.* The initial sketches were
sent to Diaghilev, and Strauss, to his annoyance, found himself faced
with a fait accompli but, having seen the Ballets Russes in Berlin, he
gradually warmed to the idea.

The dramas of their collaboration on *Ariadne* were soon to repeat
themselves. Though Kessler's name appears on the published score of
Josephslegende, as the new project was called, Hofmannsthal's fondness
for anachronism and symbolism ran riot over the scenario. In place of
an exotic, erotic Orient is a lavish setting based on sixteenth-century
biblical painting and Paolo Veronese's paintings in particular.
Sadomasochistic thrills are, it is true, present in abundance –
Potiphar's Wife goes into erotic convulsions at the thought of Joseph
being tortured with hot coals – but so is a portentous symbolism,
which completely fazed Strauss from the start. 'THIRD DANCE FIGURE
expresses the SEARCHING AND WRESTLING AFTER GOD, mingled with
moments of despair,' a passage from the scenario reads, describing
Joseph's big solo after he is brought to Potiphar's court.

By September 1912 Strauss was struggling. Hofmannsthal, to whom he played some of the sketches in December, hated what he heard and became fractious. 'In every task before us the final criterion can only be sensitivity in the manner of style, and of this I must consider myself guardian and keeper for the two of us,' he fulminated. The themes for Joseph's music, he added, were 'dressed up, dolled up, pastoral, *impossible* for this atmosphere and they put one off fatally'. Strauss kept quiet and plodded on, finally announcing in July 1913 that the revised version of Joseph's offending dance was finished. That spring they went to Italy together and talked about *Die Frau ohne Schatten*. The 'big and laborious job' of *Josephslegende* was not complete until February 1914, by which time the opening scenes of the libretto of *Die Frau ohne Schatten*, sent by Hofmannsthal as a New Year present, were in Strauss's hands. 'Simply wonderful' was his verdict, though he yet again set about asking Hofmannsthal for changes and cuts, while the latter sent yet more letters explaining the work's symbolism. The remainder of the first act arrived in April.

Josephslegende was due to open in Paris in May 1914, with Strauss conducting. As the rickety set of treaties and counter-treaties between the European Empires hardened indissolubly into the political configurations that finally led to war, Strauss arrived in the hostile French capital to oversee the first performance of the ballet he had written for a Russian company at a time when diplomatic relations between Germany and Russia had reached a frosty standstill. The première was less than a success. The choreographer was Mikhail Fokine, who had revolutionized ballet by freeing it from its trappings of Tsarist formality and utilizing movement for narrative and dramatic expression. *Scheherazade* (to Rimsky-Korsakov's Symphonic Suite), *The Firebird* and *Petrushka* (both to scores by Stravinsky) were epoch-making works in twentieth-century cultural history, demanding that ballet be perceived as a form of music-theatre of equal validity with opera. Fokine's choreography for *La Légende de Joseph* (as the ballet was called in French) does not survive, though it is clear from contemporary accounts that in seeking drama he strayed, on this occasion, too far from dance. The role of Potiphar's wife was taken by an actress, Maria Kuznetzova. Nijinsky, sacked by his lover Diaghilev for getting married, did not dance and the young Léonide Massine took his place. Most critics commented that the piece resembled a wordless play. Rolland, who had left Paris to live in Switzerland the year before, returned for the performance and commented in his diary that he thought the designs (by José-Maria Sert and Léon Bakst) were too dominant.

The score was savaged by the critics and remains buried under opprobrium. Rolland passed over it in silence. Specht declared that it should never have been composed. Even Beecham, who conducted the first London performance ten days after the Paris première, thought it 'heavy and plodding'. *Josephslegende* is uneven, but by no means a negligible work, and it should perhaps be seen as an experiment in structure, comparable in scope – if not in achievement – to the first version of *Ariadne auf Naxos*. As with *Ariadne*, its aims are radical, though its methods and intentions are the antithesis of those of Stravinsky in *Le Sacre du printemps* ('The Rite of Spring'), which had received its inflammatory première the year before. Both works represent new departures in dance music, though musical and cultural historians have dubbed *Sacre* revolutionary and seen *Josephslegende* as being anything but.

Stravinsky, composing for Nijinsky as choreographer, sought to return dance to its origins in primal, convulsive rhythm and the enactment of primitive ritual. Strauss followed Fokine's vision of ballet as music-theatre by employing a leitmotif structure to convey the mental processes of the principal characters. Potiphar's Wife's

The chaste Joseph (Rolf Arco) is led before Potiphar's Wife (Edith Kubbe) in a scene from a Berlin production of *Die Josephslegende*. The designs are closely modelled on those of the original production.

brooding ennui is initially conveyed by a heavy chordal theme that hides harmonic irresolution beneath a façade of impressive froideur. When she is sexually aroused by Joseph the theme breaks into a convulsive shuddering before the intervals that make up the dense harmonies are taken up again melodically as she attempts to seduce him. After he has rejected her, the theme converts into a grotesque parody of itself as she entertains sadistic visions of having him tortured.

Joseph is given a whole cluster of themes (mostly from the *Kythere* sketches) that are first heard in his troublesome solo, which in itself forms a self-contained symphonic suite some fifteen minutes in length, inserted into the main body of the work. Strauss's struggles with the character are audibly apparent. Human spirituality, focusing on the eternal rather than the transitory, expresses a series of fixed certainties, inimical to the leitmotif structure. Wagner's characters succeed because they are racked by doubt as their certainties are threatened. Unlike *Salome*'s Jochanaan, whose convictions are the stuff of prurient fanaticism, Joseph remains unthreatened by the sexuality of his seducer. He does not therefore develop psychologically and his music often gives the impression of having nowhere to go.

Once the première was over, Strauss returned briefly to Garmisch, then went to England where he attended the British première of *Josephslegende* in London on 23 June. Tamara Karsavina, Fokine's muse, had taken over the role of Potiphar's wife from Kuznetsova. After one rehearsal, Strauss arrived in her dressing room to suggest a change and began singing snatches of the score and dancing in front of her. Karsavina incorporated his ideas into her performance 'to his satisfaction, I think,' she wrote in her memoirs.

'I am back from London where Joseph was a great success, in spite of the fact that most of the press was angry and even the most sophisticated Englishwomen found the piece indecent,' he wrote to Hofmannsthal from Garmisch on 5 July. He was working on *Die Frau ohne Schatten*, and the first act was well under way. The text of the second had recently arrived. Now aged fifty, Strauss was regarded as Germany's greatest living composer, and accolades poured in. Oxford awarded him an honorary degree of Doctor of Music. In Munich, a street was named after him, and a commemorative plaque graced the façade of the Pschorr house where he was born.

The international political situation was rapidly worsening, although this does not appear to have impinged on Strauss's consciousness at this stage. In the Balkans, the Austro-Hungarian Empire was fracturing into chaos. Archduke Franz Ferdinand, heir to the Austrian throne, had been shot in Sarajevo by a Serbian revolutionary on 28 June. Europe waited in terrified anticipation. 'We're off to the Dolomites next week ... and shall probably spend a few days at S. Martino,' Strauss wrote to Hofmannsthal on 14 July. 'From about 25 July, I shall be back here.' The same day, Austria delivered its ultimatum against Serbia. The Strausses went on holiday. Coming back over the Brenner pass, their journey was blocked by Austrian troop transports. On 28 July, Austria declared war on Serbia and the bombardment of Belgrade began.

Hofmannsthal, who had served in the Austrian army in 1895, was still on the reserve list and was called up. On 31 July, as Austria announced general mobilization and Britain decreed it would declare war on Germany if Wilhelm II's troops moved through Belgium to attack France, Strauss sent a panic-stricken letter to Hofmannsthal's wife, begging for the address of Hugo's barracks. 'I am absolutely convinced,' he wrote, 'that there will be no world war, that the little altercation with Serbia will soon be over, and that I will receive the third act of my *Frau ohne Schatten*.' Two days later, Germany demanded free passage for its troops across Belgium. Belgium refused and on 4 August, the German army swept over the border. Cross-party divisions in the Reichstag were temporarily forgotten as left and right, in a sudden surge of patriotism, united behind the German flag. Britain opened hostilities. The Great War had begun.

4

A dead German soldier
outside his dug-out,
Beaumont-Hamel, 1916

*This great epoch serves merely as a pretext for
people to bring their mediocre products into the
open, who seize the opportunity to decry real
artists as hollow aesthetes and bad patriots,
who forget that I wrote my* 'Heldenleben', *the*
'Bardengesang', *battlesongs and military
marches in peacetime, but am now, face to face
with the present events, keeping a respectful
silence.*

Strauss to Hofmannsthal,
February 1915

War 1914–18

'Completed August 20th, 1914,' Strauss wrote on the manuscript of
Act I of *Die Frau ohne Schatten*, 'on the day of the victory of Saarburg.
Hail to our excellent and courageous troops, hail to our German
fatherland.' Strauss, like the rest of Germany, looked forward to a
German victory. 'Hugo has the damned duty not to die for the
fatherland before I get the third act, which, I hope, will earn him
more than a fine obituary in the Neue Freie Presse,' he wrote to Gerty
von Hofmannsthal, Hugo's wife, on 22 August. 'But joking aside –
these are great and glorious times … One feels exalted, knowing that
this land and this people stand at the beginning of a great
development, that they must and will assume the leadership of
Europe.' Less than a week later, the Russian army on the eastern front
collapsed before the German military machine.

Yet despite the jingoism, he was uncertain and depressed. The full
impact of the war had only just dawned on him. *Josephslegende* had
been the last major international première at a time of deepening
international crisis. The bulk of his money, tied up in England at the
suggestion of the financier Edgar Speyer, was, he now learnt,
confiscated by the British government. A projected performance of
Don Juan in London on 15 August was cancelled and Wagner's music
was removed from British repertoires. No one was particularly
interested in culture or in any diplomatic, humanitarian or pacifist
possibilities it might present. Royal subsidies were being diverted into
the war effort. Strauss's position of eminence as the German-speaking
world's leading composer-conductor, unchallenged since Mahler's
death, was being undermined as the system in which he had thrived
was gradually being dismantled. 'How are the artists treated?' he
grumbled. 'The Kaiser reduces the salaries at the Court Theatre, the
Duchess of Meiningen turns her orchestra into the street, Reinhardt
stages Shakespeare, the Frankfurt Theatre performs *Carmen*, *Mignon*
and *The Tales of Hoffmann* – who will ever understand this German

German soldiers leave Berlin for the front in the winter of 1914.

nation, this mixture of mediocrity and genius, of heroism and obsequiousness?'

He was pressurized to put his name to a manifesto of German intellectuals, defending both government and army against all criticism. Reinhardt, Hauptmann, Humperdinck, Weingartner and Siegfried Wagner had all given their signatures. Strauss refused. 'He said,' Rolland noted in his diary in October 1914, having read a report in the Budapest *Pester Lloyd*, 'that he would joyfully send back his title of doctor *honoris causa* of Oxford University if, in exchange, a British dreadnought could be handed over or sunk; but declarations about things concerning war and politics were not fitting for an artist, who must give his attention to his creations and to his work.' Later that year Rolland published his essay *Au-dessus de la mêlée* ('Above the Mêlée'), a last-ditch plea for peace, and a desperate affirmation of universal human brotherhood. The French and British branded him a coward.

Hofmannsthal, meanwhile, had been given a job as a correspondent with the Austrian War Office and was, much to Strauss's relief, away from immediate danger. Yet his duties kept him from writing and it was not until January 1915 that he was able to make any progress at all on the final act of *Die Frau ohne Schatten*. He kept it quiet that he had been suffering from severe depression; he was both anxious for Austria's future and feared the demise of European culture. The Strausses only learned of his true mental state from a mutual friend, Grete Wiesenthal, whom they met in Berlin where they had spent Christmas. 'Shouldn't we hold fast to the hope that the German Kulturland would serve Austria and lead it towards a new, more beautiful future?' Strauss wrote to Hofmannsthal on 15 January. 'Would it not be better,' he added, 'to see you involved with the eternal values of culture … and handing over the fight with everything transitory to others.'

He was working on the orchestration of the *Alpensinfonie*. Its original link with Nietzsche's *Antichrist* had evaporated during the course of composition. A Zarathustran struggle between nature and human aspiration remains – albeit in a watered-down form – in its depiction of the climbing expedition, though the work's emphasis lies less on the actual climb than on the various phenomena encountered along the way. What makes the work so fascinating is the wealth of allusion contained in the musical pictures and the symbolic use to which it is put.

The theme representing the mountain is heard at the outset, a series of fixed, brass chords which bring to mind Wagner's Valhalla. Its certainty is undercut, however, by an equally dense string dissonance consisting of every note of the B flat minor scale. The sun gradually rises and the mountaineers begin their ascent to a marching theme which strongly resembles the Nocturne from Mahler's Seventh Symphony. The link with Mahler, whose death was one of the work's triggers, is maintained throughout. Strauss's climbers are in effect himself and Mahler clambering up the whole Romantic edifice, at the centre of which Wagner is seen as an immovable mass. Wagner, as Strauss told Stefan Zweig many years later, 'was so gigantic a peak that no one could rise higher'.

The climbers enter a forest and encounter a hunt – and twelve 'off-stage' horns jubilantly peer back through the hunts in *Tristan* and *Tannhäuser* to the Trio from Beethoven's 'Eroica'. Birdsong and the sounds of a shepherd's pipe are Mahlerian throughout. The cow bells of Mahler's Sixth Symphony are drafted in and given programmatic

Strauss photographed outside his villa in Garmisch; the landscape which inspired *Eine Alpensinfonie* can be seen in the background.

significance. When the peak is finally reached, the opening theme of *Zarathustra* is hurled out, rhythmically altered (and in a different key), to be immediately followed by a meandering oboe theme which carries echoes of Mahler's Second, 'Resurrection' Symphony, before the theme associated with the rising sun blares out in all its glory.

Yet mastery of the Wagnerian edifice proves brief. The climbers are driven down by a cataclysmic storm in which each of the work's major themes is twisted out of recognition. The symphony ends with an extraordinary elegy, entitled *Ausklang*. The word's significance is ambiguous; it means 'final' or 'closing chorus', though it also carries the sense of a 'dying out of sound'. The mountain's brass theme is heard one last time before the sound drains away and the work sinks to silence, as if saying farewell. Significantly, this was Strauss's last tone-poem and the last work to which he gave the title 'Symphony'. Its première took place in Berlin on 28 October 1915. Strauss conducted, and the orchestra was the visiting Dresden Hofkapelle. No one took much notice.

By this time, he had resumed work on *Die Frau ohne Schatten*. Hofmannsthal had finally delivered the missing third act the previous April. 'Magnificent,' Strauss remarked, though he added that he considered the text too sketchy. He felt it was insufficiently lyrical, and asked for more poetry. Progress, however, was intermittent. Hofmannsthal was still plagued with war work and grieving for his terminally ill father who was to die within months. His response to Strauss's requests was slow. The text for the duet between the dyer Barak and his wife that opens Act III arrived piecemeal during June. In July, Strauss announced that he had finished the monologue for the Empress's Nurse in the second scene. By September only thirty-five minutes of music from the third act (just over half of it) was complete. By the end of the year, things had ground to a halt yet again.

He was also becoming preoccupied with his son. Franz, now seventeen, had become a fierce patriot and was anxious to join up. But much to his deep disappointment, though to his father's relief, Franz, coddled and sickly, was refused entry into the army on the grounds of health. 'It is a quite unexpected stroke of luck for you,' Strauss wrote to him on 22 November 1915, 'and for us that as a consequence of your slow physical development you will be spared from risking life and limb in this dreadful war.' Franz, however, persisted in his militarism and in 1918 he was declared 'fit only for limited service at home stations', and placed on a reserve list. He was never called.

Strauss was becoming restless. *Die Frau ohne Schatten* was still on hold. His attention wandered back to *Ariadne* and to the Prologue that Hofmannsthal had provided in 1913, in which the central figure is the young Composer whose art is threatened and compromised by external events. In January 1916 he met Hofmannsthal in Berlin. They went to a performance of the original version then on, with Reinhardt, to a club where they discussed the possible revision. They decided to go ahead immediately and Strauss flung himself into the project with enthusiasm. The initial sketches were ready by May. The new section, the Prologue, together with a substantial revision of the opera itself, was finished seven weeks later. Leo Blech suggested to Strauss that he might consider casting a soprano or mezzo-soprano in the role of the Composer after the fashion of Octavian in

Rosenkavalier, an idea he accepted with alacrity. Hofmannsthal was soon fulminating that Strauss's 'theatrical opportunism' was leading him astray. 'To prettify this particular character, which is to have an aura of "spirituality" and "greatness" about it … strikes me as, forgive my plain speaking, odious … if only I were able to bring home to you completely the essence, the spiritual meaning, of these characters.' Strauss, fed up with 'essence' and 'spiritual meaning', held firm and Hofmannsthal backed down. When he finally heard the score he confessed to finding it 'enchanting'.

The première took place on 4 October 1916 in Vienna. The conductor was Franz Schalk, a former assistant of Mahler's. Selma Kurz sang Zerbinetta and Jeritza repeated the title role. During rehearsals, the soprano cast as the Composer, Marie Gutheil-Schoder, was taken ill. Her understudy was the young Lotte Lehmann, who was kept on in the role at Strauss's insistence, even when Gutheil-Schoder had recovered. It was the first success in what proved to be one of the most remarkable operatic careers of the century, and she joined Jeritza on Strauss's list of muses.

If the revised *Ariadne* made Lehmann a star, it did little for Strauss's fortunes, and the second version initially met with the same indifference as the first. The work must have seemed incongruous. The German economy was a disaster, crops had failed and the country was bracing itself for famine. Public and political opinion began to split and polarize with the left favouring peace and reconciliation and the right-wing nationalists making strident demands for total mobilization of the populace in defence of the fatherland. A new artistic avant garde began to form at this time, its sentiments embittered by atrocity. Painters such as Max Beckmann and composers like Paul Hindemith were developing a fierce and open political engagement as a result of their experience of the horror of active service. Few cared about what Strauss was doing in Vienna. The revised *Ariadne* had to wait nearly half a century to take its place in the mainstream repertory, of which it now forms an integral part, though the continued absence of the original is a matter for considerable regret.

The second version may be seen as a response to outward circumstances. Comparison of the two versions reveals a subtle, though marked, shift in emphasis. In the original musical tradition is

Ariadne with her attendant nymphs in the revised version of *Ariadne auf Naxos*, at Salzburg in 1964. The eighteenth-century chandeliers of Ita Maximanova's sets strongly convey the sense that this is an 'opera within an opera'.

held up to withering scorn as both Zerbinetta and Jourdain make fun of the Composer's work. The second version, however, puts musical tradition back on its plinth as the 'holy art' which the Composer exalts to one of Strauss's most ecstatic outpourings of melody – significantly in the 'Eroica' or *Heldenleben* key of E flat – and is consequently held up as an eternal constant in the face of temporal chaos.

Several important changes to the subsequent 'opera' reinforce the shift. The cat-calling on-stage audience has been abandoned and Zerbinetta's role has undergone substantial alteration. Her rondo, transposed down a tone, is now shorn of the improvisatory cadenza with which it originally ended. Her second aria, mockingly praising the arrival of Bacchus, is cut altogether and a further change is introduced at the very end. Strauss originally gave the last vocal word to Zerbinetta and her disruptive Harlequinade, before ending with the theme associated with Jourdain. In version two, Zerbinetta only makes a brief appearance during the final love duet, into which her voice weaves its way elegantly, before Strauss brings the work to a close with a mighty orchestral peroration. The Composer's opera, interrupted and unfinished in 1912, is completed despite disruptions in 1916. The 'holy art' of music has survived the machinations of those who would destroy it.

Zerbinetta's character undergoes a similar process of change in the new Prologue. The other characters comment that she remains the same person off-stage as on, yet Zerbinetta, faced with the Composer, who is sexually drawn to her, briefly reveals her inner loneliness behind the bravura façade. She is looking for one man to whom she can be faithful, she tells him. Strauss's music, seductively tender, leaves us in no doubt that she is sincere. Her function as the spirit of misrule and individualism is consequently undermined.

The compositional style of the Prologue itself follows naturally out of *Rosenkavalier*. Recitative and aria flow into one another imperceptibly. Fragments of exquisite melody arise and then are tantalizingly whisked away from the listener. The orchestration is supple and translucent. Although the subsequent 'opera' weakens the impact of the 1912 original, the Prologue remains one of Strauss's greatest creations. During its course, the Composer, usually at moments of crisis, hears fragmentary tunes inside his head and mournfully regrets that there is no longer time to incorporate them in his opera. They derive from the jettisoned incidental music from *Der Bürger als Edelmann*, though this, too, was soon to be resuscitated. Having agreed that the opera should be separated from the play, Hofmannsthal then mooted the resurrection of Molière with an expansion of the original incidental music and Strauss grudgingly complied. Reinhardt was once more drafted in to direct and *Der Bürger als Edelmann*, with the original balletic interlude restored, opened at the Deutsches Theater in Berlin in April 1918. It was a resounding flop and was withdrawn before the end of its projected two-month run. Undeterred, Hofmannsthal thought of turning *Bürger* into an opera. 'I would suggest that we stop doctoring it,' was Strauss's response, and that was the end of it as far as Hofmannsthal was concerned, though Strauss arranged a concert suite of the incidental music which was first performed in Salzburg in 1920. Thereafter in his correspondence with Hofmannsthal, Strauss referred to the project as 'your beloved *Ariadne*'. It was Hofmannsthal's favourite among their collaborative works and he fondly called it 'a hapless child'. Before long, Strauss would be using similar language to describe *Die Frau ohne Schatten*.

Strauss found the resumption of work on his epic difficult. He and Hofmannsthal were arguing again. After his return to fluid, bittersweet comedy in the Prologue to *Ariadne II*, he was struggling to pull Hofmannsthal away from the world of heavy-handed symbolism. Early in 1916 he told Hofmannsthal that for their next subject he wanted 'either an entirely modern, absolutely realistic domestic and character comedy ... or some amusing piece of love and intrigue ... Say a diplomatic love intrigue in the setting of the Vienna Congress.' Hofmannsthal was dismissive. 'The things you propose are to my taste truly horrid,' he retorted, 'and might put one off becoming a librettist for the rest of one's life.'

Strauss had other ideas. 'I have a definite talent for operetta,' he wrote back. 'After all I'm the only composer nowadays with some real humour and a sense of fun and a marked gift for parody. Indeed, I feel downright called upon to be the Offenbach of the twentieth century, and you will and must be my poet.' His letter provoked a response of utter fury from Hofmannsthal. Strauss had swamped his precious text for *Rosenkavalier* in music that was too heavy. Offenbach, he raged, would never have allowed his choruses to be 'rattled off in burlesque fashion' as Strauss had done. Having dashed off his reply, he thought twice and did not send it.

Strauss, still hankering after change, plodded on with *Frau*, finally completing it in June 1917. Both he and Hofmannsthal were well aware that an opera of such complexity and length (an uncut performance runs to nearly five hours including intervals) would remain unperformed until after the war. Strauss's attitude to the work was ambivalent. He called it his 'child of sorrow' and in later life referred to it as 'my greatest opera', but though it contains some remarkable music and certain sections represent perhaps his finest achievement in orchestral sonority, his initial worries about a lack of red-bloodedness hold true. The libretto remains daunting and abstruse and there are moments in the score, notably in the problematic third act, where his inspiration dips.

Die Frau ohne Schatten, Hofmannsthal told Strauss, 'would be related to *Die Zauberflöte* as *Der Rosenkavalier* is to *Figaro*.' Mozart's six principal characters each consequently find their equivalent in

Hofmannsthal's complex synthesis of symbols. Tamino and Pamina become the human Emperor and his spirit Empress. Papagena and Papageno mutate into the figures of the dyer Barak and his unnamed, shrewish Wife. Mozart's Queen of the Night, initially presented sympathetically but then revealed as a monster, finds her counterpart in the sinister figure of the Empress's Nurse. Sarastro is turned into the unseen deity Keikobad, the Empress's father, who is initially stern but gradually shown to be manipulating the action for the sake of the characters' wellbeing.

Hofmannsthal's handling of these six central figures brings to the fore a number of conservative attitudes which lurk behind his previous librettos but which are now given prominence. Erotic though it is, *Rosenkavalier* preserves the status quo of moral convention in that two of the three members of the central triangle, Octavian and Sophie, move towards marriage while the mistress, the Marschallin, is effectively expelled. In *Die Frau ohne Schatten*, moral conservatism completely dominates, and woven into the text is a critique of both Freudian sexual attitudes and the Nietzschean philosophy of individualism.

In his *Three Essays on the Theory of Sexuality* Freud argued that desire is independent of both aim and object and that its goal is pleasure. Hofmannsthal posits an opposing view: sexuality is only valid when allied to the capacity for procreation, and the moral imperative of humanity lies in its duty to reproduce. His two central couples are childless and their state is treated throughout, worryingly, as an emblem of human deficiency. The Empress's failure to become pregnant, despite nights of passionate sex, is seen as threatening to rob her husband of his humanity; after a year, he must be turned to stone unless she acquires the shadow which indicates potential motherhood. The altruistic Barak's marriage is similarly sterile because his wife (the character based on Pauline) treats him with contempt for his lack of self-assertion. The Empress's trial set for her by Keikobad, her unseen father, consists of overcoming the temptation to destroy the human couple for the sake of her own personal fulfilment: she is given the opportunity to buy Barak's Wife's shadow, but she gradually becomes aware that the price – the complete collapse of the dyer's marriage – is too high. Barak's Wife similarly has to resist the allure of the phantom (and hence fraudulent) figures who offer purely sexual gratification.

Behind this lies a complex metaphysical structure. Keikobad's pervasive influence hints at the presence of an externally imposed destiny. Humanity is portrayed as having what Hofmannsthal called a *Präexistenz* (pre-existence): the two couples' Unborn Children, potentially to be sacrificed, are portrayed as capable of psychic contact with their future parents, whose destiny they can influence. The libretto also overturns one of Nietzsche's key images. Nietzsche saw man as a rope over an abyss leading to the *Übermensch*. At the end of Act I, the watchmen of the opera's unnamed city call on 'the husbands and wives who make love in one another's arms' to remind them that they are 'the bridge over the abyss across which the dead return to life'.

On Strauss's side, *Die Frau ohne Schatten* ushers in a similar element of conservatism, a retreat towards a less liberal view of sexuality. With the exception of *Daphne* and *Capriccio*, Strauss's operas after *Frau* bolster the institutions of marriage and the family against threatening forces within and without. A certain ambivalence in *Frau* remains, however, evinced by the fact that the Empress, the key character, is musically more interesting when still a spirit than when she acquires the humanity she seeks. As Keikobad's daughter she once possessed the ability to change her shape at will – into a bird, as she nostalgically recalls, or a gazelle, in which form the Emperor hunted her down. Strauss uses the images of her previous incarnations to create a character portrait of great subtlety. If you look at the score, her vocal line appears to refuse to anchor itself to the stave, frequently swooping above it or below it, effectively detaching the character from the earth. Birdsong ripples through her voice the moment she appears. In her acquisition of a shadow and the humanity that goes with it, she also acquires musical homogeneity and becomes just another soprano in the static final ensemble rather than a unique enchanted being.

Strauss let himself be led by Hofmannsthal's ideas of what the music should sound like, though he did not closely follow his librettist's instructions. Hofmannsthal wanted 'heroic recitative' for the spirit world and 'real conversation such as only the Master of *Rosenkavalier* can compose' for the humans. Mankind, however, is introduced with dense, clangorous textures reminiscent of *Elektra*, whose vocal successor Barak's Wife unquestionably is. If the Empress's music hovers above the stave, hers is anchored to it as if earthbound, often sinking below it, though when she is tempted by the Nurse with erotic visions, her voice soars into the Empress's stratospheres.

As the two worlds interact, Strauss's orchestral and harmonic palettes become richly subtle. Keikobad is omnipresent. His motif is hammered out by the lower brass in the opera's opening bars then constantly shifts shape, anchoring both worlds together. The clamour associated with humanity gradually lightens to take on the richness of the spirit world's orchestration as dignity is revealed behind its façade of apparent squalor. The Nurse, a malign diplomat between the two worlds, is tracked by groups of solo instruments that frequently provide a point of contact between them. Her motives – utter contempt for mankind and terror at the supernatural – belie her apparent self-control. Her final rejection by the spirit world provokes from Strauss the most extreme bitonal dissonances in his output, proof that he could progress beyond the harmonic language of *Elektra* if he wanted to. Only the ending, where Strauss's struggles become

Adolf Mahnke's orientalist design for the 1939 Dresden production of *Die Frau ohne Schatten*. Middle-Eastern folk tales were one of the sources of Hofmannsthal's heavily symbolic parable of marriage and procreation.

audible, seriously disappoints. The moment the Empress has acquired her shadow, inspiration drains from the score. The impression one takes away from the opera's last twenty minutes is of overwhelming bombast, indicating that Strauss felt he had come to some sort of dead end.

By the time *Frau* was finished, the libretto of his next opera, which Strauss wrote himself, was complete; it was, in effect, the domestic drama for which he had pestered Hofmannsthal and which the latter had failed to provide – though he had a hand in its genesis. In 1916, while dismissing Strauss's proposals as 'truly horrid', Hofmannsthal had suggested Hermann Bahr as a suitable author for the new text. Bahr, a playwright of considerable skill, is now best known as the critic who in 1914 coined the term 'Expressionism' to describe the avant-garde art movement which included such painters as Erich Heckel, Wassily Kandinsky and, later, Oskar Kokoschka. Bahr's wife, Anna Mildenburg, one of the great mezzo-sopranos of her day, had sung Klytemnestra in both Vienna and London.

When Strauss and Bahr met in Salzburg in August 1916, the subject Strauss proposed was a marital comedy, effectively a pendant to *Frau* depicting the Mieze Mücke episode which had threatened his own marriage fourteen years earlier. When he found the first draft unsatisfactory, Bahr asked him for suggestions for the dialogue and was so impressed with the results that he suggested Strauss go ahead and write the libretto himself. The finished product, according to Strauss's memoirs, earned Reinhardt's comment that he could 'produce it as a play without altering a line.' The original title, *Das eheliche Glück* ('Wedded Bliss'), was eventually changed to *Intermezzo*, an eighteenth-century term signifying a comic interlude between the acts of a serious opera, though for Strauss it had the added meaning of a temporary break in his collaboration with Hofmannsthal, with whom he hoped to resume work soon. In the end, he worked on *Intermezzo* for several years and did not complete it until 1923.

In January 1917 he went to Switzerland to conduct *Ariadne* in Berne. Through Hans Huber, director of the Basle Conservatoire, he tried to contact Rolland – still under a cloud of public disapproval and now living in Geneva – in order to send him an invitation to one of his performances. But Rolland, who was well aware of what a public encounter between Germany's most famous composer and a disgraced French pacifist might do to the reputations of both, would only agree to meet Strauss in private. Undeterred, Strauss wrote to Rolland direct, repeated his invitation, adding that they might have supper 'in some quiet spot'. Rolland wrote back saying that a serious bout of flu prevented him from making the journey. Strauss did not answer his letter until he returned to Garmisch in mid February, but his reply is telling. 'It is precisely we artists,' he wrote, 'who should freely keep our gaze fixed on all that is beautiful and noble, and who should put ourselves at the service of truth which … must after all, one day emerge from the thick tissue of lies and of falsehoods with which the world in delirium seems to be enveloped at the present time.'

Strauss's letter clearly shows that he, like Hofmannsthal, was anxious for the future of European culture during these troubled times, and for the international community of artists that formed its basis. This led to both men becoming involved with the founding of the annual Salzburg Festival, which eventually became a focal point of cultural preservation both before and after the Second World War. Mozart's birthplace had been hosting intermittent festivals as early as 1877, though nothing had been permanently established. The prime mover behind the project was Max Reinhardt who, in 1917, sent a proposal to the Austrian government. In 1918 an 'artistic advisory committee' was formed consisting of Strauss, Reinhardt and Franz Schalk, joined the following year by Roller and Hofmannsthal, whose enthusiasm was boundless and whose artistic influence was soon to prove dominant.

That year Strauss turned to the composition of lieder for the first time in twelve years. At the time he was involved in a complex legal wrangle with one of his publishers, the Berlin publishing house of Bote & Bock, which published both the *Sinfonia Domestica* and his last completed set of songs. A clause in his contract with them stipulated that he submit a second group of six songs. Fulfilling this now entailed some embarrassment, as Strauss had been trying different firms, and had reached a mutual understanding with Adolf Fürstner.

His return to lieder stemmed not from publishers' demands, however, but from his attraction to another singer, Elisabeth Schumann, who became, along with Jeritza and Lehmann, one of his soprano muses. Strauss worked with her regularly as an accompanist and the two were close friends; there were persistent rumours of an

affair between them, but no proof of this exists. But if he was not
infatuated with Schumann herself, Strauss was certainly infatuated
with her voice and, early in 1918, he set six poems by Clemens
Brentano with Schumann in mind.

Bote & Bock now began to exert pressure, but Strauss was
unwilling to let them have the *Brentano Lieder* and set about looking
for a suitable alternative. In 1913 Alfred Kerr, one of the critics who
had savaged *Ariadne*, had sent him a book of his own poems, *Die
Harfe* ('The Harp'). Strauss, familiar with Kerr's lacerating wit, asked
him for some scurrilous verses on the music publishing trade. Kerr
was happy to oblige and in March 1918 Strauss received the text of
Krämerspiegel ('The Tradesman's Mirror'), a satire of unwonted
viciousness in which the leading German publishing houses (with the
exception of Fürstner) were each lampooned in their turn by means of
puns on their names. Strauss's settings consist of little more than a
series of entertaining vignettes, but one song stands out, the eighth,
which is ushered in with an exquisite piano nocturne reminiscent of
Schumann. Strauss later purloined it to form the great 'moonlight
interlude' from *Capriccio*.

Predictably, Bote & Bock refused to publish the set and threatened
legal proceedings. Strauss now had no choice but to comply with their
wishes, and dashed off the six Op. 67 songs to satisfy them; they
include the three *Ophelia Lieder*, based on *Hamlet*, which are his last
musical depiction of mental instability and amongst his finest. The
vocal line meanders over constantly unresolving discords, pausing
occasionally before swooping into shrill, screeching laughter or singing
snatches of manic, folksy waltzes. Bote & Bock withdrew their lawsuit
and Fürstner published the *Brentano Lieder. Krämerspiegel* did not
appear in print until Paul Cassirer's art publishing house, famous for
its championship of the Expressionists, brought out an illustrated
edition in 1921.

Even more significant than Strauss's return to lieder composition
was his contemplation of a career move that would have long-standing
consequences. In 1918, he went to Vienna to conduct *Elektra, Ariadne*
and *Rosenkavalier* at the Court Opera. The Intendant, Hans Gregor,
was due to retire and suggested Strauss might like to quit Berlin and
his guest conductorship in favour of the Austrian capital. Strauss,
whose relationship with the Berlin Opera had been under strain for

some time, seized the chance. On 23 May, he wrote to
Hofmannsthal: 'I have pursued in my mind many recollections of my
pleasant stay in Vienna, and in particular have discussed with my
wife the possibility that, in the event of Gregor's departure, I might
share in a possible Schalk directorship, perhaps as co-director, in such
a way that I would spend two or three winter months in Vienna over
a number of years.'

Hofmannsthal pondered carefully before responding and did not
broach the subject until the following August. His letter was frank.
Fifteen years ago, he argued, Strauss would have been 'the ideal person
to bring about the urgently needed renaissance of the Vienna Opera,
but I don't believe you are that today ... I believe, when it comes to
engaging artists, making decisions, friends etc., in short in handling
the policy of the theatre, the advantage to your own works would be
uppermost in your mind and not the advantage of the institution.'
Strauss took this broadside in his stride, arguing that he had always
wanted 'the de facto supreme artistic control of a big Court Opera
House on the artistic side'; he was really only a summer composer; he
could infuse the repertoire with new life; besides, Pauline had always
wanted to live in Vienna. By September Hofmannsthal had come
round and was discussing 'our ideas' with the new Intendant, Leopold
von Andrien-Werburg. When Schalk was officially appointed Director
on 10 November (two days before the abdication of the Austrian
Emperor), he knew he would eventually be sharing the burden with
Strauss, even though the latter's appointment was kept secret for
a while.

As the war drew to its close, Germany's internal political situation
was hurtling towards a crisis. The polarization between right and left
had become extreme, with the nationalists forming the
Vaterlandspartei (Fatherland Party) and jingoistically demanding that
power pass into the hands of the viciously autocratic General
Ludendorff. By January 1918 unrest had spread to the cities. The
country's main industrial plants were placed under military control
and a state of siege was proclaimed in Berlin.

On 8 August, the war machine finally collapsed and defeat was
now inevitable. The Bismarckian constitution was rapidly dismantled.
On 28 October, the balance of power passed from the Kaiser to the
Reichstag and Germany, for less than two weeks in its history, became

World War I had a
profound effect on Hugo
von Hofmannsthal, for
whom it represented the
demise of European
civilization. The theme of
cultural renewal in times of
crisis dominates his later
librettos for Strauss.

a constitutional monarchy. On 8 November, the Bavarian socialists proclaimed a Republic. The rest of the country followed suit and on 9 November, Wilhelm was forced to abdicate. The Armistice was signed two days later.

'My best beloved!' Strauss wrote to Pauline in early November from Coburg where he was conducting. 'The war is over, definitely over! But what is to come may be worse … I am still holding my head high in the hope that Germany is too 'diligent' to fall into such a complete decline … Bismarck's dream has suffered a rude awakening at all events, and 200 years of Prussiandom are at an end. Let's hope that it will be replaced by better times. I don't believe that it will … We will have to think over everything calmly, although I wouldn't know what else to do, even now, other than carry on as usual for as long as possible, according to plan, for as long as theatres and concerts keep going and pay fees. If you love me then there isn't much the world can do to harm us.'

Strauss playing skat, his
favourite card game, which
he depicted in his 1924
opera *Intermezzo*. His
partners are the conductor
Hans Knappertbusch (left)
and his old friend Eugen
Papst (right).

I cannot bear the tragedy of the present time.

Strauss to Rolland, 1924

Weimar 1919–33

On 19 January 1919 Germany went to the polls. The socialists were victorious, though they failed to gain an overall majority. Friedrich Ebert was elected president on 10 February, and the Weimar Republic, named after Goethe's city out of a belief in German humanism, came into being. Its democracy was fragile from the outset. Clause 48 of the constitution allowed the president the right to suspend civil liberties when he saw fit and to take whatever steps deemed necessary to restore law and order. The Republic's parliamentary history consisted of a series of rickety coalitions and counter-coalitions that led to repeated stalemates, new elections, new governments and a constantly shifting balance of power.

The government was further weakened by its failure to reform the judiciary, the civil service and the army's officer corps, where the imperial spirit still reigned and where resentment at Germany's defeat festered like an untreated wound. These relics of the old regime, anxious for their survival, favoured the rise of the political right and the nationalists. Communism was widely perceived as constituting the most dangerous political threat to the newly formed Republic, a sentiment which the Nazi Party, founded in 1919, knew how to exploit right up to the Republic's tragic end. Though extremists at both ends of the political spectrum instigated violence, the fear of 'international Bolshevism', combined with a biased judiciary, ensured that the political left was isolated, while the right gained in strength. The Treaty of Versailles and the Allies' imposition of massive war guilt payments destroyed public morale, while the polarity between left and right gradually hardened into totalitarian stridency. The Republic, begun amid scenes of violence, ended in the worst nightmare humanity has ever known. In between came the great, doomed flowering of German modernism and sexual liberalism which, retrospectively, made the Weimar Republic an icon of progressive culture. Strauss, the former servant of the old regime, struggled to steer a course through both the chaos and the glory.

He attempted to 'carry on as usual', as he had promised Pauline he would, though he was unable to ignore the civil unrest for long. In February 1919 he travelled from Garmisch to Berlin to fulfil a conducting engagement. When he arrived in Munich, the atmosphere was jittery and uncertain. On 21 February Kurt Eisner, leader of the Bavarian Independent Socialists, had been assassinated by a right-wing fanatic. Members of the Leninist Spartacus League were inflamed by the suppression of their abortive January revolution in Berlin and had taken to the streets. Strauss, unable to leave the station, waited for

Despite the suppression of the 1918-19 revolution, the German Communist Party continued to hold massive rallies in Berlin until the Weimar Republic collapsed in 1933.

'things to happen' as he told Pauline. Nothing did. He reached Berlin in safety, though he found the city in the throes of a massive strike organized by the Communists. Violence broke out, when the Freikorps (Free Corps) – a band of thuggish, right-wing volunteers recruited by the government to both maintain civil order and pacify the army – moved in on the protesters. Over a thousand people were killed, many shot on suspicion of carrying arms. 'I've just come back from the theatre where it should have been *Fidelio* but wasn't as the lights were out,' he wrote to Pauline. 'There was a lot of shooting today, the government troops won at Alexanderplatz and did a thorough cleaning out of the Spartacists.'

The Staatsoper, as the Berlin Court Opera was now renamed, wanted to renew his contract on condition he become a salaried employee. 'So it's all one to me,' he told Pauline, 'whether I conduct or not.' Still fantasizing about writing operetta, he drafted a scenario for a political satire to be called *Revolution*, which he sent to Kerr in the hope he might provide a text. He told Kerr: 'National Assembly, Old Comrades' associations, party politics, while the people starve, a *souteneur* [pimp] as Minister of Education and Culture, a burglar as Minister of War, a murderer as Minister of Justice, could form the background.' Nothing came of it. Satire was becoming the dominant mode of the political left rather than the medium of the 'old guard' which Strauss now represented in the public eye.

The formal announcement in March of his post in Vienna came as little surprise in Berlin, though it caused a scandal in the Austrian capital, which was suffering from the effects of galloping inflation. Strauss was appointed 'artistic supervisor' (as opposed to Schalk's title of 'Head of the Opera House') and was to give his services to the House from December to May each year, for a retainer of 80,000 krone plus 1,200 krone for each performance he conducted. Virtually the entire staff of the Opera House joined forces to produce a petition protesting that the salary was 'too high for an impoverished country like Austria', that Strauss would use the House to promote his own works at the expense of the standard repertory, and that he would interfere with the Vienna Philharmonic's subscription scheme by giving concerts at the Opera. Maria Jeritza and Selma Kurz refused to sign. Schalk attempted to remain aloof, but then decided in Strauss's favour.

Strauss kept his cool, stayed in Garmisch and politely stated that, in the face of such opposition he was prepared to withdraw his offer of the première of *Die Frau ohne Schatten*. This caused the pro-Strauss faction, which consisted of most of the Viennese intelligentsia, to swing into action. An open telegram, signed by Hofmannsthal, Mahler's widow Alma, Alfred Roller, Richard Specht, Stefan Zweig and Arthur Schnitzler among others, was dispatched urging him to reconsider. Specht vociferously castigated the Opera House's management at one of his public lectures, and a performance of *Parsifal* was nearly abandoned when Vienna's opera fanatics in the standing room at the back of the stalls began chanting 'We want Strauss!' That decided the matter. 'So you're going to Vienna? Where the people are so deceitful,' a Berlin acquaintance quipped. 'People are deceitful everywhere,' was Strauss's response, 'but in Vienna they're so pleasant about it.'

Vienna eventually proved to be a far from pleasant experience. The long-awaited première of *Die Frau ohne Schatten* went ahead as planned on 10 October 1919. The critics were harsh and the public indifferent. The libretto was attacked as being deliberately obscure, and Strauss was now perceived as being adrift from his time. The opera's course remained chequered and it was not until Dresden staged a new production in 1927 that *Frau* made any headway (it was only accepted by a wide public after Strauss's death).

By December the Strausses were installed in an apartment on the Mozartplatz and on 20 January the following year, Strauss made his official début conducting *Lohengrin*, the work which Mahler had also chosen for his first performance in 1897. It was, perhaps, an unwise move, as Mahler's years in Vienna were now held up, retrospectively, as the city's 'Golden Age'. The Viennese press, opposed to Mahler in his day, were soon making snide comparisons, usually to Strauss's disfavour. In his first season he also conducted *Fidelio, Tristan, Die Zauberflöte, Ariadne* and *Der Rosenkavalier*. He was partly fulfilling his intentions of overhauling and germanifying the repertoire that he had expressed to Schalk in a letter of December 1918. 'It is not necessary,' he wrote, 'to give *Traviata, Masked Ball, Mignon, Faust* every week. That's why I'm coming to Vienna, to make a new modest try at a repertoire which is lofty and German.' But he was by no means true to this resolve, restoring Puccini to the Vienna repertory after a wartime absence and insisting that *Carmen* be staged as a vehicle for Jeritza.

His attitude to new music was more circumspect. Favouring the tonal post-Romantics, he introduced the reactionary Hans Pfitzner's arch-conservative *Palestrina* into the repertoire (surprisingly, since the jealous Pfitzner loathed him) and championed music by Zemlinsky, Franz Schreker and Korngold. He was suspicious, however, as was Hofmannsthal, of the great flowering of Weimar and Austrian modernism. 'I would also have performed Schoenberg and Krenek,' he later wrote, 'for I do not subscribe to the point of view that the novelties which I perform should be personally pleasing to me.' He and Schoenberg – with Wolzogen as a mutual friend – had briefly been close in Berlin at the turn of the century. In 1902 Strauss (unaware of the rival versions by Debussy and Fauré) had suggested Maeterlinck's *Pelléas et Mélisande* as a suitable subject for the young Austrian. When Schoenberg began to move away from tonality, strain began to enter his relationship with Strauss when the latter, troubled by his music and aware that it might provoke an alarmist reaction on the part of the conservative Berlin public, turned down the Five Orchestral Pieces for performance. In 1911, shortly after Mahler's death, Strauss had been appointed trustee of a foundation set up in Mahler's name to help struggling composers. Alma Mahler suggested Schoenberg as a possible candidate for a grant. Strauss agreed, though he added in his letter that he thought Schoenberg would 'do better to shovel snow than scribble on music paper'. Alma, maliciously, showed the letter to Schoenberg, and the subsequent rift between the two men never healed. 'As for what I may have learned from him in the past, I thank God that I misunderstood it,' was Schoenberg's comment. It was Mahler, not Strauss, who became the hero of the post-war avant garde.

Ernst Krenek, even more than Schoenberg, came to epitomize the progressive spirit of Weimar liberalism by pulling down the barriers between 'serious' and 'popular' culture and introducing jazz elements into his stage works. Hofmannsthal dismissed his masterpiece, the opera *Jonny spielt auf* ('Johnny Strikes Up'), as textually and musically weak. In retrospect his judgement is tragic, given that it was Krenek, more than any other composer, who was regarded by the Nazis as the embodiment of what they termed cultural 'degeneracy'. Strauss similarly failed to see that the modernists were in fact carrying on the tradition of revolutionary individualism that he had explored in his early tone-poems and operas. 'Why do you compose like that?' he also once asked the young Paul Hindemith, offended by the latter's stridency. 'You don't need to – you have talent.' He never conducted works by Hindemith either.

Yet it is much to Strauss's credit that he took no public part in the sinister ideological squabbles that were taking place in the musical press in which hideous rhetoric, eventually drafted into Nazi ideology, was being spouted. In 1919 Pfitzner published *Die neue Ästhetik der musikalischen Impotenz: Ein Verwesungssymptom* ('The New Aesthetic of Musical Impotence: A Symptom of Putrefaction'), a repellent tract denouncing atonality as a manifestation of 'Jewish Bolshevism' which had 'placed the alien madness of destruction and demolition in the German mind'. Despite his abiding concern with the issue of composers' rights, Strauss tried to keep aloof. 'Haven't I the right, after all, to write what music I please?' he told Rolland. 'I want to create joy. I need it.'

The inflationary mess of the Austrian Republic, meanwhile, was beginning to put the Vienna Opera under financial strain. A tour of South America between August and November 1920 briefly bailed the company and was such a success that they were invited to return to Brazil at the government's expense. Strauss's own finances remained parlous, however, and he decided to make a concert tour of the States as an accompanist for Elisabeth Schumann and as a guest conductor with the New York Philharmonic and Philadelphia Orchestras.

He and Schumann, with his son Franz in tow, sailed in October 1921. Though he was now less than a star in Germany and Austria, Strauss had lost none of his glamour as far as America was concerned. As in 1904, the press were waiting and the public both expectant and enthusiastic. In New York, crowds watched the motorcade which took them to a reception at City Hall. 'Strauss drives through New York like a King,' Schumann wrote in her diary. In the following two months, he took part in more than forty concerts, mostly with Schumann, though he also conducted singers from the Metropolitan Opera's roster of stars in performances of orchestral versions of his songs.

The tour was stressful. Schumann noted in her diary how Strauss frequently flew into rages in the morning ('his bad time') and took

them out on Franz. 'By midday his mood is brightening,' she
commented. 'Then he too is sorry for his insensitivity – and in the
evening, he is enchanting.' By the end, he had made $50,000 (about
10,000,000 Marks at the current exchange rate), and had collected
money from orchestra members to distribute to European musicians
affected by the war. The sum involved was comparatively small, which
led to snide remarks in the press.

The following summer, the Salzburg Festival took off in earnest.
The official opening had taken place two years earlier, when
Hofmannsthal's *Jedermann* ('Everyman', an adaptation of the medieval
mystery play) was the sole work performed. In the summer of 1922 the
Vienna Opera moved into the Landestheater for a Mozart season
consisting of *Don Giovanni, Die Entführung aus dem Serail, Figaro*
and, most important of all, *Così fan tutte*, which Strauss had been
championing for so long. Thanks to his efforts and as a result of the
Salzburg performances the opera finally achieved its full recognition
and was soon taken up by every major opera house in Europe. During
the preceding rehearsal months, Strauss discovered another singer in
the form of Rose Pauly, a young Hungarian Jewish soprano who had
made her operatic début as Aida in Hamburg in 1912 at the age of
seventeen. Entrusted with the role of Donna Anna in *Don Giovanni*
(which she had to learn in three days), she nervously visited Strauss in
Garmisch. 'He took kindly to me from the beginning of my career,'
she later remembered, 'and remained a wise and benevolent adviser.'
Her voice was rich and dramatic, and steady as a rock. She was the
first singer successfully to essay the Dyer's wife in *Frau*, and Strauss
regarded her Elektra as definitive.

In Vienna, tension was beginning to flare between Strauss and
Schalk. Strauss's absences were already cause for considerable concern.
His habit of giving singers leave to perform elsewhere (particularly if it
was in one of his own operas) was throwing the casting system into
chaos. Strauss also began to be cavalier about the House's finances out
of the belief that quality of performance was more important than
cash. 'I am here to lose money,' he grandly stated on one occasion
when shown the budget. Such an attitude may have been acceptable
before the war, when the monarchical system of patronage kept
theatre coffers full and Strauss was capable of bypassing imperial dicta,
but now it was firmly frowned upon. The Viennese press had also

moved against him. In addition to being compared unfavourably with Mahler, Strauss was attacked for not championing new works and accused of favouring his own music at the expense of others. Much of this was untrue. His arguments that new music would not be accepted by the notoriously conservative Viennese public cut no ice. And with the exception of *Josephslegende*, allotted nineteen performances after its Vienna première in 1922, his works featured no more frequently in the repertory than they did anywhere else.

The tension finally broke in 1924, a year which marked a turning-point in several areas of Strauss's life. It began well enough with Franz's marriage to Alice von Grab, the daughter of Strauss's Jewish friend Emmanuel, to whom he had been close – they shared a passion for skat – since their first meeting in Prague in 1907. Strauss was a regular guest in Grab's country house and had taken his family there for a holiday in the summer of 1919 during which Franz met Alice, who was then fifteen. In 1923, while Strauss was on his second tour of Brazil with the Vienna Opera, the pair announced their engagement. They were married in Vienna on 15 January 1924. Strauss wrote a

Franz Strauss with his wife Alice, née von Grab. Alice was devoted to her father-in-law and after his death founded the Strauss Archive, housed in the composer's Garmisch Villa.

Hochzeitspräludium ('Wedding Prelude') for the service. One Viennese wit remarked that the occasion signified the burial of Strauss's anti-Semitism (*Grab* means 'grave' in German). Though traces of an anti-Semitic attitude still survived, Strauss's prejudice had lessened with time and experience. He and Alice adored one another from the start, and remained touchingly devoted.

His contract, meanwhile, was up for renewal. To coincide with his sixtieth birthday, the city built him a house on a plot of land on the Jacquingasse, loaned to him and his heirs until sixty years after his death. He and Pauline moved in that April, and Strauss duly signed his contract. He overplayed his hand, however, by inserting a clause insisting that Schalk should be retired at the end of the 1924–5 season, and the feud between the two escalated. In February they had had a blistering row over Strauss's taking leave of absence to conduct *Salome* in Rome. Strauss added fuel to the flames by complaining about the House's lack of funds. The Austrian Ministry of Education, faced with Strauss's demands, dithered. He ignored their objections, thinking he was safe.

His sixtieth birthday was a national event in both Germany and Austria. Dresden named a square after him. There were Strauss weeks in Berlin and Munich, as well as Vienna, which made him an

Strauss's house on the Jacquingasse in Vienna; the architect was Michael Rosenauer.

Two of the dancing pralines from Strauss's 1924 ballet *Schlagobers* ('Whipped Cream')

honorary citizen. The Vienna celebrations were dampened by disaster when Strauss presented the city with a return gift in the form of a new ballet, *Schlagobers* ('Whipped Cream'). The scenario, his own, was intended as a homage to the legendary Viennese confectionery and features a young confirmation candidate stuffing his face full of chocolate in a local coffee shop. Such is his greed that he becomes violently ill – Strauss's cue to provide a dream sequence (not unlike Tchaikovsky's *Nutcracker*) in which one episode represented a Viennese patisserie being stormed by a procession of armed candymen in rebellion against their maker. In a city in which many remembered the horrors of bread queues and food riots in the years immediately after the war, the whole spectacle was greeted with considerable alarm and the ballet was a resounding failure.

Schalk finally seized his chance while Strauss was away that summer. He renegotiated his own contract with a clause stipulating that he should have 'sole responsibility' for the company during Strauss's absences. Strauss remained ignorant of this when he returned to Vienna at the end of September for a revival of *Der Bürger als Edelmann*, which proved no more successful than it had been on its first outing in Berlin. He left almost immediately for Dresden where *Intermezzo* was in rehearsal. While there, he received a visit from Ludwig Karpath, adviser to the Education ministry on the Austrian national theatres, who informed Strauss of the contents of Schalk's contract to which he demanded his assent. Strauss refused and, possibly thinking he could fight bluff with counterbluff, handed in his resignation. It was accepted on the spot. He had been manoeuvred out, and for a long time afterwards it rankled. In 1926, the fences were mended a bit when he returned to Vienna as a guest to conduct *Elektra*. The house on the Jacquingasse remained at his disposal. During the Third Reich, he was going to need it.

Intermezzo, a qualified success, opened on 4 November 1924. It remains dogged by the controversy which surrounded it from the beginning. No one in the first-night audience could miss the autobiographical implications. Josef Correck, playing Hofkapellmeister Robert Storch, wore a mask that made him look like Strauss and the set for the Storch family home was modelled on the Garmisch villa. Pauline, astonishing as it may seem, knew nothing of the subject matter and was furious. Lotte Lehmann, who created the role of Christine Storch, encountered Frau Strauss after the performance and said she thought the opera was the most wonderful compliment her husband could have paid her. 'I don't give a damn,' Pauline snapped back. That night in their hotel, she stormed at Strauss for exposing their private life in public and continued berating him the following day while they drove back to Garmisch in a thunderstorm.

Lotte Lehmann, 'the ideal interpreter of my operas', as Christine Storch, and Theodor Stark as Baron Lummer, in the tobogganing scene from the Berlin première of Strauss's autobiographical opera *Intermezzo* in 1924

Many critics since have rounded on Strauss for his portrait of Pauline as a snobbish, self-dramatizing shrew, 'a horror, simply dreadful', as Storch's skat-playing cronies describe her behind his back. In some respects, such criticism ignores the subtlety of the portrait and the irony that lies beneath it. Christine's temper may be vicious, but underlying it are the loneliness and insecurity that make her an easy prey for a young opportunist like Baron Lummer, who (to the most insidiously beautiful waltz that Strauss wrote) instigates a platonic flirtation with her in the hope of relieving her of her money. Strauss's own self-portrait as Storch is a similarly telling depiction of a man who is, at times, irritatingly placid, slow to express emotion and, like Barak, not always capable of standing up to his wife. The genuinely awkward moments in the text of *Intermezzo* lie elsewhere: the Baron is allowed a dramatic importance in the first act that is not followed through; Bubi, who sides with his father throughout, is given an overly sentimental portrait; worst of all is an ugly anti-Semitic gibe near the beginning – the maid Anna remarks that Storch never seems to stay in one place for very long. 'I suspect,' Christine retorts, 'that he has Jewish blood in his veins.'

Qualms about the opera's subject matter have frequently led to dismissal of the score, but Schoenberg, for one, rated it a masterpiece. Strauss had originally conceived the work in terms of film, asking Hermann Bahr for a succession of 'cinema scenes' depicting his

Intermezzo was set in a reconstruction of the Strausses' own milieu. Here Strauss and Pauline (third and fourth from left) are photographed at a tobogganing party at Rodeln, near their villa in Garmisch.

marriage. The whole has a cinematic fluidity as the brief scenes flash past at astonishing speed (some lasting no more than a couple of minutes), and are linked by symphonic interludes which give the impression of continuous motion and momentum.

The vocal style reverts back to the *Ariadne* Prologue, in that speech becomes welded to song and is frequently indistinguishable from it. Lyricism is reserved for a few brief, telling moments. Strauss, adamant that every word of the text should be heard, prefaced the score with a volley of instructions to conductors as to how it should be treated. The fine shading between speech, recitative and lyricism must be stressed throughout. There is no room for anyone to play the prima donna or show off on stage. The cast must remember that they represent genuine human beings. 'By turning its back upon the popular love-and-murder interest of the usual opera libretto,' the preface ends, 'and by taking its subject matter too exclusively from real life, this new work blazes a path for musical and dramatic composition which others after me may perhaps negotiate with more talent and better fortune.' The opera's move away from symbolist extravagance mirrors the emergence of the *Neue Sachlichkeit* or 'New Objectivity' movement in German art, which stressed the acute observation of social realism as opposed to the emotive subjectivism of Expressionism. Strauss, usually accused of being behind the times after World War I, is far from being so in *Intermezzo*, which is essentially a modernist experiment, albeit one which had few imitators.

By 1922 he and Hofmannsthal were working together again. The war had shattered Hofmannsthal's morale and the subsequent inflationary chaos placed him under severe financial constraints. His only means of financial survival was to sell his paintings. He began to suffer again from severe depression, which left him unable to read without showing symptoms of acute stress. Having been taken ill in March of every successive year, he began to dread each approaching spring, convinced that it would mean his death.

He had continued to ply Strauss with proposals in an attempt to arouse his interest, but in vain; their first collaboration after the break was in fact on another of Strauss's adaptations, this time of Beethoven's incidental music for *Die Ruinen von Athen*, a ramshackle play by the German Romantic dramatist August von Kotzebue. Hofmannsthal redrafted the text and Strauss interwove sections of the original score with extracts from Beethoven's ballet *Die Geschöpfe des Prometheus* ('The Creatures of Prometheus'), a theme from which had found its way into the 'Eroica'. The unsteady resulting amalgam was first performed in Vienna in September 1924. It flopped.

While they were working on *Die Ruinen von Athen*, other plans took shape. Hofmannsthal's letters make reference to the 'symbolic nuptials of Faust and Helena', Helena being Helen of Troy whose mythic beauty is one of the temptations put in front of Goethe's hero by Mephistopheles. Hofmannsthal had first pondered the significance of the figure of Helen in 1920 and in February 1922 he submitted a draft scenario to Strauss. By 1923 he was writing enthusiastically to Strauss about 'Greek Operetta'. Strauss, with fond memories of Jeritza in Offenbach's *La Belle Hélène*, gave his consent, believing that he was finally going to receive the text for the operetta of his dreams.

What followed, however, was a rerun of much that had gone before. Hofmannsthal soon admitted to having problems in producing 'a lighter kind' of text according to Strauss's requirements. Strauss, having finished *Intermezzo* in Buenos Aires, wrote on his homeward journey that he hoped the libretto would be waiting for him when he returned to Garmisch, 'preferably with entertaining ballet interludes: a few delightful elf or spirit choruses would be most welcome.' Hofmannsthal was dithering and told Strauss to expect 'something ... like a Puccini opera', then advised him to 'handle it as if it were merely an operetta – it's bound to be by Richard Strauss in the end.' Having received Act I in October, Strauss was soon writing in glowing tones reminiscent of his delight on receiving the text of *Rosenkavalier*. 'Most of it virtually sets itself to music,' he commented. 'It's coming on unbelievably fast.'

By the end of the month, the cracks were showing. They had initially decided that the opera was to be a Singspiel, a work in which arias and choruses are linked with spoken dialogue in place of recitative. It was soon apparent that certain numbers 'cannot be treated in a light character'. By the following March, the trappings of operetta, dialogue and all, were deemed to be 'dispensable'. The piece was turning into yet another vast symbolic phantasmagoria and was starting to be worryingly abstruse.

Act I of the opera, nevertheless, was finished in July 1924. Act II proved to be a nightmare. Hofmannsthal's depression grew worse and

his finances were becoming desperate. In an attempt to raise money he
started writing the titles for a silent film adaptation of *Der
Rosenkavalier* by the great director Robert Wiene, whose Expressionist
classic *The Cabinet of Doctor Caligari* had helped bring the German
film industry to international attention. Strauss, meanwhile, fazed by
Hofmannsthal's introduction of a set of new characters in Act II,
suddenly began to suffer from composer's block. Work on the score
dawdled on over the next few years and the opera, named *Die
ägyptische Helena*, was not finished until October 1927.

As with *Ariadne*, there were fights over the première, which was set
for Dresden the following year. Hofmannsthal, like Strauss, had firm
ideas that Jeritza should sing the title role and also wanted Richard
Tauber as Menelas, Helena's husband (Hofmannstahl uses the original
Greek form of 'Menelaus' throughout). Jeritza, however, demanded
too high a fee and Dresden was not prepared to put up the money. In
her place, Strauss chose Elisabeth Rethberg (vocally less wayward than
Jeritza but neither a great actress nor a great beauty), which provoked
another furious letter from Hofmannsthal, who considered his work
undermined. In the end, a compromise was reached. Dresden would
give the première on 6 June with Rethberg as Helena, Curt Taucher as
Menelas and Fritz Busch conducting. Five days later, on his sixty-
fourth birthday, Strauss would conduct the piece in Vienna with
Jeritza. The two premières went ahead as planned. Strauss fulsomely
described the Vienna performance as 'perhaps the greatest triumph of
my life', though the critics were unanimous in considering the piece
dated and mediocre. Their assault continued through the year when
the opera opened in Berlin and New York. 'Splendidly vacuous,' raged
the *New York Herald Tribune*. 'At best [Strauss] can only borrow from
himself, at worst he can but remember his inferiors.' Nowadays few
would be quite so damning about the score, though many still find
the text a serious stumbling-block.

Die ägyptische Helena is a parable of sex and marriage in the
aftermath of war. Hofmannsthal's source material was an odd addition
to the Trojan myth, originally invented by the poet Stesichorus, who
strove to reconcile a dichotomy in Homeric legend. Menelaus dragged
his adulterous wife from the smoking ruins of Troy vowing revenge,
yet in the *Odyssey* Telemachus encounters them in Sparta contentedly
reconciled and apparently oblivious to preceding traumas.

Strauss with Elisabeth
Rethberg, creator of the role
of Helena, at the first-night
party of *Die ägyptische
Helena* on 6 June 1928

Stesichorus's theory was far-fetched. At the moment of her seduction
by Paris, Helen was spirited away to Egypt. In order that her
reputation might remain untarnished, the gods substituted a phantom
Doppelgänger in pursuit of which the war was actually fought. On his
return to Greece, the gods reunited Menelaus and Helen by wrecking
their ship on the Egyptian coast and engineering a meeting between
husband and wife at which point the phantom melted into air.
Hofmannsthal's adaptation conflates the two Helens, real and
phantom, into one while the shipwreck becomes the work of the
benevolent sorceress Aithra, the mistress of the god Poseidon, who
hovers off-stage instigating the proceedings, not unlike Keikobad in
Die Frau ohne Schatten.

Poseidon has provided Aithra with a bizarre selection of magical
equipment – a talking conch-shell which, like a telephone (the
German word *Muschel* means telephone ear-piece as well as shell),
brings her news of the outside world, and a plethora of potions; these
act as tranquillizers and antidepressants, with which Aithra lures
Helena and Menelas into a temporary sense of false security. While
they are both drugged, Aithra reinvents Stesichorus' story and
convinces Menelas that the Helena he wants to kill is a phantom
rather than his real wife; his anger consequently evaporates and he
rediscovers the depth of his desire for his wife. But Aithra's plan

Leonie Rysanek as Helena ecstatically recalls her reunion with Menelas (Bernd Aldenhoff), while the latter sleeps at her feet in the 1956 Munich production of *Die ägyptische Helena*.

misfires. Their brief second honeymoon is interrupted by the arrival of Altair and Da-ud in Act II. The latter bears an alarming resemblance to Paris, is promptly attracted to Helena – and history begins to repeat itself. Helena, whose longing for a genuine reconciliation with her husband has been clear from the beginning, refuses to let either herself or her husband live a drug-induced lie and rejects Aithra's ministrations. Menelas, forced to recognize that the 'phantom' Helena he desires and the real Helena whom he wants to kill are one and the same being, finally comes to terms with his abiding love for his wife. The sense of acceptance of self and others, together with the continuity of their pre-war past, is further stressed by the arrival of their daughter Hermione, who completes their reconciliation. As with *Die Frau ohne Schatten*, the complex phantasmagoria resolves itself into a hymn to marriage and a conservative statement that the family unit rather than the individual is the way forward.

Strauss's score, though not always able to cope with Hofmannsthal's complicated ideas, is sensual and allusive. The emphasis on potions suggests *Tristan* and the plot of *Helena* reverses Wagner's erotic fantasy, in which marriage founders into adultery as a result of Brangäne's substitution of a love philtre for the poison which Wagner's hero and heroine, unable to face their desire for each other, are willingly prepared to consume. In *Helena*, rejection of the potions' powers leads to marital reconciliation after adultery. When the shipwrecked couple reach Aithra's palace, a long silence is broken by a bass clarinet playing a theme associated with Helena herself, but bearing an alarming resemblance to the opening motif of Wagner's opera. Helena's erotic allure is suggested by a phrase which resembles Dalila's 'Softly awakes my heart' from Saint-Saëns's *Samson et Dalila*, an opera which the young Strauss raved about to Ludwig Thuille. Her great aria after her reunion with Menelas is one of Strauss's most sensually charged creations.

Strauss's difficulties with Act II are audible, however, and much of the orientalism which characterizes the music associated with Altair seems bogus when set beside *Salome*. Da-ud's music in particular caused considerable comment. Fritz Busch thought it was banal and told Strauss so. 'That's what's wanted for the servant girls,' was Strauss's comment. 'Believe me, dear Busch, the general public would not go to *Tannhäuser* if it didn't contain "O Star of Eve".' Busch was shocked. Strauss's comment is wide of the mark, however, for the beautiful Paris look-alike, Da-ud, who is about to be violently destroyed like half the young men of Europe ten years previously, is characterized by music of touching simplicity which looks back to Sophie and Octavian, and forward to the best of *Arabella*. Though Strauss generally disliked tenors, the anguished, confused Menelas is the finest role in his output for a Wagnerian *Heldentenor*.

Hofmannsthal saw Menelas as the central figure in the opera, and returned to the splits and contradictions that made up his damaged, shell-shocked personality in an essay entitled *Literatur als geistiger*

Raum der Nation ('Literature as the Spiritual Space of the Nation'), published in 1927. 'Everything,' he wrote, 'must be drawn into one, making a unity of the exterior, for only for those who are whole in themselves will the world become a unity.' The essay goes on to assume a political tone. 'The isolated, titanically searching ego … breaks through to a supreme community by uniting in itself that which for centuries has split a people lacking in the common bond of a culture … The process of which I am speaking is nothing other than a conservative revolution unknown to European history. Its goal is … a new German reality in which the entire nation participates.' The tone – vague, idealistic and almost mystical – hides a plea for a unifying culture that transcends the ideological divisions and splits which were tearing both the Weimar Republic and Austria apart. Hofmannsthal was well aware of the danger of speaking out in this way. Though his family was Catholic by creed, his Jewish origins were well known. As early as 1920, his work had been pilloried by the anti-Semitic writer Adolf Bartels as being extraneous to German-language culture.

Strauss's own political views were now beginning to cross the dangerous borderline between conservatism and totalitarianism. As early as 1916, Hermann Bahr had noted that his Nietzscheanism was taking on a political aspect. 'He is opposed to universal suffrage,' Bahr noted in his diary, '[He] wants a true aristocracy, a selection of the strong – believing that everyone can be strong if he disciplines himself.' Some commentators have read an encroaching nationalism into his *Drei Hymnen* ('Three Hymns') to poems by Friedrich Hölderlin, written in 1921. The lines 'Love … bleeds on the flag of victory, jubilant for the fatherland' followed by 'you my fatherland, holy, enduring! See, you have remained!' may point to Strauss's political mood at this time, though his choice of text is not, in itself, suspect. Despite being set by Brahms and admired by Nietzsche, Hölderlin's poetry had languished in obscurity since his death in 1843. Rediscovered during the early years of the twentieth century, his by no means unique mystic vision of Germany as a second flowering of Hellenic culture appealed to both literary progressives and reactionaries alike.

By 1924 Strauss was clearly confused by the state of European politics. While he was in Italy conducting *Salome*, Mussolini, a fan, sent him a photograph signed 'To Richard Strauss, with profound admiration, Mussolini, Rome, February 1924'. When Rolland met Strauss in Vienna the following May, he found him 'very preoccupied by nationalist follies, by our threatened European civilization. Civilization, for him, is concentrated in Europe, a tiny little Europe, three or four nations. And they are destroying themselves … He appears to be absolutely indifferent to national questions and to national quarrels.' By 1928, however, a more extreme note had crept in. In June, he and Kessler had dinner with Hofmannsthal at his house in Rodaun, near Vienna. 'Among other things,' Kessler noted in his diary on 14 June, 'Strauss gave forth his droll political views, the necessity of a dictatorship etc. Nobody took it seriously.'

Hofmannsthal and Strauss had already embarked on what proved to be their final collaboration, *Arabella*, a bittersweet comedy set in Vienna in 1860. 'I have no work,' he wrote to Hofmannsthal in 1927 as *Helena* was nearing completion. 'So please, write some poetry. It may even be a 'second *Rosenkavalier*' if you can't think of anything better. If the worst comes to the worst, a little stop-gap job – a one act piece – to keep my hand in.' Hofmannsthal initially bridled at the idea of a 'stop-gap job', though he took Strauss's words to heart. He turned to a manuscript abandoned two years previously, a comedy called *Der Fiaker als Graf* ('The Cabman as Count'). 'It takes place in a ballroom, and offers enchanting possibilities,' he wrote to Strauss. It had 'a touch of *Rosenkavalier* about it, a most attractive woman as the central figure, surrounded by men'. A few weeks later, however, he decided that *Der Fiaker als Graf* was 'too flimsy' a subject for an opera, and told Strauss he intended to combine the material with an adaptation of his own short story *Lucidor*, to produce 'almost an operetta', which would not only form a sequel to *Rosenkavalier* but would also rival Johann Strauss's *Die Fledermaus* in its brilliance.

He read his scenario the following December. Strauss was worried that the dramatic balance between the characters was uneven. The hero, the Croatian nobleman Mandryka in love with the titular heroine, Arabella, was too dominant. What was needed was a central female figure, someone with whom audiences would identify as they had with the Marschallin. This time Hofmannsthal took Strauss's criticisms calmly, and their working relationship passed onto an even footing for the first time since *Rosenkavalier*. Strauss, for his part, was soon buried in Viennese libraries researching Slavonic folk song and Croatian costume.

The first draft of Act I was completed in April 1928. Strauss found it splendid ('I find we understand each other better every year,' he told Hofmannsthal), though he was worried by the character of Arabella herself, which he found weak. With *Helena* launched on her chequered career, Strauss and Hofmannsthal were finally able to devote more of their time to the new opera. Progress was slow, though both were content. A draft of the complete text was finished by December. Strauss wanted yet more changes. Hofmannsthal dutifully wrote and rewrote according to his instructions. Things took a brief turn for the worse in the spring of 1929 when Hofmannsthal was taken ill with a severe attack of gastric influenza which lasted several weeks. Strauss, too, was unwell, went to Italy to recuperate and then on to the spa town of Karlsbad for the annual cure he was now in the habit of taking. He was still unsatisfied with the text of the first act. It lacked lyricism, he argued, and should end with a big aria for Arabella. 'The aria after all,' he wrote, 'is the soul of opera. Separate numbers with recitatives in between. That's what opera was, is and should remain.' Hofmannsthal sent the text of the missing monologue on 10 July. On 14 July, Strauss sent a telegram : 'FIRST ACT EXCELLENT. MANY THANKS AND CONGRATULATIONS.'

By the time it arrived in Rodaun the following morning, Hofmannsthal was dead. On 13 July, for reasons which have never been fully established, his son Franz had shot himself. For two days, Hofmannsthal sat in silence in his study, desperately trying to grapple with his grief. On the day of the funeral, as he bent down to pick up his hat, he told his wife Gerty that he was feeling unwell. 'Why are you looking at me?' he asked her, and collapsed. He had suffered a massive stroke and died without recovering consciousness. His funeral took place at Rodaun on 18 July. Franz Strauss and Alice attended. Strauss, suffering from shock, wrote to Gerty: 'No musician ever found such a helper and supporter. No one will ever replace him for me or the world of music … The wonderful libretto which he sent me so shortly before his tragic end and for which in my supreme happiness I was only able to thank him in a brief telegram will remain a last, glorious page in the work of this noble, pure, high-minded man.' He was true to his word and set the text of *Arabella* in tribute.

The libretto's last two acts were unrevised at Hofmannsthal's death, and although Strauss made some verbal changes, he refused to alter its basic outline. Shying away from the depth of his grief, he let other projects – an adaptation of Mozart's *Idomeneo* and a National Hymn for Austria – distract him from the score. It was not completed until 1932.

Arabella is essentially a terminal work, an opera which says farewell to an era as well as looking forward to the 'conservative revolution' of which Hofmannsthal dreamed. It takes place on Shrove Tuesday as Carnival gives way to the seriousness of Lent. Imperial Vienna, already affected by the passing of time in *Rosenkavalier*, has now become subject to its ravages and is in decline. 'The atmosphere of *Arabella*, quite close to our own time as it is, is more ordinary, less glamorous, more vulgar,' Hofmannsthal had written to Strauss just before he died, comparing the two operas. The febrile world of the Weimar Republic, celebrating its final Carnival before catastrophe, colours the libretto, which was completed in 1929, the year in which the Wall Street Crash destroyed the fragile German economy.

In *Arabella* monetary chaos rules to the point where moral distinctions have become blurred. The aristocratic Waldners are holed up in a hotel, the parents' penury endangering the emotional happiness of their daughters. Arabella, the elder, beautiful and self-assured, is effectively to be sold in marriage to the highest bidder in an attempt to save the family fortunes, either to one of her father's former military colleagues, or to one of three Counts. Zdenka, the younger daughter (and the central character of Hofmannsthal's *Lucidor*), has been brought up as a boy in order to save money. She obsessively desires Matteo, Arabella's rejected former suitor. Arabella is looking for 'the right man' (*der Richtige*) and wants to marry for love. The Carnival itself has a double significance: for Arabella it is the last day of her girlhood and its end symbolizes the approach of the adult responsibility of bailing her family out of its difficulties; for the other characters the Carnival implies the temporary collapse of moral norms and class boundaries – the pivotal second act takes place at the annual Viennese Cabmen's Ball, at which social distinctions are abolished, and servants, for a single night, are accorded the same status as their masters.

Into this emotionally charged world comes Mandryka, a stranger from the outer edges of the Empire, the rescuer of the Waldner

In this scene from the 1955 Metropolitan Opera production of *Arabella*, the heroine (Eleanor Steber) is introduced to Mandryka (George London), while her parents (Ralph Herbert and Blanche Thebom) look on approvingly.

family fortunes and at the same time the catalyst that forces this crumbling society to confront itself. 'There can be no more subterfuges,' Arabella remarks when she first meets him. He and Arabella are meant for one another (he is her *Richtige*), but before they can finally accept each other their love founders on mutual misunderstandings that first break, then strengthen, their ideals. Mandryka overhears Zdenka arranging a tryst with Matteo in her sister's name, assumes that Arabella is a slut and lets himself be drawn into the Carnival frenzy instigating a flirtation with Fiakermilli, the Cabmen's provocative mascot. Arabella herself, faced with her sister's devotion to Matteo, must also confront her own selfishness. At the ball Mandryka tells Arabella that the custom in his village is for a woman to present the man she loves with a glass of pure water drawn from a well behind her father's house. In the final scene, Arabella brings him the drink as a symbol of forgiveness and also as a reminder that he must learn to trust her and accept her for who she is. Behind this gentle plea for mutual understanding is

Hofmannsthal's mystic view of the 'nation' renewing itself by means of transcending its own divisions.

Strauss's music captures the libretto's mood exactly. The surface beauty hides feverish textures. Carnival dances flicker in and out of the score. Waltzes and polkas fragment before they have even begun, their giddiness gradually undercut by the gentle seriousness contained within the wealth of references to Slavonic folk song which musically link Arabella and Mandryka and which gradually supplant the score's superficial sophistication. Vocally, Fiakermilli is Zerbinetta's second cousin, though comparison of the two women underlines the shift in Strauss's stance. The coloratura soprano, the embodiment of iconoclasm in 1912, has, by 1932, come to portray a parodistic tart.

Arabella has its faults. Strauss's insistence on setting Hofmannsthal's unfinished draft unchanged except for points of verbal detail leads to a second act which musically shoots its bolt too soon and leads to a very weak finale (he was aware of this and later authorized a cut which dovetails it into the beginning of Act III). Though his initial worries about the heroine being too weak a central character are unfounded and Arabella herself is perhaps his most appealing heroine since the Marschallin, the dramatic conflict within the opera is comparatively slight and its dependence on nuance and subtlety is by no means universally persuasive. Mandryka's appearance as the solution to the Waldners' problems occasionally strains credibility: though human love and understanding assume ethical primacy, the presence of Mandryka's bank balance allows Hofmannsthal to avoid the issue of what the implications might be were Mandryka not rich. Hofmannsthal's subordination of symbolism to psychology for the first time since *Rosenkavalier* has also led to the opera being dismissed, ironically, as novelettish and sentimental, while the idea of *Arabella* as *Rosenkavalier*'s sequel has frequently led to unfavourable comparisons between the two. On its own terms *Arabella* can be deeply moving, doubly so if one bears in mind that it forms Strauss's musical tribute to his librettist. The rest of Strauss's career as an opera composer was chequered by his search to find a suitable equal.

A natural successor to Hofmannsthal soon presented himself in the form of one of the great figures of twentieth-century German literature, the Austrian-Jewish novelist and biographer Stefan Zweig. Zweig had been hovering on the edge of Strauss's circle for a while, though the two had never met. He was a close friend of Rolland, whose works he translated into German. He was also one of the signatories of the Viennese petition in Strauss's favour, and had worshipped him from afar. Ten years previously he had drafted the scenario of a Ballet Pantomime for Strauss but had never had what he believed to be the temerity to send it. It was Zweig's publisher, Anton Kippenberg, who effected the introduction, calling on Strauss during the summer of 1931 to suggest Zweig as a possible collaborator.

They met at Munich's Vier Jahreszeiten Hotel the following November to discuss two proposals which Zweig had already outlined. The first was his old ballet scenario, clearly written with the Nietzschean Strauss in mind. It was to be a form of ritual theatre 'which comprises all contrasts of the arts, from the tragic to the lighthearted, from the Apollonian to the Dionysiac'. Strauss preferred

Stefan Zweig (1881–1942), the Austrian-Jewish novelist, whom Strauss hoped would become his second Hofmannsthal

Zweig's other proposal, a comedy based on Ben Jonson's *Epicoene, or The Silent Woman*. They decided to go ahead.

The first chunk of the libretto of *Die schweigsame Frau* reached Strauss in June 1932. 'More suited to music than either *Figaro* or *The Barber of Seville*,' he told Zweig. 'I am burning to get started on it in earnest.' But Zweig was working on the final chapters of a biography. *Arabella*, meanwhile, was still incomplete. Fritz Busch and Alfred Reucker, the Intendant of the Dresden Opera, were quietly insistent that *Arabella* should have priority over any new work. Strauss's last Hofmannsthal opera was duly completed in October and dedicated to Busch and Reucker.

Around them, the Weimar democracy was crumbling. By 1932, the Nazis had obtained 230 seats in the Reichstag and were consequently the largest party though without an overall majority. Strauss was already playing a strange game, displaying the ambivalent behaviour that would characterize his future relations with the Third Reich, as if he were trying to placate the political far right in order to preserve himself and promote his work. In 1931 he had been asked to provide a piece for the annual Vienna Philharmonic Ball. He unearthed the last movement of *Lebende Bilder* ('Living Pictures'), a set of *pièces d'occasion* written in his Weimar days in 1892 to celebrate the golden wedding of Grand Duke Karl and his Duchess Sofie. One of the pieces depicted a German victory over the Swedes during the Thirty Years War. Strauss submitted it to Vienna and republished it in 1932 under the title *Kampf und Sieg* ('Battle and Victory').

The fantasy of stability which dictatorship appeared to offer exercised a continuing appeal. In 1932, he was once again in Italy. He and Franz were granted an audience by Mussolini, who promised his help in obtaining an Italian première for *Die Frau ohne Schatten*. Il Duce sought Strauss's advice on the rebuilding of the Rome Opera and Strauss recommended that musicians should be consulted in place of architects: they, after all, knew more than builders what was wanted. The following morning, Mussolini's architect arrived at his hotel to discuss his ideas. Strauss was impressed.

On 17 January 1933, Zweig delivered the completed text of *Die schweigsame Frau*. Strauss, who was working on a revision of *Helena* with Lothar Wallerstein (the director of the Vienna première), was delighted with it. It was perfect, he told Zweig; not one word needed to be changed. Less than a fortnight later, on 30 January, Hitler was offered the Chancellorship. The Nazis had made no secret of their desire for what they called a *Machtergreifung*, a seizure of power, and had manipulated the flawed democracy of Weimar in order to achieve it. That night, a remarkable piece of political theatre was stage-managed in Berlin as 100,000 uniformed men tramped in rigid torch-light procession through the streets before the new Chancellor who stood on his balcony. They sang the Horst Wessel Song, the national song of the Nazi party during the Third Reich, named after a martyr to their 'national revolution'. Democracy began to perish and Strauss would soon be forced to face the most horrific of realities.

6

The Olympic torch is ceremonially carried through the streets of Berlin, prior to the opening of the 1936 Games, for which Strauss wrote the celebratory Olympic Hymn.

I made music under the Kaiser and under Ebert — I'll survive under this one as well.

Strauss to his family after the Nazi takeover of power

The Third Reich 1933–45

Strauss's activities during the Third Reich, which constitute the most controversial aspect of his life and career, have produced a variety of responses ranging from vilification to extravagant excuses on the grounds that he was a morally unimpeachable victim of circumstance. The truth is somewhere in between. Strauss's behaviour throughout the period fluctuated according to the pressure of external events. On occasion, he acted out of self-interest or, even worse, personal spite; there were also other times when he was, without question, deliberately persecuted and emotionally blackmailed. He seemed unconcerned that so many of the friends and artists he admired were forced into exile, yet his devotion to his family – to his Jewish daughter-in-law Alice and his grandsons Richard and Christian above all – was wholly admirable. Some of his works from the period betray elements of compromise with the regime. Others reveal a struggle to evolve a personal style of expression which the Nazis would be unable to affect.

Though his political stance had gravitated towards the right during the Weimar Republic, he had not made statements which can be construed as proto-fascist rhetoric, unlike Pfitzner. Strauss never joined the Nazi Party or put any of the proscriptions of Nazism into action. But it is also true that he never publicly condemned the regime, even after its collapse. His actions suggest that he may have confused Nazism with imperial autocracy and behaved initially as he had done during the Kaiserreich, alternately serving the regime and flouting its dicta. No assessment of his life and achievement during the period, however, can fail to take into account a number of factors, the chief of which was his inability to understand the Nazis' attempted obliteration of the dividing line between politics and art. Nazism was politics as theatre, its rallies extravagant uniformed spectacles, the public enactment of collective ritual, designed from the beginning to be seen, photographed and filmed; yet if its stagecraft turned politics into art, its aesthetic theories attempted the opposite.

There could be no such thing as apolitical art during the Third Reich. All art was to become totally subject to the dictates of the regime and autonomous expression was to be nullified.

Hitler came to power on 30 January 1933, not as an outright dictator but as the leader of a right-wing coalition. Two months of organized terror followed, which led to the passing of laws (the Enabling Act of 23 March) to put an end to civil unrest and enable the formation of the one-party state. Germany's artistic community, it was soon apparent, was not immune.

On 7 March 1933 Fritz Busch (the dedicatee of *Arabella*) arrived at the Dresden Opera House to take a rehearsal of Verdi's *Il trovatore*. He was not Jewish but was outspoken in his condemnation of the regime. The SA (*Sturmabteilung*, Storm Troopers) moved in and brought the rehearsal to a halt. The Reichskommissar for Saxony promptly decreed that any musical event leading to public disorder could be banned. The staff of the Opera House were coerced into signing an indictment to the effect that Busch lacked artistic merit and, in spite of contacts in the Nazi party (Busch's wife had previously been a friend of Emmy Sonnemann, one of Goering's mistresses), he

Strauss in the dining room of his Garmisch villa, with his son Franz and grandsons Richard and Christian

was forced to resign along with Reucker. Strauss threatened to withdraw the première of *Arabella* in protest but the theatre held him to his contract.

On 16 March, the Reichskommissar's decree was invoked to prevent Bruno Walter appearing in Leipzig. Walter, due to conduct in Berlin four days later, applied for police protection and was refused. The Propaganda Ministry informed the Berlin Philharmonic that the concert in Berlin might only go ahead if an Aryan took Walter's place. Strauss was in the city to conduct *Elektra* at the Staatsoper, and was pressurized to conduct by Walter's agent, who was Jewish, and by Hugo Rasch, music editor of the Nazi newspaper *Völkischer Beobachter*. Strauss, who had never been kindly disposed towards Walter, agreed to take his place, donating his fee to the orchestra. Within days the press were vociferous in his support. On 1 April, Hitler received a telegram from America signed by a number of resident musicians, including Toscanini (an exile from fascist Italy) and Fritz Reiner, openly denouncing the Nazis' anti-Semitic policies. The *Völkischer Beobachter* claimed that Strauss's actions represented a 'salute to the new Germany'. The *Neue Zeitschrift für Musik* praised him for having been 'undeterred by a threatening letter from hateful Jewish Americans'.

'Politics pass, the arts live on, hence we should strive for that which is permanent and leave propaganda to those who find it fulfilling and satisfying,' Zweig wrote hopefully in April. That month the Nazis imposed a tax of 1,000 Marks on anyone crossing the German border into Austria. Zweig had been a regular visitor in Garmisch but from now on their meetings would be few and far between.

Strauss continued to play into the Nazis' hands. The year 1933 was the fiftieth anniversary of Wagner's death. On 17 April, the *Münchener neueste Nachrichten* published an open letter of protest against Thomas Mann, whose anniversary lecture on Wagner had condemned his anti-Semitic dismissal of Mendelssohn's music. Furthermore, Mann deplored the fact that Wagner's music had become a vehicle for nationalism. Recent evidence suggests that the letter of protest was organized by the conductor Hans Knappertsbusch. Strauss had been stung by Mann's criticisms in the past and was also fond of Knappertsbusch, whose card-playing skills were considerable. He put his signature to the letter.

Strauss at Bayreuth with
Wieland Wagner, the
composer's grandson,
who later became one of
the most influential post-war
opera producers

That summer Toscanini withdrew from the Bayreuth Festival.
Wagner's widowed daughter-in-law Winifred, a Nazi Party member
since 1926 and a close friend of Hitler, invited Strauss to conduct
Parsifal in Toscanini's place, to which he agreed. It was his first
invitation from Bayreuth since his relationship with the Wagner
family had cooled, and he had not conducted at the Festival for thirty-
nine years. In gratitude Winifred sent him a page of Wagner's sketches
for *Lohengrin*. 'My modest help for Bayreuth,' he wrote to Winifred,
'was only a respectful payment of the great debt of gratitude stored
up in my heart for all that the great master gave to the world and to
me in particular.'

Hitler was in Bayreuth that summer and he and Strauss met.
Strauss, thinking of composers' rights, proposed that a royalty of one
per cent should be imposed on all Wagner performances, the proceeds
to be given to the Festival. Hitler objected, arguing that there was no
precedent. Bayreuth was later funded directly from Nazi coffers under
his direct control.

In June, Hitler gave the Propaganda Ministry, headed by Goebbels,
the right to take control of 'all areas that influenced the mind,

including complete control of cultural affairs'. This was a triumph for Goebbels, for he had been feuding for some time with his rival Alfred Rosenberg, the party ideologue, who was angling for authority over the Reich's cultural life. In 1929, Rosenberg had formed the Kampfbund für deutsche Kultur, an organization whose aim was the defamation of modernism and the promotion of nationalist cultural values. The group's official mouthpiece, the journal *Die Musik*, was consistently violent in its opposition to Strauss, who had also come under attack from other quarters. In *Musik und Rasse* ('Music and Race'), published in 1932, the Nazi musicologist Richard Eichenauer wrote: 'He [Strauss] is predominantly Nordic, but who is brave enough to claim this with regard to his music? He is the shining representative of the internally hollow times which … have changed the art of the soul for the art of nerves.'

Goebbels also disliked Strauss's music, but he was prepared to use him for his own purposes. It would be singularly fortunate for the Nazis if Germany's most famous composer could be seen to be on their side, particularly since many of the country's greatest musicians were leaving or had left. Strauss had made no protest against this tragic exodus. 'Unfortunately we still need him,' Goebbels wrote in his diary, 'but one day we shall have our own music and then we shall have no further need of this decadent neurotic.' His plans were for a central organization, the Reichskulturkammer (Reich's Culture Chamber), to put Hitler's dictates into action. On 22 September, the new Chamber, divided into seven areas of Music, Fine Arts, Theatre, Literature, Press, Radio and Film, was established by law. On 1 November, it was announced that anyone involved with the 'production of cultural material' was legally bound to take up membership of the chamber overseeing their specific field of activity. Strauss was nominated president of the music section, the Reichsmusikkammer. 'I was not consulted,' he later wrote. 'I accepted this honorary office because I hoped that I would be able to do some good and prevent worse misfortune, if from now onwards German musical life was going to be, as it was said, "reorganized" by amateurs and ignorant place-seekers.' His motives for acceptance may be taken at face value: he saw in the Reichsmusikkammer the potential for an extension of his work with the Genossenschaft deutscher Tonsetzer, and a chance to campaign for alterations in copyright law in composers' interests, including his own. He indicated his gratitude to Goebbels by writing a song and dedicating it to him. *Das Bächlein* ('The Brook'), to a text attributed to Goethe, depicts water (and consequently new life) gushing forth from an underground source. 'He who summoned me from stone,' the final couplet reads, 'he, I think will be my guide.' The word 'guide' in German is *Führer*.

The new Culture Chamber was formally inaugurated on 15 November with much speechifying and a performance of Strauss's highly imperial *Festliches Präludium* ('Festival Prelude'), written in 1913. Strauss chose to head the composers' section personally and by May 1934 had achieved one of his principal aims in having copyright law extended from thirty to fifty years after death. He now enjoyed, or so he thought, a status similar to that which he held in the Kaiser's Germany; he was, once more, the star of a state system and officially Germany's greatest composer. In 1934, his seventieth birthday was celebrated with a certain style, and Strauss weeks were held throughout Germany. Hitler and Goebbels both sent him signed photographs.

Initially Goebbels allowed the Chamber a token autonomy, partly to allay suspicions of excessive state control. It was not long, however, before Strauss was acting in ways of which the Nazis disapproved. He was frequently absent from the Chamber's Berlin headquarters, and a number of decrees were consequently passed in his absence: the use of foreign-sounding pseudonyms was forbidden; only German pianos could be used in performance; all musicians working abroad should be vetted and, if need be, their travel permits revoked. He refused to take a stand against the avant garde, as the Nazis hoped he would. The critic Fritz Stege lambasted him in the press for permitting the performance of atonal works. 'The Reichsmusikkammer,' Strauss retorted, 'cannot forbid works of an atonal character, for it is up to the audience to judge such compositions.'

More important and greatly to Strauss's credit was his visible unwillingness to act under Article 10 of the implementation decree of 1 November 1933. This permitted the Chamber to expel members arbitrarily and turn down membership applications if the candidate failed to possess what was considered to be the necessary 'reliability and suitability'. In effect this was intended to complement the Civil

Service Restoration Act of 7 April which forbade Jews from holding public office and offered an opening to the Reichsmusikkammer to act on blatantly anti-Semitic principles. Significantly, the article was only ever invoked during Strauss's absences from Berlin; his signature does not appear on any of the anti-Semitic material produced by the the Reichsmusikkammer and his actions, on occasion, suggest he might have thought he was capable of quietly subverting the Nazis' anti-Semitic policies. Rosenberg's mob was vociferous in its demands that Mendelssohn's incidental music for *A Midsummer Night's Dream* be replaced by music by an Aryan composer. Strauss flatly refused the task (which was eventually undertaken by Carl Orff). He was also anxious that Mahler's works should still be played. A minor official in Frankfurt attempted to block a performance of Debussy's *Nocturnes* conducted by Furtwängler. 'Tell Councillor Spiess,' Strauss told Furtwängler, 'that nothing stands in the way of a performance of *Nocturnes*, any more than any of the symphonies of Mahler, which he has not yet ventured to include in the programmes.'

Disillusionment soon set in. It became apparent that he had been appointed as a figurehead and that he was not taken seriously. 'Nothing is accomplished by these meetings,' he wrote to the conductor Julius Kopach in 1934. 'I hear that the Aryan law is to be sharpened and that *Carmen* is to be forbidden. I have no wish to take part in such embarrassing blunders … My extensive and serious proposals for reform were declined by the minister [Goebbels] … Time is too precious for me to participate in such dilettantish rubbish.'

He was, however, already compromised artistically. *Arabella* opened in Dresden on 1 July 1933, without Busch and without Lehmann, whom he had in mind for the title role and who had already announced she would not sing in Germany while the Nazis remained in power. The conductor was Clemens Krauss, whom Strauss had first heard when he was an assistant in Vienna in 1922 and whom he consistently championed. This was in some respects a fortunate choice, for Krauss was also much admired by Hitler, a fact which Krauss, though not a member of the Nazi Party, was occasionally content to exploit in Strauss's favour. Krauss's wife, Viorica Ursuleac, sang Arabella. She became another of Strauss's soprano muses, though this may have been by default. Although a singer of considerable stature, she possessed neither the magnetic glamour of Jeritza, the subtle warmth of Lehmann, the exquisite brilliance of Elisabeth Schumann nor the vocal opulence of Rose Pauly (all four sopranos left Strauss's orbit for exile over the coming years, though they continued to perform his work). *Arabella*, however, was popular with the public, if not with the critics, and it became one of the most frequently performed of Strauss's operas during the Third Reich, though it made little headway elsewhere until after World War II. The Nazis could not overlook the popularity of Strauss's collaborations with Hofmannsthal. The librettos of Mozart's operas, written by Jewish authors, were eventually rewritten by Nazi musicologists but Hofmannsthal's texts remained unaltered.

By 1934 Strauss was aware that his relationship with Zweig was under threat. Nazi law now explicitly forbade Strauss's collaboration with a Jew, although Zweig, an Austrian citizen, was technically out of its reach. In August of that year, when Strauss returned to Bayreuth for a revival of *Parsifal*, Goebbels arrived unannounced and told him that his collaboration with Zweig was an embarrassment to the government. Strauss said he had no wish to embarrass anyone and offered to cancel the première of *Die schweigsame Frau*. Goebbels decided that Hitler should have the last word and a copy of Zweig's text was sent to the Führer. Hitler announced that not only did he have no objections, but that he and Goebbels would attend the first performance. Within days, however, the Reichsmusikkammer edict preventing German musicians working abroad was invoked against Strauss, forcing him to withdraw from performances of *Fidelio* in Salzburg. Strauss was forbidden to attend unless he went as an ordinary member of the audience, which he did. *Elektra* was in the repertoire. He went on stage to acknowledge the applause, and was later seen talking publicly to Zweig and Bruno Walter. The following winter he began work on a hymn, commissioned by the Olympic Committee (which was heavily subsidized with Nazi money) for the next series of games, due to take place in Berlin in 1936. 'I kill the boredom of the Advent season by composing an Olympic hymn for the proletariat,' he wrote to Zweig. 'I, of all people, who hate and despise sport.'

The score of *Die schweigsame Frau* was now finished. In Zweig's text Strauss had found the kind of breezy, brilliant comedy that he had been trying to extract from Hofmannsthal for years, though the handling of the subject matter is, in many respects, disappointing. The bittersweet irony that adds profundity to *Rosenkavalier* and *Arabella* is conspicuous by its absence. In its place is a brittle humour that slides towards caricature, hugely entertaining in itself but narrow in its range after his previous operas. The gravitation towards 'numbers' opera, first audible in *Helena*, is now even more apparent. Elements of Italian *opera buffa* are relentlessly invoked in both plot and characters. The story closely resembles Donizetti's *Don Pasquale*, while the Dickensian-sounding Sir Morosus, the barber Schneidebart and the unnamed Housekeeper closely resemble Bartolo, Figaro and Marcellina from Rossini's *Il barbiere di Siviglia*.

In the context of its times, however, the opera has a terrible irony, for buried beneath its surface froth is a parable about music under threat. Morosus dreams of a world without sound, distrusts music, will only marry a 'silent wife' and disinherits his nephew Henry for joining an opera company. He is tricked, however, into contracting a marriage, which turns out to be bogus, with the company's coloratura soprano. As with Zerbinetta, Strauss equates the voice with the spirit of misrule, and the seemingly docile Aminta (named after the legendary shepherdess of Italian Pastoral) brings nothing but chaos, ear-splitting cacophony and a vast barrage of operatic allusions in her train. Strauss's score spins out quotes one by one – *Faust, Zauberflöte,*

Maria Cebotari as Aminta in the 1935 Dresden première of *Die schweigsame Frau*, at the moment when the 'silent wife' mutates into a shrieking harridan

Meistersinger, Freischütz, Rigoletto, his own *Frau ohne Schatten.* Aminta has a raucous singing lesson during which she purports to sing an aria by opera's perceived originator Monteverdi (Strauss parts company with the seventeenth-century original in the second bar). The reconciliatory ending is gorgeous, though the words, in the context of the early years of the Third Reich, can only bring with them hideous sadness. Music is beautiful, Morosus claims, once it has stopped. By the Reich's last months, only the Berlin Philharmonic would be permitted to play.

By that time it was obvious to Zweig that their collaboration was untenable. He was working with a man who held an official post in a regime which openly persecuted his own people. Strauss's own actions were adding to the tension between the two. His suggestion that it might be better to withdraw *Die schweigsame Frau* for fear of causing embarrassment to the government hurt Zweig, though he was not prone to dramatic displays of feeling. Strauss then proposed that the two should collaborate in secret and lock their works in a safe 'that will be opened when we both consider the time propitious'. Zweig was unequivocal in his response: 'It seems inappropriate that something in your life, in your art, should be done in secrecy,' he wrote to Strauss. 'I am aware of the difficulties that would confront a new work if I were to provide the text … I will be happy … to assist with advice anybody who might work for you, to sketch things out for him – without compensation, without boasting about it, simply for the pleasure of serving your great art.'

Strauss was panic-stricken that his new Hofmannsthal was withdrawing from him. 'I will not give you up simply because we happen to have an anti-Semitic government,' he wrote in touching desperation. 'Do a few more beautiful things for me (I will never find another writer), and we will keep the matter confidential until we both think the time is right to come out with it.' Zweig held firm. He was prepared to allow more suitable, non-Jewish writers to adapt his own material; he would even oversee their texts, but he would not compromise either of them by writing another libretto himself.

In 1935 the Nuremberg Laws were passed, which deprived the Jews of citizens' rights. This coincided with a clampdown on artistic freedom and a greater involvement by Goebbels in the Reichskulturkammer. The première of *Die schweigsame Frau* was fixed for 24 June in Dresden, where the new music director was Karl Böhm, a staunch Nazi supporter. Strauss continued to refuse Zweig's offer of supplying him with a substitute librettist and overseeing his work. 'Don't recommend any other librettist to me,' he wrote to Zweig on 24 May. 'It's a pity to waste the writing paper.' Zweig decided to lay his cards on the table. On 15 June he wrote to Strauss (who was overseeing rehearsals), reminding him how he was widely perceived abroad as having compromised himself by standing in for Bruno Walter and then Toscanini in 1933. Strauss's reply was both explosive and insensitive. 'This Jewish egoism!' he wrote to Zweig on 17 June. 'It's enough to make one an anti-Semite! Do you think that I have been guided in any of my actions by the thought that I am German? … Do you believe that Mozart consciously composed as an Aryan? … For me the populace only exists from the moment it becomes an audience. Whether they are Chinese, Bavarians, New Zealanders or Berliners, it's all the same to me, so long as they've paid the full price of admission … Who has told you that I have become so deeply involved in politics? … Because I pose as President of the Reichsmusikkammer? … I would have taken on this tiresome honorary office under any government.' He posted the letter the same day in the hotel letterbox. It was intercepted by the Gestapo and sent to Martin Mutschmann, assistant to the Nazi governor of Saxony. By the beginning of July a copy was in Hitler's hands.

On 22 June, two days before the première, Strauss, playing skat with some friends in his hotel, casually asked if he could see the playbill for *Die schweigsame Frau*. Friedrich von Schuh (son of Ernst and the Dresden Opera's business manager) handed him a proof copy. Strauss saw immediately that Zweig's name had been omitted and, enraged, threatened to walk out. Paul Adolph, the Intendant, agreed that the librettist's name should be reinstated. The première itself was a success, although Hitler and Goebbels did not attend.

Strauss was evidently uneasy. On 3 July, back in Garmisch, he confided his thoughts to paper in one of a series of private memoranda, which he wrote during the Third Reich. 'It is a sad time,' he wrote, 'when an artist of my rank has to ask a brat of a minister what he may set to music and what he may have performed … I almost envy my friend Stefan Zweig, persecuted for his race, who now definitely refuses to work with me in public or in secret … To be

honest, I don't understand his Jewish solidarity, and regret that the
artist in Zweig cannot rise above political fashions. If we do not
preserve artistic freedom ourselves, how can we expect it from soapbox
orators in taverns?'

Three days later, Strauss was visited by Otto von Keudell, an
assistant of Secretary of State Walter Funkel, who produced the
intercepted letter and ordered him to resign from the
Reichsmusikkammer on the grounds of 'ill health'. He did so at once.
Die schweigsame Frau was officially banned after four performances.
Paul Adolph was summarily dismissed for having reinstated Zweig's
name on the publicity material. On 10 July, Strauss wrote a second
memorandum, summarizing the circumstances that led to his
dismissal. The ending reads as follows:

I was condemned [in the Viennese press] as a servile, self-seeking anti-
Semite, whereas in truth I have always stressed at every opportunity to
everyone of importance how much (to my disadvantage) I consider the
Goebbels-Streicher Jew-baiting a disgrace to German honour ... I openly
acknowledge here that I have received so much support, so much selfless
friendship, so much generous help and intellectual stimulus from Jews that
it would be a crime not to acknowledge it all with gratitude. It is true
that I have had adversaries in the Jewish press ... But my worst and most
malicious enemies were 'Aryans'. I need mention the names of Perfall ...
Felix Mottl, Franz Schalk, Weingartner [widely believed to have been
behind the anti-Strauss petition in Vienna in 1919], and the whole Party
press: the Völkischer Beobachter *and the rest.*

Three days later, however, he wrote a grovelling letter to Hitler.

My Führer ... I hold my removal from the Reichsmusikkammer
sufficiently noteworthy to feel obligated to recount to you, my Führer, in
brief, the whole development of the affair ... I willingly admit that
without a precise explanation and taken out of the context of a long
artistic correspondence, without knowledge of its previous history nor the
mood in which the letter [to Zweig] was penned, the contents of this letter
could be easily misinterpreted and misunderstood ... In the above-
mentioned letter, there are three passages which have given offence. I have
been given to understand that these were that I have little comprehension

*of anti-Semitism, as well as the concept of the people's community, and of
the significance of my position as President of the Reichsmusikkammer. I
was not given the opportunity for a direct and personal explanation of the
sense, content and meaning of this letter which, briefly, was written in a
moment of ill-humour against Stefan Zweig and dashed off without
further thought ... My whole life belongs to German music and to an
indefatigable effort to elevate German culture. I have never been active
politically nor even expressed myself in politics. Therefore I believe that I
will find understanding from you, the great architect of German social
life, particularly when, with deep emotion and with deep respect, I assure
you that even after my dismissal ... I will devote the few years still
remaining to me only to the purest and most ideal goals. Confident of your
high sense of justice, I beg you, my Führer, most humbly, to receive me for
a personal discussion, to give me the opportunity to justify myself in person
... Your forever devoted, Richard Strauss.*

Hitler never replied. Strauss's successor at the Reichsmusikkammer,
Paul Raabe, a Party member, was appointed almost immediately and
at the end of August the Chamber issued an edict stating that no Jew
was permitted to play in a German orchestra. Strauss maintained an
appearance of aloofness, but his next move was significantly rebellious.
In 1934 he had been nominated President of the International Society
of Composers, founded to break down national barriers between
musicians. Strauss arrived in Vichy for the Society's first festival in
September 1935, two months after his dismissal. In addition to
performing music by 'our composers', he chose to conduct works by
the French-Jewish Paul Dukas who had died a few months earlier. His
gesture did not go unnoticed. The German ambassador walked out of
the performance.

Strauss had finally capitulated to Zweig's demands that he work
with a different librettist. In 1934 they had met to discuss future plans.
Strauss was reading *The World History of Theatre*, by one of Zweig's
friends, the Viennese cultural historian and theatrical archivist Josef
Gregor, and was much taken by the idea of Calderón's play *La
Redención de Breda* ('The Redemption of Breda'), depicting the
peaceful surrender of the Dutch city to a Spanish army of occupation
after an eight-year siege in 1625. Zweig suggested changing the date
and setting to the last day of the Thirty Years War, and by 21 August

had produced the draft of an impressive scenario entitled *24. Oktober 1648*. It was at this point that Zweig began to suggest more politically suitable librettists to continue his work. After Strauss had vehemently rejected several writers, Zweig began to push Josef Gregor forward. Gregor was not Jewish and the Nazis could have no objection to a collaboration between the two. Strauss finally agreed to a meeting. It took place in a hotel in Berchtesgaden – where Hitler had his mountain retreat – on 7 July 1935, the day after Strauss's dismissal from the Reichsmusikkammer.

Gregor presented Strauss with six scenarios, of which, he claimed, the composer selected three: *24. Oktober 1648* was one, *Daphne* was a second and the third remains unidentified, though it may have been *Die Liebe der Danae*. Gregor was a well-meaning but sycophantic man, determined to impress Strauss (who did not much care for him) and anxious to be seen as a second Hofmannsthal, which he was not. The verse of his librettos is dull and uninspiring. What theatrical impact they have derives largely from Strauss, who nagged him until he was satisfied, which was not very often. 'I don't believe I will ever find music for it,' he railed, when *1648* was delivered. 'These aren't real people. The Kommandant and his wife, they're on stilts … The dialogue of the two Kommandants … is how two schoolmasters would hold a conversation on a given subject: "30 Years War."'

Strauss in 1938 with Josef Gregor, who became his librettist at Zweig's suggestion

Gregor was installed for a while in one of the towers in the
Garmisch villa, where Strauss was able to follow the progress of the
libretto as he worked on it. The title was soon changed to *Friedenstag*
('Peace Day'). It is possible that Strauss's harassment of Gregor was
motivated by the desire to force him to return the libretto to Zweig,
but the latter was only prepared to supervise from the wings. His
single intervention consisted of revising the offending text of the duet
for the two Kommandants. Strauss and Zweig were now
corresponding under pseudonyms for fear of official discovery. Strauss
called himself Robert Storch (his alter-ego from *Intermezzo*) and
instructed Zweig to sign his name Henry Morosus (the opera-loving
nephew from *Die schweigsame Frau*). Gregor occasionally carried
letters across the border. Strauss was becoming increasingly anxious
that his mail was being intercepted (which is certainly possible,
though there is no concrete evidence to support his fears).

Adolf Mahnke's design for
the 1938 Dresden
production of *Friedenstag;*
the local Gauleiter
considered the work to be a
'highly political opera'.

The music of *Friedenstag* was completed in June 1936, a year which saw the establishment of an uneasy truce between the composer and the government. On 1 August Strauss conducted the Olympic Hymn at the Berlin games in Hitler's presence. In November, the Dresden company made a visit to London for a season at Covent Garden; *Rosenkavalier*, conducted by Karl Böhm, was chosen as the opening work. Strauss sat in a box with the German ambassador, Joachim von Ribbentrop, and went on stage at the end of the performance to acknowledge the applause. Four days later he conducted *Ariadne* himself. He travelled abroad to conduct as much as he could, and the Reichsmusikkammer made no attempt to stop him.

In September he began work on the score of *Daphne*, which was destined from the beginning to be *Friedenstag*'s companion piece. 'The more I read it, the less I like it,' was Strauss's initial comment on Gregor's text, and he sounded off to Zweig once more about his new librettist's 'schoolmaster banalities'. Gregor was eventually made to revise the text twice but Strauss remained unsatisfied. The ending caused particular trouble. Gregor was adamant that *Daphne*, like *Friedenstag*, should end with a choral finale. Strauss was equally adamant that a choral depiction of Daphne's transformation into a tree was singularly inappropriate. He consulted Clemens Krauss, who came up with the answer. 'The miracle of transformation occurs: *only with orchestra alone!*' he wrote to Gregor on 12 May 1937, when work on the rest of the score was already well underway. 'At most at the very end: after the tree is complete, she might wordlessly – nothing but sounding nature – sing eight bars of the laurel motive! Do you like that?' Gregor had little choice but to comply. The score of *Daphne* was finished on Christmas Eve 1937 in Taormina, Sicily, where Strauss was convalescing from an illness.

Though intended as a pair, *Friedenstag* and *Daphne* soon parted company. The two operas had different dedications – *Daphne* to Karl Böhm, *Friedenstag* to Krauss and Ursuleac. Krauss, appointed music director in Munich in 1937, was determined that *Friedenstag* should have its première during his first season and pressurized Strauss to allow the opera to be performed separately. The première duly took place on 24 July 1938, coupled with Beethoven's *Die Geschöpfe des Prometheus*. Krauss conducted and Ursuleac took the leading role of Maria. The producer was the young Rudolf Hartmann, whom Strauss deeply admired. In one sense, it was a musical homecoming. *Friedenstag* was, after all, the first Strauss opera to have its première in his native city.

Friedenstag is a curious opera and one open to the consistent misinterpretation that it is essentially an anti-fascist work. Much of the pacifist mythology surrounding the opera can be traced back to a statement Strauss made in 1949 when *Friedenstag* was broadcast on French Radio. 'I want to consider it as a good omen that my artistic vision of 1938, conjuring up that peace so much desired … can radiate over the world from the city of light that is Paris.'

This is quite different to statements made at the time of the opera's composition and première. In 1936 there had been talk of staging the work in Dresden. A copy of the text was accordingly sent for approval to Martin Mutschmann (he who had purloined Strauss's letter to Zweig the previous year). 'Highly political opera libretto,' was Mutschmann's comment. 'This is what we need.' 'You see,' Strauss wrote to Pauline. 'I'm always up to the minute. Since *Salome* it's always been the same.' Strauss's heart may not have been in the opera, and he certainly distrusted militarism, but there is little question that *Friedenstag* is a work which suited the ideology of the party that had recently dismissed him from office; at the time of the première it was, in fact, widely acclaimed as the first opera to coincide with Third Reich ideals. Though the charge of opportunism, frequently made against him, does not always survive analysis, it does so here.

The opera enacts the process of fascist emergence, the fashioning of 'new brothers' (invoked in the work's final chorus) out of war and economic chaos. The libretto repeatedly mentions the siege of Magdeburg in 1631, the most horrific incident of the Thirty Years War and synonymous in German culture with military disaster, in which the city's Lutheran population were first threatened then massacred by Catholic forces. The tragic chaos of Weimar is starkly recalled in the opening scenes in which the populace, screaming for bread and food, become vociferous in their demands that the unnamed city in which the opera takes place should surrender to its enemies.

The Kommandant, however, is a man of principle determined to die for a cause. He promises the citizens a signal which will herald the arrival of peace, though he plans in secret to blow the citadel and everyone in it to bits rather than give in. His devoted wife Maria, the only named character in the work, decides to die with him. His plans are foiled when a distant cannon shot leads the Kommandant to think that battle has recommenced, but this is, in fact, the signal that a truce has finally been declared and the war is over. The enemy army marches into the city and the Kommandant and his opposite number are reconciled. The jubilant choral finale has questionable undertones, however. Fascism demands that the individual be subsumed into the collective, and Gregor's stage directions read: 'The walls open, the tower sinks. Bright sunlight floods in. Everything is a single surging sea of people.' At this point Strauss's singers step out of character; opera is turned into cantata as, for the first time in the work, everyone sings in unison: 'What now shakes us, what now blinds us are signs that shall never end. The future will carry us easily over bridges which we dare not now tread.' During the finale, Strauss, who has previously given us a sharp depiction of the city's plight with a wonderful aria for the unhappy Maria and a great duet for the heroine and her husband, plunges towards fascist kitsch as Beethoven's Ninth Symphony collides with a tune of overwhelming banality reminiscent of a Nazi marching song.

On 12 March 1938, four months before the opera's première, Hitler's expansionist policies had been put into action with the Anschluss, the annexation of Austria. Two months after the first performance, the Munich conference took place. Clutching a piece of paper, Neville Chamberlain made his disastrous speech about 'peace in our time', while the Nazis entered the Sudetenland. *Friedenstag* mimetically enacts the process. The enemy Holsteiner (from the north) marches with full military accoutrements into the opera's unnamed southern city to be received with open arms as many Austrians welcomed the Nazis. Though Strauss and Gregor could not have been aware of the resonance of this when they wrote the work, *Friedenstag*'s resemblance to recent events was undoubtedly an important factor in its initial success – Hitler, perhaps significantly, did not hear it during the course of its first run in Munich, but attended the première in Vienna, now capital of the renamed *Ostmark*. The figures of the Kommandant, his wife and those soldiers prepared to remain in the citadel and obliterate themselves for the sake of their cause were held up as embodiments of the Nazi ideal. But after 1939, militarism masquerading as peaceful takeover was no longer

Hitler, Goebbels and Martin Bormann (far right, standing) at the Vienna première of *Friedenstag* on 6 June 1939, after the annexation of Austria. The performance formed part of the official celebrations of Strauss's seventy-fifth birthday.

the order of the day. Germany was at war, and the opera was quietly dropped from the repertoire all over the Reich. Since then its outings have been few and far between.

Daphne proved remarkably different. For the première, in Dresden on 15 October, the double-bill format was restored, though *Friedenstag* was placed second. Karl Böhm conducted. At the dress rehearsal, Pauline, usually vocal and obstreperous on such occasions, sat through the piece in silence, then walked up to Böhm and kissed him. To the end of her life, she maintained that the opera was her favourite among her husband's works. At Garmisch Strauss frequently played extracts from his own music for his family at the piano, and the closing scene of *Daphne* was the music he played most often. The work's significance was clearly deeply personal, as if, after the compromising public statement of *Friedenstag*, he felt he could return to private territory.

Though it lacks dramatic bite, *Daphne* is among the most lyrically beautiful of Strauss's scores, exquisitely orchestrated with a textural clarity absent from his music since his evocation of the Empress's spirit world in *Die Frau ohne Schatten*. The choice of subject matter, and Strauss's handling of it, is significant. The myth of Daphne, turned by the gods into a laurel tree in order to escape the sexual attentions of Apollo, was the subject of the very first opera, Jacopo Peri's *Dafne*, performed in Florence in 1597 or 98 (the score is regrettably lost). Strauss is therefore hinting at the origins of the form and his own place in the continuity of operatic tradition. Onto the basic myth Gregor has grafted images which essentially derive from Nietzsche's *Die Geburt der Tragödie aus dem Geiste der Musik*. They make their last explicit appearance in Strauss's work, though Gregor follows Hofmannsthal's ambiguous stance in subverting them and calling them into question. Daphne's drama is played out against the enactment of a feast of Dionysus, which Apollo interrupts. The boundaries between Apollonian serenity and Dionysiac frenzy first blur and then crumble: Apollo acts throughout with obsessive irrational violence, while Leukippos, a follower of Dionysus and Apollo's rival for Daphne's affections, is gentle and shy. Daphne's

The feast of Dionysus in the 1964 Munich production of *Daphne*

rejection of both leads to catastrophe (Apollo peremptorily kills Leukippos in a fit of blind rage, though he is immediately contrite), followed by the extraordinary finale in which the jingoism of Nazism is, by subtle implication, overturned. Apollo requests that the gods join Daphne to the eternal nature which she worships by turning her into the tree whose leaves will permanently symbolize heroism and victory. When Daphne's transformation begins, however, a very different set of values are evoked. She calls upon humanity (*Menschen*) to take her not as a symbol of victory but as a sign of undying love. It is precisely at this point that the words cut out and the great orchestral finale, among the most rapturous of Strauss's creations, begins. When Daphne's voice is finally heard once more, she has passed beyond words to become pure sound. The finale asserts the permanence of music as an expression of love and looks ahead to Strauss's own return to absolute music at a point in his life when the Nazis had made his existence unbearable.

In 1938 his relationship with the regime took a further, hideous, twist. If he thought there was safety in compromise, he was soon

Strauss and Goebbels at the opening of the Reichs-musiktage in Düsseldorf on 28 May 1938

found to be wrong. In April, to celebrate Hitler's birthday, Mussolini finally fulfilled his promise of mounting *Die Frau ohne Schatten* in Rome. In May, Strauss took part in the first of the annual Reichsmusiktage in Düsseldorf, a parade of Nazi-endorsed compositions, which included *Arabella*, Pfitzner's 1921 nationalist cantata *Von deutscher Seele* ('From the German Soul') and new works by Werner Egk who later claimed he was writing subversive anti-Nazi satire. The same month also saw the opening, in Düsseldorf, of the *Entartete Musik* exhibition, a collection of scores, photographs and recordings of the work of musicians deemed by the Nazis to be 'racially degenerate'. Schoenberg, Berg, Krenek, Hindemith, Weill and Klemperer were represented, and obscene graffiti about 'Jewish Bolshevism' and the 'niggering of art' was splattered on the walls. Strauss chillingly remarked that he thought *Salome* should be included; his Jews, after all, sang atonally (which is not, in fact, true). With *Friedenstag* and *Daphne* successfully launched in October in Dresden, he returned to Italy.

The persecution of the Jews now began in earnest. In July, Goering issued a series of decrees ordering the confiscation of all Jewish property and the enforced closure of all Jewish businesses before the year was out. On the night of 9 November – twenty years to the day after the proclamation of the Weimar Republic – the horrendous pogrom known as Kristallnacht took place. In Garmisch, Strauss and Pauline were treated with suspicion by the local populace on account of their Jewish daughter-in-law, Alice, and the family was ostracized. Strauss's grandsons, Richard and Christian, were harassed and bullied at school. Franz had meanwhile joined the Nazi party.

The subject of Strauss's collaboration with Zweig had been raised at SS meetings as early as the previous May and on Kristallnacht, the Nazis arrived to arrest Alice. She and Franz were away, apparently at their hunting lodge. Instead, Richard and Christian were dragged in tears to the town square where they were forced to spit publicly on other Jews who were held there. Strauss returned from Italy as soon as he heard what had happened and bombarded every official he could think of with letters, even going so far as to write yet again to Hitler. The Chancellery eventually announced that the boys should be treated as Aryans, but that they would not be eligible for party membership, military service or public office.

Under the circumstances, it is not surprising that the opera on which Strauss was now working turned out to be uneven. This was *Die Liebe der Danae*, the composition of which was begun early in 1938 and completed in June 1940. The librettist was officially Gregor, but various people had a hand in shaping the text. Strauss demanded that Gregor rework a scenario on the subject, written by Hofmannsthal in 1920, which Strauss had initially rejected. Gregor tried to combine his own scenario with Hofmannsthal's, much to the annoyance of Strauss who objected to most of Gregor's alterations and flung draft after draft back at his hapless librettist. By November 1937, they were on version two of the libretto based on the fourth draft of the scenario. The following year, Strauss plunged into composition though he remained dissatisfied. Clemens Krauss was drafted in to help and Strauss accepted his proposals for the shape of the final act. This nearly led to a rift between Strauss and Gregor, who took understandable umbrage, began to suffer from writer's block and proceeded to stay away from the première of *Daphne*. Strauss was forced to apologize, soothed Gregor's wounded feelings with a request for a potential ballet (nothing came of it) and finally managed to draw from him a text for the final act which came close to his wishes.

While he worked on the score, his anxiety continued to grow. He maintained his taciturn, professional exterior but he was becoming depressed in his attempts to keep his family safe. In June 1939, as Europe slid towards war, he went to Vienna to conduct a concert for his seventy-fifth birthday. He included the *Domestica* in the programme. During the performance he kept glancing round at his family who were sitting in a box. Afterwards he broke down in the artists' room, muttering 'Now it's all over' between sobs. In 1940 he broke off work on the score of *Danae* to compose a piece, commissioned by the Japanese government, to celebrate the 2600th anniversary of the founding of the Imperial dynasty. Strauss told both the Nazis and the Japanese officials that he was accepting the commission to ensure his family were left alone. He gradually became convinced that *Danae* would be his last work and that he would never hear it. The première, he told Gregor, was not to take place until two years after the war, in other words 'after my death. So that's how long you will have to possess your soul in patience.' Krauss, he agreed, was to be its first conductor, but for a while he continued to refuse him permission to use the score.

Strauss's darkening mood when working on the opera profoundly affected the finished piece, while his gathering sense that *Danae* was to be posthumous infuses the score with a retrospective element that looks back first to his own earlier work, then further back to Mozart and Wagner. The tone of the opera, subtitled 'Cheerful Mythology in Three Acts', becomes increasingly serious as the opera progresses. Two acts of forced humour and variable inspiration give way to a third act of considerably greater subtlety. Gregor, like Hofmannsthal, was fascinated by Baroque theatre, and in *Danae* two well-known Greek myths combine; Danae, seduced by Jupiter in the form of a shower of golden rain, meets and falls in love with Midas, the king whose touch turns everything to gold, much to the annoyance of Jupiter who still wants Danae for himself.

As the opera proceeds, the dramatic allusions proliferate. Midas, Danae and Jupiter are Octavian, Sophie and Ochs at one remove. The bridegroom's deputy yet again carries off the bride, presenting her with a golden twig in place of a silver rose (the values of gold being fraudulent and illusory throughout, there is much vacuous tinkling in the orchestra). As in *Daphne*, though here much more explicitly, the sexual attentions of a wooing god are rejected and with them his rule of law. Danae prefers love in poverty with Midas to soulless grandeur with Jupiter and her punishment for having 'chosen the fate of humanity', as Jupiter contemptuously describes it, is transformation into a statue like the Emperor in *Die Frau ohne Schatten*. Midas, falling in love with Danae's portrait, echoes Tamino in *Die Zauberflöte*, while Jupiter is a comic counterpart of Wagner's Wotan, a god caught in his own self-created constructs, who eventually returns to earth disguised as a wanderer in order to face the effects of the havoc he has caused. In the opera's final scene, Jupiter accepts his own defeat in the face of human emotion and realizes, like Wotan, that he is facing 'the end' (*Das Ende* – the phrase is borrowed from *Walküre*). Quietly, he bids Danae farewell to music infused with the nostalgic sadness that redeems the opera from the superficial cheer that characterizes much of the earlier sections of the score. By the end Strauss has forged a remarkable empathy with the initially unsympathetic Jupiter, whose farewell he may well have seen as prefiguring his own withdrawal from the world of music.

Strauss did not withdraw. Within weeks of completing the score of *Danae* he began work on its successor which, after passing through various transmutations, was eventually called *Capriccio*. This was his last completed stage work. Though far greater than *Danae*, it has a number of points in common with it. Firstly, the sense of retrospection that underlies *Danae* is now brought centre stage. Secondly, it has its origins in the unearthing of a previously rejected sketch. This was *Prima la musica e poi le parole*, by the Abbé Casti, which Zweig had first suggested in 1934 having discovered the original text (a libretto for Mozart's rival Salieri) in the British Library. Zweig considered the original 'too slight' to stand on its own, though he used the idea of Casti's text as part of his plan to push Strauss in Gregor's direction and a draft, assiduously written by the latter under Zweig's supervision, reached Strauss in June 1935. He had angrily rejected it (there is a reference to it in the letter intercepted by the Gestapo), after which the subject was temporarily dropped.

In 1939, however, Strauss surprised Gregor by asking him to reconsider *Erst die Worte, dann die Musik* ('First Words, Then Music' – which is Casti's title about face), though he was more fascinated by the implications of the title than by Gregor's handling of the material, which bore a strong resemblance to *Ariadne auf Naxos*: a group of travelling players were to arrive at a medieval castle to put on an entertainment for the local aristocracy under the supervision of their director. Gregor and Zweig both had Max Reinhardt in mind as a model. Reinhardt, like Zweig, was now in exile, though his personality (interwoven with character traits of both Strauss and Hofmannsthal) hovers over the figure of La Roche in the final version. Gregor revised the text, which Strauss dismissed as disappointing. Gregor struggled and began to flounder. Strauss yet again consulted with Krauss and with Rudolf Hartmann, who by now was working as a director in Munich. A meeting between the three men in Garmisch, in October 1939, just over a month after World War II broke out, produced the necessary results; Krauss wrote a scenario which matched Strauss's expectations. A few days later Gregor was quietly removed from the project and Krauss took over. When Strauss began work on the score in July 1940, the libretto was not yet complete, and what followed was very much a close collaborative effort with the composer and his conductor-turned-writer working in tandem. The libretto was completed on 18 January 1941. Just over a month later, Strauss finished the score. There is no question that Strauss saw *Capriccio* as a highly personal work, as well as a terminal one. 'Isn't this D flat major [the key of the final chord] the best winding up of my life's work in the theatre?' he asked Krauss in 1944, when the conductor was gently pressuring him to think of another opera. 'One can only leave one testament behind.'

Like *Ariadne, Capriccio* is an opera about opera, though on this occasion it has an ingenious cyclic structure. Following Casti's original scheme, the characters decide to write an opera themselves. As the piece progresses it becomes clear that what is being heard is the work the characters have created; the final chord effectively throws the listener right back to the beginning to start the whole process again. The setting is France in the last years of the *ancien régime,* when Gluck's reforms were leading to fierce discussion of the relative importance of words and music within opera itself. The composer Flamand and the writer Olivier are both in love with the young, widowed Countess Madeleine. She in her turn is drawn to both, though the libretto frequently equates her not with music (*Musik* in German) but with sound or tone (the word *Ton* translates both). 'Word and sound' (*Wort und Ton*), her lovers remark, 'are brother and sister,' and the Countess indeed has a brother, a man of words, in love with the actress Clairon. *Capriccio* explores their creative dependency, leading to what is arguably the greatest soprano monologue in Strauss's output, in which Madeleine, pushed to choose between her two admirers and consequently to decide the ending of the opera they have written about her, finds herself emotionally torn in two. *Wort und Ton* are indivisibly linked like *Tristan und Isolde* for whom the word '*und*' binds them forever into a unity (a quote from Wagner's opera is heard as Flamand first improvises to Olivier's words), and the question of their relative values is unanswerable. At the end of the opera, Madeleine, both its inspiration and the heroine that Flamand and Olivier have created, still cannot make up her mind.

The 'conversation piece for music', as the opera is subtitled, consists of a series of dialogues in which operatic history is surveyed and assessed, mostly to fluid recitative punctuated by brief flights of

lyricism. There is a touching, though oblique, allusion to
Hofmannsthal: Olivier writes a sonnet – declaimed by Clairon, set to
music by Flamand and sung by Madeleine in the final scene – the text
of which is drawn from the French poet Ronsard, one of the writers
about whom Hofmannstahl had written his university thesis. When the
conversation progresses to a suitable subject for the opera which Olivier
and Flamand will write, Strauss presents themes from *Ariadne* and
Daphne only to dismiss them, then allows an astonishingly beautiful
melody to take their place, derived from the Schumannesque interlude
from Strauss's own *Krämerspiegel*. It is first heard when the Countess
remarks that the theatre is a reflection of life. 'We see ourselves,' she
says, 'as if through a magic mirror.' Strauss allows the melody to
increase in fullness with each repetition until it becomes the glorious
'moonlight' interlude that precedes Madeleine's final monologue.

The 'conversation piece for
music', *Capriccio*, Strauss's
operatic testament, at the
Cuvilléstheater in Munich
in 1964

   It has been argued that *Capriccio* represents a burying of Strauss's
head in the metaphorical sand by writing a drawing-room comedy in

the shadow of Dachau (the camp is in a Munich suburb) while the world was at war. *Capriccio* does, however, represent a response, albeit ambivalent, to contemporary events. At one point La Roche harangues the assembled company. 'I follow the eternal laws of theatre,' he shouts. 'I preserve the good that we possess. I still expect the works of genius of our age. Where are the works that can speak to the heart of the people? Where are they? – I cannot find them, however hard I search.' Strauss's frustration and unhappiness are apparent in the text. The tirade continues with a plea for humanity, echoing the conclusions of *Daphne* and *Danae*: 'I want to populate my stage with people [*Menschen*]. With people who are like us, who speak our language.' Yet compromise remains in *Capriccio* and its expression is ugly. Madeleine's brother suggests the Trojan War as a potential subject for Flamand and Olivier. 'We've got enough Egyptians, Hebrews, Persians and Romans in our operas,' is La Roche's response.

It is possible this line was inserted to push the work past the Nazis, though we shall never know for certain. Getting *Capriccio* staged was a complex nightmare, for shortly before it was complete, Strauss yet again became a pawn in a game between two members of the Nazi hierarchy. This time the players were Goebbels and Baldur von Schirach, the former head of the Hitler Youth and now Gauleiter (district commander) of Vienna. Despite Strauss's composition of the *Japanische Festmusik* ('Japanese Festival Music') in 1940, his family remained subject to harassment. When the art- and music-loving Schirach announced he wanted to turn Vienna into the cultural capital of the Reich, Strauss declared himself willing to help on condition that his family be allowed to live in peace. By the end of 1941, Strauss, Pauline, Alice, Franz and their children were living once more in the house on the Jacquingasse, and Strauss was taking part in music festivals organized by Schirach featuring the works of many composers who were out of favour in Berlin as well as conducting Mozart to 'Aryanized' librettos.

The situation remained uneasy. Strauss had promised he would not make any public anti-Nazi remarks, but Pauline could be outspoken in her contempt. She told Schirach that once the war was over, he would always be welcome in Garmisch, 'but as for the rest of the gang … ' Franz and Alice were at one point arrested and had to

spend two days in Gestapo custody, until they were released on
Schirach's orders. Even so, Strauss, in gratitude to the Gauleiter for
his protection, allowed the String Sextet which opens *Capriccio* to be
played in Schirach's house on 7 May 1942. Earlier that year he had
tactfully set two poems by Josef Weinheber in honour of the poet's
fiftieth birthday. Weinheber was a fervent Nazi who finally
committed suicide when the war turned against Germany. Strauss
chose texts, however, which are free from fascist connotations. One of
them describes the Belvedere district of Vienna in which he and his
family now lived.

Strauss's association with Schirach inflamed Goebbels. In February
1942 Strauss was summoned to the Propaganda Ministry and publicly
humiliated, in front of a group of other composers, over a letter which
he had written. The letter, which appears not to have survived,
contained slighting remarks about Franz Lehár (who, as Albert Speer's
memoirs prove, was one of Hitler's favourite composers) and ended
with the words 'It is not for Dr. Goebbels to interfere.' 'You have no
conception of who you are,' Goebbels screamed. 'You dare refer to
Lehár as a street musician?! … Lehár has the masses and you haven't!
Stop your claptrap about the importance of serious music, once and for
all. It will not serve to raise your own standing. Tomorrow's art is
different from yesterday's! You, Herr Strauss, belong to yesterday!' When
the onslaught was over, Strauss broke down in Goebbels's outer office.
'If only I'd listened to my wife and stayed in Garmisch,' he sobbed.

That *Capriccio* reached the stage in Strauss's lifetime was largely
thanks to Krauss, who wanted the première to take place in Munich as
part of a Strauss Festival to be held in October 1942. Strauss had his
doubts that the work would appeal to a broad public and described it
to Krauss as 'a dainty morsel for cultural gourmets, not very
substantial musically'. But Krauss had no doubts about its validity and
managed to obtain Goebbels's consent for the première to go ahead by
requesting that the Propaganda Minister act as 'official patron' of the
performance. Out of sheer vanity, and perhaps to score points against
Schirach, Goebbels agreed. The first performance accordingly took
place on 28 October and was enthusiastically received. Audiences
braved the now nightly Allied air-raids to attend. Since the war, the
opera's popularity has steadily increased and Strauss's fears that it
might prove uninteresting for the general public were unfounded.

It was soon apparent that Schirach's protection was neither adequate nor extensive enough. Though his influence unquestionably played a part in Alice's survival and the safety of her children, Schirach was either unable or unwilling to intervene in the tragedy that overtook the rest of her family. On 1 October 1941, Jewish emigration was forbidden and the Reich's borders were closed to those who still had the power to escape. On 14 October, the deportations to the gas chambers began. Alice's mother, Marie von Grab, was safe in Lucerne. The remainder of her family, including Alice's grandmother, Paula Neumann, had been stripped of their possessions and by the end of 1941 were being held in the ghetto in Prague. Marie von Grab was anxious that her mother join her in Lucerne. Though Frau Neumann already possessed a Swiss visa, the Nazis refused to let her go. In the summer of 1942, members of the Grab-Neumann family were taken from Prague to the concentration camp at Theresienstadt, the so-called artists' camp, where the Nazis, on occasion, put up a show of respectable treatment in order to deceive the International Red Cross. Other members of the family were taken to the ghetto in Lódz. Strauss wrote to the SS in Prague asking for their freedom. His letters were never answered. He appealed to Schirach and to Hans Frank (the music-loving governor who butchered occupied Poland, an admirer of Strauss's music and an even greater fan of Pfitzner). They too professed themselves powerless.

In 1943 Frau Neumann was also taken from Prague to Theresienstadt. In desperation, Strauss drove to the gates of the camp. 'My name is Richard Strauss,' he said to the guards. 'I want to see Frau Neumann.' They turned him away, telling him he was insane. Twenty-six members of Alice Strauss's family were among the millions exterminated by the Nazis as part of the Final Solution. When Paula Neumann died in Theresienstadt, her possessions were returned to the Strauss family. Among them was a photograph of a young Jewish boy, possibly a relative of Frau Neumann's, which Strauss kept on the desk of his study.

During this bleak period he turned away from opera back to absolute music. Before he did so he made one last tentative stab at a tone-poem, *Die Donau* ('The Danube'), which was intended as a tribute to the Vienna Philharmonic on the occasion of their centenary in February 1942. The tone-poem was to end with a choral finale,

The concentration camp at Theresienstadt, where members of Alice Strauss's family were held before being transported to the extermination camps, and where her grandmother, Paula Neumann, died

setting another of Weinheber's poems. He could not complete it. 'Emotion is not as easily turned into music as in the days of the old masters,' he wrote to the orchestra in an apologetic letter. By the end of the year, however, he was writing to Viorica Ursuleac that he had 'just completed a little horn concerto, the third movement of which … has come out particularly well'. The 'little' Second Horn Concerto (it is actually longer than the First) ranks among his masterpieces and ushers in the series of small-scale, largely instrumental works with which his career began to draw to a close.

In some respects, the concerto follows on from *Capriccio*. Eighteenth-century influences dominate, the three-movement form and the small forces at once suggesting Mozart. There is, however, not a whiff of pastiche from beginning to end and the Concerto's most extraordinary qualities, shared by many of the works which followed, are a sense of timelessness and a mixture of exhilaration and unbearable poignancy, qualities shared only in musical history by Verdi's *Falstaff*. The Concerto begins the period in Strauss's career which is usually described as his 'Indian Summer'. Strauss, aged seventy-nine and surrounded by unspeakable horror, suddenly found a new lease of creative life which lasted to the end.

The reasons for this sudden upsurge remain a mystery. Strauss, who so often hid the depths of his emotions behind a mask of humour, was characteristically modest and witty about his last works.

'My life's work is at an end with *Capriccio*,' he told Willi Schuh in 1943. 'The music that I go on scribbling for the benefit of my heirs, exercises for my wrists … has no significance whatsoever from the standpoint of musical history.' Like the elderly Verdi, he clearly saw his final works as private statements, as music written for himself and not to please a public.

Nostalgic memories of his youth and a need to turn away from contemporary nightmare have been suggested as Strauss's motivations for undertaking the Second Horn Concerto. His father's horn playing, together with his own love of the instrument, may well have influenced the piece, though perhaps the most significant factor is that, like his own Daphne, a return to wordlessness signified a new freedom of expression. The similarity of the opera's finale to the melismatic style of Strauss's late instrumental works has been the subject of frequent comment. In surrendering her voice, Daphne moves out of the sphere of both human and divine influence to a place where she can no longer be harmed. Programme music, such as Strauss's tone-poems, and opera are both dependent on literature. Words, for Strauss, had been the source of both triumph and disaster. In returning to absolute forms, he was safe from political interference and at the same time free to express himself as he liked. In the Second Horn Concerto that freedom is first tentatively expressed in the horn's questioning opening theme before relaxing into the elegiac, arching melody of the slow movement and then finally scampering off in unashamed glee in the rondo finale.

The stress caused by their continuing anxieties for Alice and her family took their toll on Strauss and Pauline in the winter of 1942–3. Both were ill with repeated bouts on influenza. While recuperating, Strauss returned to another musical form from his youth and began writing a work for wind ensemble, his first Sonatina for Wind Instruments. He nicknamed it *Aus dem Werkstatt eines Invaliden* ('From the Workshop of an Invalid'). The following summer he and Pauline went back to Garmisch where he turned once again to the figure of Daphne, extracting a new text from Gregor as a replacement for the jettisoned choral finale. Gregor had been understandably upset at his removal from *Capriccio*, though he had followed Strauss in gravitating towards Schirach's circle. His tract, *Das Theater des Volkes in der Ostmark* ('The Theatre for the Nation in the Ostmark'), published in 1942, is dedicated to Schirach. Strauss's request for a new text healed the breach between the two men and undoubtedly eased Strauss's conscience over his treatment of Gregor. The finished cantata, *An den Baum Daphne* ('To the Tree Daphne'), is a piece of exquisite beauty in which the chorus, repeating themes from the opera, apostrophizes the wordless singer of 'the song of love, of eternity' before itself passing for a while into wordlessness. It is also possible that while Strauss was working on the cantata he was thinking of Zweig. His former collaborator had committed suicide along with his wife in Rio de Janeiro on 22 February 1942. 'I hope that my friends might see the dawn,' he wrote in his suicide note. 'Being too impatient I go before them.'

In Garmisch the Nazis continued to exert pressure. Rationing meant that there was rarely enough petrol for the car. A minor official, one Windeisen, at one point demanded that Strauss's chauffeur, Theodor Martin, join up at once and that the Strausses take in evacuees. The conversation turned into a row when Strauss began referring to 'Herr Hitler'. Windeisen demanded he speak of 'the Führer'. 'I call people by their names, I say Herr Hitler,' was Strauss's retort. Windeisen then launched into Nazi spin and told Strauss he had to make sacrifices for the fatherland. 'No soldier needs to fall on my account,' was Strauss's response. 'I did not want this war, it is nothing to do with me.' Windeisen stormed out of the house, declaiming 'Other heads than yours have already rolled.'

Strauss, panic-stricken, threw himself on the mercy of Hans Frank, who arrived by chance later in the day to pay an admiring call. Windeisen's orders were promptly countermanded. Frank later invited Strauss to visit him in Poland. Strauss demurred (though he did send Frank the manuscript of a song) and managed to keep out of his way. Windeisen never harassed Strauss again, though by January the following year, news of the incident had reached Hitler. On 24 January, Martin Bormann issued a communiqué ordering that 'The personal association of our leading men with Dr. Strauss shall cease. However the Führer, to whom Reichsminister Dr. Goebbels referred the question, decided today that no obstacles should be put in the way of the performance of his works.' Obstacles were nonetheless put in his way. The porter's lodge at Garmisch was commandeered. Strauss was arbitrarily refused permission to travel to Switzerland to take his annual

cure. His health began to suffer, as did Pauline's. By the summer of
1944, when they celebrated their golden wedding, she was virtually an
invalid and had spent months in bed with pneumonia and erysipelas,
an acute infectious disease causing inflammation of the skin.

Around them the Reich was crumbling. The little that survived of
German culture was now being physically decimated by war. On
2 October 1943, the Nationaltheater in Munich was bombed in an air
raid. Strauss was devastated. 'This is the greatest catastrophe of my
life, for which there can be no consolation,' he told Willi Schuh,
recalling how the theatre, where his father had served as first horn for
forty-nine years, had witnessed the premières of *Tristan* and
Meistersinger. He wrote a few pages of *Trauermusik* ('Funeral' or
'Mourning Music'), then set them aside.

Vienna was still a comparative oasis, and he briefly returned to
mark his eightieth birthday on 11 June 1944. The Nazis guardedly gave
permission for official celebrations, though they refused actively to
encourage them and publicity was minimal. Goebbels sent a polite
telegram of congratulations, but no more. Pfitzner, who was seventy-
five that year, was now being talked of in some Nazi circles as 'the
greatest composer of our time', and stayed with Hans Frank in
Kraków castle, while the latter oversaw the extermination of millions.
In Strauss's honour, Karl Böhm, now music director in Vienna,

'The greatest catastrophe of
my life', Strauss's description
of the Allied bombing of the
Munich Nationaltheater on
2 October 1943

committed *Daphne* to disc in May, then conducted *Ariadne* as a birthday tribute. The performance was broadcast and the tapes later used as the basis of a recording. Strauss conducted the Vienna Philharmonic in a programme which consisted of *Till Eulenspiegel* and the *Sinfonia Domestica*, using a heavy, striped presentation baton which the orchestra had given him.

Clemens Krauss was also determined to celebrate Strauss's eightieth birthday. Since 1941 he had been artistic director of the Salzburg Festival and had finally persuaded Strauss to lift his ban on *Die Liebe der Danae*. A date was set for the summer of 1944. Hartmann was engaged as director and Ursuleac was to sing *Danae*, with the young Hans Hotter (the first Kommandant in *Friedenstag*) as Jupiter. Krauss struggled with the project against almost insuperable odds. A fire at a

A scene from the public dress rehearsal of *Die Liebe der Danae* at Salzburg on 16 August 1944. The opera's première did not take place until after Strauss's death.

Leipzig printing works in 1943 had destroyed the orchestral parts
which had to be prepared again from scratch. The set for Act II was
ruined in an air-raid on Munich. Because of lack of electricity, the
costume makers were brought from Munich to Salzburg to continue
their work in makeshift huts. Even so, the première did not take place.

On 6 June, the Allied forces landed in Normandy. On 20 July,
Claus Schenk von Stauffenberg, the head of the German Resistance,
failed in his attempt to assassinate Hitler. On 1 August, Goebbels
announced the immediate closure of all theatres and concert halls
within the Reich. In Salzburg, Goebbels's order was promptly
countermanded by the local Gauleiter and work on the new opera was
allowed to continue up to and including the official dress rehearsal on
16 August. The audience consisted mostly of convalescent soldiers.
Strauss arrived in Salzburg on 7 August. There is no evidence that
Pauline accompanied him and it is possible that she was still too ill to
travel. During rehearsals he made few comments, though on one
occasion, he rose to his feet while the orchestra played the interlude
depicting Jupiter's renunciation of his love for Danae, and walked to
the rail of the orchestra pit, where he stood listening until the opera's
final scene had finished. When it was over, he was in tears. 'Perhaps
we shall meet again in a better world,' he told the players. Rudolf
Hartmann led him gently from the building and through the streets of
Salzburg back to his hotel. *Danae* was not heard again in his lifetime.
The first public performance finally took place in Salzburg on 14
August 1952. Krauss yet again conducted.

On 25 August 1944, Goebbels declared 'total war against the
enemies of the Reich', and his edict commanding the closure of
theatres and concert halls was now fully enforced. Only the Berlin
Philharmonic (under the auspices of Hermann Goering in his role as
the capital's Gauleiter) was exempt. The orchestra continued to
perform Wagner and Bruckner while the Nazis continued to play out
their own obscene *Götterdämmerung*.

By the autumn Vienna was being bombed. Strauss ordered his
family back to Garmisch, though his grandson Richard remained in
Vienna for a while as a factory worker. Strauss's finances were in a dire
state. His works continued to be published – Fürstner's business had
been transferred into the name of the 'Aryan' Johannes Oertel –
though his foreign royalties were now frozen. He began copying his

manuscripts in the hope of being able to sell them in future. 'It stops me thinking about other things,' he wrote to Richard in Vienna, 'now that I don't even have an occasional game of skat to divert me and poor Mama needs a lot of comforting.' Pauline's health was starting to improve, though she remained sickly. The Gestapo had yet again attempted to move in on Alice and a warrant for her arrest was delivered at Garmisch Nazi headquarters. The Strausses were tipped off, and Alice contemplated escape to Switzerland before deciding to stay. The warrant was never served. One local official always made sure it remained at the bottom of his in-tray.

In December 1944, Romain Rolland died at his home in Vézelay in Burgundy. It is unlikely that Strauss knew of his death until after the war. In honour of Rolland's sixtieth birthday in 1926, Strauss had sent him a song, dedicated to 'The heroic fighter against all the wicked powers working for the destruction of Europe'. Thereafter, their friendship had drifted. Rolland, a pacifist to the end, had sought a solution to humanity's problems in the work of Marx and Gandhi. In 1938 he abandoned his Swiss exile to return to France, determined that he would not live through another European conflagration branded a coward. The Nazis interned him for a while as an enemy of the Reich, only allowing him to be released when his health, never strong, was dangerously undermined. Before he died, he managed to obtain smuggled copies of the scores of *Friedenstag* and *Daphne*. He passed over the former in silence. Of *Daphne* he wrote, 'It is wonderful to see how that old man grows younger with each new year.'

Despite Strauss's frequent voicing of his fears that his life's work was at an end, he continued to compose. He wrote a second Sonatina for Wind Instruments, produced the definitive version of a suite of waltzes from *Rosenkavalier* (having intensely disliked arrangements by other composers) and resurrected a short waltz he had written in 1939 to accompany a film about Munich which never materialized (the project was called off by Hitler and Goebbels before the film was shot). He added a central section in a minor key and called the piece *München, ein Gedächtniswalzer* ('Munich, a Memorial Waltz').

His most important work from the period was begun shortly after his return to Garmisch from the *Danae* dress rehearsal. He had been rereading Goethe and decided to set a text from the latter's *Zahme Xenien*. The words were apt: 'Nobody can know himself or divide himself from his inner being, yet every day he has to test … what he is and what he was, what he can and what he may. Yet nobody can really know the composition of the world … just think: 'It's been all right till now, so it may well last to the end.'

He abandoned the setting when a commission arrived for a work for string orchestra from the Swiss conductor Paul Sacher, and he reworked his sketches as a study for twenty-three solo instrumentalists incorporating the material of the abandoned *Trauermusik*. He interrupted work on the *Adagio*, as he called it, twice (to compose the Second Wind Sonatina and prepare the *Rosenkavalier* Suite), only returning to it in January 1945 while the concentration camps were liberated and the bombs continued to fall.

On the night of 13–14 February Dresden, the site of all his most important premières, was flattened. 'I am in despair,' he wrote to Gregor. 'My lovely Dresden – Weimar – Munich all gone!' By 8 March, the short score of the work, now entitled *Metamorphosen* ('Metamorphoses'), was complete. The title derives from Goethe's use of the word to describe a work in progress gradually emerging after a long period of gestation, though there are also inevitable links with Ovid's poem of the same name (in which the legend of Daphne makes its first appearance). Few would doubt that the finished piece, perhaps the most remarkable expression of grief in the history of music, ranks among Strauss's masterpieces and among the greatest of all compositions, though it has caused considerable controversy. Strauss gave few clues as to its significance, and *Metamorphosen* has been variously interpreted as an elegy for Hitler and the Third Reich (which is at variance with Strauss's attitudes and the suffering he and his family endured), a work of mourning for the demise of German culture, a piece expressing anti-Nazi resistance, and a confessional apologia on Strauss's behalf for his initial involvement with the regime.

What is certain about *Metamorphosen*, however, is that it deals with images of the foundering and betrayal of heroic ideals, and a number of pointers and allusions in the score make this clear. In structure the work is essentially a series of variations on a theme in which the theme itself is stated last – though Strauss always claimed that the concept only occurred to him partway through composition. The theme of *Metamorphosen* which finally emerges from the preceding material is the Funeral March from Beethoven's 'Eroica'

which trudges wearily beneath its final cadences with the words IN
MEMORIAM engraved in the score. Equally important is an allusion to
Tristan und Isolde, which makes its first appearance partway through.
Strauss, however, alludes not to Wagner's central couple, but to the
tragic figure of King Mark whom the lovers have betrayed. Tristan is
referred to throughout the opera as 'the hero without equal', yet Mark
rounds on him with a very different language. 'Did you have to do
this to me?' he pleads. 'Was Mark's shame the price for countless
services?' Buried in the harrowing stream of sound are references to
the complete shattering of Strauss's early heroic ideals as well as his
sense of betrayal at the hands of the culture he had served, which had
finally foundered into barbarism and atrocity.

The score was completed on 12 April. On 30 April, Hitler
committed suicide in his bunker in Berlin. Admiral Dönitz assumed
command of the armed forces. On 7 May, Germany finally
surrendered and the Nazi government was forcibly dissolved on 23
May. The four powers – America, Britain, France and Russia –
assumed control of the defeated Germany. The greatest nightmare in
human history was finally over.

7

'We have gone hand in
hand through pain and joy':
Strauss with Pauline at the
official celebrations of his
eighty-fifth birthday in
Garmisch, 11 June 1949

*I ask myself why I am being called back into an
existence in which I have outlived myself.*

Strauss to Willi Schuh, December 1948

Aftermath and Rehabilitation 1945-9

On 30 April 1945, the Allies arrived in Garmisch. Early that morning Strauss's grandson Richard, safely back from Vienna, espied American tanks in a nearby field. At eleven o'clock, a jeep full of soldiers drew up outside the villa with an order that the house be evacuated within fifteen minutes. Strauss went to the door. 'I am Richard Strauss,' he said, 'the composer of *Rosenkavalier* and *Salome*. Leave me alone.' The squad's leader, a Major Kramer of Dutch descent, was a keen music lover. Within minutes an acquaintanceship was struck up and the soldiers were soon inside the house eating venison stew. When they left, a sign saying 'Off Limits' was put up outside. There would be no further attempts to requisition the property. A few days later, Strauss and his family had dinner with the American district commander.

Musicians serving in the forces were soon visitors in Garmisch, among them the pianist Joseph Kalm and the critic Irvin Kolodin. 'How are my friends in America?' Strauss asked them, recalling that he had heard a short-wave broadcast of *Der Rosenkavalier* during the war. Kalm sat at the piano and played Gershwin's *Summertime*. 'Very pretty,' Strauss remarked. 'Did you compose it?' On other occasions his visitors were less respectful. A German-speaking Mr Brown arrived in the company of a friend who was a journalist. They seemed charming. The two men, Strauss and Alice sat in the garden while Strauss chatted amiably. Mr Brown turned the subject round to Strauss's experiences in the Third Reich. 'My last opera *Die Liebe der Danae* was simply ignored,' Strauss remarked. 'And you must know what difficulties I had on account of Stefan Zweig's libretto. *Die schweigsame Frau* was a wonderful text – and I had no idea in 1933 that there would be those racial laws.' Mr Brown pressed him further. Strauss expressed understandable pride in how his daughter-in-law had remained 'the only free Jewish woman in greater Germany'. He said how grateful he was for the protection of Schirach and Hans Frank ('So cultivated! He protected my operas!'). Schirach and Frank were awaiting trial in Nuremberg: Schirach was sentenced to twenty years' imprisonment.

Frank was executed. Mr Brown turned out to be the disguised Klaus Mann, son of Thomas. He printed the text of his conversation with Strauss in the American Army magazine *Stars and Stripes*. The article was widely interpreted as betraying Strauss's complicity with the regime, which Strauss never publicly condemned, even after its destruction. In his private memoranda, however, he voiced his true sentiments. 'From May 1 onwards,' he wrote, 'the most terrible period of human history came to an end, the twelve-year reign of bestiality, ignorance and anti-culture under the greatest criminals, during which Germany's 2,000 years of cultural evolution met its doom.'

If Strauss's encounter with 'Mr Brown' proved detrimental, his meeting with another GI was remarkably fortuitous. This was John De Lancie, a former oboe player from the Pittsburgh Symphony Orchestra. Like everywhere else in Germany, conditions in Garmisch were extremely difficult: the Strausses were often without simple necessities like soap, which De Lancie provided when he could. He and Strauss frequently had long discussions about music and literature. On one occasion De Lancie asked if Strauss had written anything specifically for the oboe. A brusque 'No' was the reply. De Lancie let the subject drop, though his words sank in. As one of his 'exercises for my wrists', Strauss wrote an Oboe Concerto, one of the

When the Allies arrived in Garmisch, many GIs were fascinated by Strauss, who is seen here with an American soldier in the garden of his villa.

greatest of his later works, a continuous ecstatic outpouring of exquisite melody, the music of a man who has just emerged from a nightmare.

He soon realized that he would have to face one of the Tribunals set up to investigate the activities of those who had worked with the regime. He had held public office, collaborated and colluded, and he was under suspicion. He was also worried by the prospect of privations during the coming winter. Germany was functioning on a black market economy. Food could only be purchased at astronomical prices, and there was no fuel. It was going to be impossible to heat the villa. As both his own and Pauline's health was far from good, friends suggested that the couple should go abroad. He applied for permission to travel to Switzerland, but the authorities stalled and it was only when Swiss and American friends agreed to stand surety for him that he and Pauline were allowed to leave. Franz, Alice and the children, however, were forbidden to accompany them and remained in Garmisch.

He packed the scores of the tone-poems he had been copying into one of his cases, together with the manuscripts of the Second Horn Concerto and the as yet incomplete Oboe Concerto and, early on the morning of 9 October, he and Pauline left for Bregenz in Austria, then proceeded to the Swiss border. Their papers were not in order and they were nearly turned back. They were rescued, according to an entry in Strauss's diary, by Prince Friedrich of Saxony, who found them beds for the night, and took them the following morning to see the French commander, Count D'Audibert. The manuscript of the Weinheber songs was placed in D'Audibert's hands, a score of the *Alpensinfonie* was inscribed there and then for the Bibliothèque Nationale in Paris, and they were allowed to proceed. On 11 October, they finally arrived at the Hotel Verenahof in Baden-bei-Zürich. The scores were deposited in the hotel safe as security against unpaid bills. 'This is heaven,' he wrote in his diary. 'We can pass the rest of our days in peace and quiet, in the company of good people and friends.' The Oboe Concerto was finished days later.

The idea of Switzerland as an earthly paradise quickly wore off, however, as Strauss realized how tarnished his reputation had become. There were, it was true, local successes. *Metamorphosen* was first performed by Paul Sacher in January 1946. Strauss conducted the final rehearsal himself but refused to attend the première. It is possible that he considered the work so intensely personal a statement that he shied away from the idea of its being heard in public. The Oboe Concerto was first performed the following month, though the soloist was Marcel Saillet and not 'that Chicago oboist', as Strauss erroneously called De Lancie.

Elsewhere his association with the Nazis was held against him: the *Basel Nationalzeitung* published an article decrying his presence in the country; when the Zurich Opera revived *Arabella*, in 1946, there were attempts to block the casting of the soprano Maria Cebotari, Aminta in the original *Die schweigsame Frau*. One local soprano was up in arms at the idea that a woman who had sung under the Nazis should now be performing in Zurich. One great admirer was the actor Lionel Barrymore who invited Strauss and Pauline to visit him in Hollywood and promised to help them overcome any potential difficulties with American immigration. Barrymore's offer, however, was suddenly withdrawn: Strauss had had such bad coverage in the American press that he considered it not to be in the composer's interests to travel to the States. Strauss didn't always help himself by making tactless remarks. 'The Nazis were criminals,' he was overheard saying in a Zurich restaurant. 'I have always known that. Imagine, they closed the theatres and my operas could not be given.' His unhappiness is understandable, but, as Klaus Mann pointed out, his remarks to the effect that he saw Nazism as an affront to himself and a deliberate attempt to block his work were inappropriate after Auschwitz. When *Die schweigsame Frau* was finally allowed her voice again after the war, Strauss wrote to the conductor Joseph Keilberth to thank him for rescuing the opera 'from the concentration camp'. The murder of Alice's family, along with details of Franz's party membership, remained family secrets, like Josephine's madness so many years before. Until her death in 1991, Alice Strauss discouraged any mention of their experiences during the Third Reich.

The Swiss climate did much to improve Strauss's health but lack of money remained a problem. His royalties were frozen. The manager of the Verenahof hotel had caused offence and panic by insisting that the scores in his safe be valued. Strauss was making desperate attempts to sell his manuscripts. In order to find a purchaser, he wrote to Hugo Burghauser, a former bassoonist with the Vienna Philharmonic, now with the Metropolitan in New York. 'My son will soon become a millionaire as a result of my operas,' he wrote, 'but now I am in urgent need of money.' He still tried to help his family. Visitors brought him luxuries – cakes, sweets, pralines and marzipan. He hoarded them to send to Garmisch, though communications in Germany were poor and few of his food parcels got through.

Even so, when financial offers came that might have compromised his work, he rejected them. In December 1945 he received a visit from Ernst Roth, an Austrian émigré resident in London, who worked for the music publisher Boosey & Hawkes. In 1942 the publisher had – without Strauss's knowledge – acquired the British rights to his works from Fürstner. Roth communicated an offer from the Hungarian-born film director Alexander Korda, who had become one of the great figures of the British film industry. Korda wanted to make a film of either *Rosenkavalier* or *Salome*, offering Strauss a fee of £20,000 for the rights, but could not guarantee that the operas would remain uncut or unaltered. Strauss turned the offer down. Roth was still anxious to help him and in 1947 suggested the idea of a London Strauss Festival to the composer's erstwhile champion Sir Thomas Beecham. Aware that Strauss's presence might lessen some of the opprobrium he had received in the press, Beecham invited him to attend. That year a cultural thaw in relations between Britain and the German-speaking world began: the Vienna State Opera made a famous visit to Covent Garden, during the course of which Krauss conducted *Salome* with Cebotari in the title role; Bruno Walter was reunited with the Vienna Philharmonic at the Edinburgh Festival where a performance of *Das Lied von der Erde* put Mahler back on the European musical map.

Strauss arrived in London on 4 October 1947, having flown for the first time in his life. Willi Schuh went with him, as Pauline was too ill to travel. His arrival caused quite a stir. One reporter asked him what his plans for the future were. 'Well, to die,' he replied. He stayed at the Savoy, where the food was not to his liking and where yet again he had to remind the staff that no, he was not the composer of the *Blue Danube*. He and Schuh walked round the National Gallery and the Wallace Collection, and Strauss revealed that his old anticlerical self was still intact. 'The only purpose of life is to make art possible,' Strauss told him. 'Christianity had to be invented … in order to make possible the Colmar altar [by Matthias Grünewald], the Sistine

Madonna [by Raphael], the *Missa solemnis* [by Beethoven] and *Parsifal.*'

The Festival opened on 5 October, with performances of *Der Bürger als Edelmann, Don Quixote,* the closing scene from *Feuersnot* and an orchestral fantasia of extracts from *Die Frau ohne Schatten,* which Strauss had prepared the previous year. This was conducted by Norman Del Mar, a former horn player who later wrote a comprehensive three-volume study of Strauss's entire output. During rehearsals the old man listened attentively, then walked up to the conductor's desk and began to examine the score. 'All my own fault,' he gloomily remarked and walked away.

Two weeks later, Strauss himself conducted the Philharmonia in a packed Albert Hall, in a programme which consisted of *Don Juan,* the *Burleske,* the *Rosenkavalier* waltzes and the *Sinfonia Domestica.* At one point during rehearsals, he stopped the orchestra. 'No,' he said. 'I know what I want and I know what I meant when I wrote this. After all, I may not be a first-rate composer, but I am a first-class second-rate composer.' After the concert, a woman approached him. It was Gerty von Hofmannsthal. He cried when she told him her name. The Festival ended with a cataclysmic broadcast of *Elektra* with Beecham conducting, and a BBC Symphony concert during which Strauss conducted *Till Eulenspiegel.* On 31 October, he flew back to Switzerland for a tearful reunion with Pauline, whom he had desperately missed on his travels. In his pocket was a cheque for just under £1,000 as payment of outstanding royalties.

Many photographs of Strauss taken late in life show him apparently happy, but his last years were in fact blighted by financial worries, weak health and accusations of Nazi collaboration.

He and Pauline now lived at the Palace Hotel in Montreux. The town proved a safe haven and they were much cheered by the fact that they were at last able to receive visits from Franz and Alice. Their existence had, for a while before then, been itinerant. Pauline's temper, as fierce as ever, led to arguments with a succession of hotel managers, and the Strausses were frequently asked to leave.

Travelling from Germany to Austria and Switzerland had initially been hazardous. Alice had reached Vienna in the autumn of 1945 in order to salvage what she could – mostly Strauss's correspondence and private papers – from the house in the Jacquingasse, which had first been commandeered by the Russians, then turned into a British Officers' mess. The following year, after an arduous journey (which involved sleeping on railway station benches), she reached Lucerne where she was reunited with her mother and sister – two members of her family who had escaped the Holocaust. Strauss and Pauline gave her dollars to smuggle back to Germany (which she did in a vacuum flask) and sent sugar, coffee, sardines and sewing needles, which were in short supply.

Strauss continued to compose. Thinking of Burghauser's beautiful bassoon tones, he produced another exquisite miniature, the Duett-Concertino for clarinet, bassoon, harp and strings, in 1947. He also started another stage work. Gregor, who was struggling for survival in Vienna and to whom both Strauss and Marie von Grab had sent food parcels, was hankering after another commission. He had his chance in 1947, when Strauss was approached by Father Stephen Schaller, head of the Benedictine school in Ettal (where Christian was now a pupil), requesting a piece for school performance. Asked to provide a suitable text, Gregor decided on a subject drawn from the works of Christoph Martin Wieland, an early contemporary of Goethe of whom Strauss was fond. *Die Abderiten, eine sehr wahrscheinliche Geschichte* ('The Abderites, a Very Probable History') is set in the imaginary town of Abdera in Thrace, whose inhabitants, like *Till Eulenspiegel*'s Burghers of Schilda, were mythically stupid. Gregor chose one episode from Wieland's book, which became the basis of *Des Esels Schatten* ('The Donkey's Shadow'), a vicious satire on bureaucracy and legal obfuscation. A dentist hires a donkey from a drover to take him to a nearby town. The weather is stifling, and the dentist cools himself by resting in the shadow of the tethered donkey.

The drover, however, institutes legal proceedings on the grounds that the donkey's shadow forms no part of his contract with the dentist. Strauss, almost predictably, disliked the text the moment he read it, dismissed it as 'frogs' droppings', sacked Gregor yet again and approached the musicologist Hans Adler for a revised version. Many have assumed that Strauss subsequently lost interest in the project, though he tinkered with the score during the following two years and told both Adler and Schaller that he intended to complete it. It remained unfinished at his death, though a version based on his sketches was first performed in Ettal in 1964. It has never entered the repertoire and remains largely ignored.

Suffering from depression, he buried himself in books and scores, pored over *Tristan*, read Wagner's writings once more, studied art history, philosophy and Oriental classics. During one of his visits in 1948, Franz attempted to alleviate his mood. 'Papa, do stop writing letters and brooding,' he said. 'It doesn't do any good. Write a few nice songs instead.' A few months later, during a second visit, Strauss placed some manuscripts on a table in Franz's room. 'Here,' he told Alice, 'are the songs your husband ordered.' He had little need of Franz's encouragement, for the group of songs had occupied him on and off for the last two years.

In 1946, he first read Joseph von Eichendorff's *Im Abendrot* ('In the Sunset'), was struck by the aptness of the words to his and Pauline's situation and, on 3 April, copied the text into his sketchbook. The poem depicts an elderly couple, faithful and loyal to each other, who contemplate the waning light of the sun as it sinks behind a mountain landscape. 'We have gone hand in hand through pain and joy,' the poem reads. 'The air is already growing dark in the valley. Only two larks rise upwards … Come close and let them flutter. Soon it is time to sleep, so that we do not lose each other in this solitude … How tired we are of wandering. Can that, perhaps, be death?'

A year later, he was sketching a version for soprano and orchestra. He changed the final line to read 'Can this, perhaps, be death?' The song was completed on 6 May 1948. It begins with a huge arching orchestral phrase which quietens and darkens as the song progresses until the voice fades out and only the two skylarks are left trilling in the gathering gloom, their happiness echoing that of the central couple as they contemplate the end. As the soprano asks her final, irresolute question, the transfiguration theme from *Tod und Verklärung* is gently quoted by the orchestra before being subsumed into the texture.

Knowing the song could not stand alone, Strauss turned to the poetry of Hermann Hesse to find its companions and selected four poems with the initial intention of making a set of five, though he only finished three – *Frühling* ('Spring'), *Beim Schlafengehen* ('Going to Sleep') and *September*, the last of which he completed on 20 September 1948. Hesse's poems also speak of the approach of death, of human transience in the face of the permanence of natural beauty and of the need for rest after exertion. In *Beim Schlafengehen* the human soul soars free in sleep after the narrator has spoken of 'greeting the starry night like a tired child'. Strauss sets the words to a rapturous ascending phrase preceded by a slowly unwinding violin solo that ranks as one of the most beautiful things in his output.

Taken together, the group has deservedly become one of the most widely performed and best loved of his works, though even so, the songs are something of a mystery. They are generally accepted as constituting Strauss's own requiem, a final farewell, intended from the outset as a posthumous testament, but the title, *Vier letzte Lieder* ('Four Last Songs'), was invented after his death by Eugen Roth. Strauss may also have wanted to adhere to his original idea of five songs rather than four: they were inspired by his love for Pauline, and during their composition he also orchestrated *Ruhe, meine Seele*, one of the songs which formed his wedding present to his wife. It is possible that he intended this to be the fifth song in the series, though it has never been included in performance. Though the *Vier letzte Lieder* are also regarded as his final hymn to his idealized soprano voice, it is also possible that they were written for a specific singer. The great Wagnerian soprano Kirsten Flagstad was a regular guest in Switzerland after the war. She always maintained that Strauss had contacted her with a view to giving the première in his lifetime and that she had stipulated that Furtwängler should conduct. There is no evidence in Strauss's correspondence to support this, though Flagstad and Furtwängler did give the first performance in London in 1950. There was to be one last song, *Malven*, to a text by Betty Knobel, published in 1948: Strauss set the poem as soon as it was written. He sent it to Jeritza in New York, inscribed 'To beloved Maria, this last

rose.' The manuscript was not discovered until after her death
in 1982.

In June 1948, after repeated postponements of hearings, his name
was finally cleared by the de-Nazification tribunal. It was noted that
his dismissal formed part of Goebbels's reappraisal of the
Reichsmusikkammer and its move towards the implementation of
entrenched anti-Semitic policies. Strauss had already accepted an offer
of citizenship from the Austrian government in 1947. He was now free
to travel where he wished, but he elected to remain in Switzerland for
a while. His health had become a matter of some concern. In April
1946 he underwent a successful operation for appendicitis and made a
quick recovery. At the end of 1947, however, he began to suffer from
persistent bladder infections, which eventually necessitated major
surgery in December 1948.

He began to hanker after Garmisch. The Swiss authorities
announced they were only prepared to renew his resident's permit for
a short time. In the hands of the Allied powers, West Germany was
beginning to make its economic recovery and conditions were rapidly
improving. On 10 May 1949, just over a month before his eighty-fifth
birthday, he and Pauline finally returned home.

He was growing weaker, and he knew it. 'All my life I've been used
to my body obeying me, and now I have to obey it!' he grumbled
when he realized he could not travel to some of the planned birthday
celebrations. He was unable to go to Paris, where *Friedenstag* was
incongruously broadcast on the eve of an international peace
conference. Instead he sent the musicologist Gustave Samazeuilh a
letter containing his exculpatory statement about the opera's contents.
The broadcast was one of many: most Western European radio
stations devoted the evening of 11 June to his works.

The day began with many local people in Garmisch turning up on
his doorstep to offer congratulations and flowers. Later that morning
with the press out in force, a concert of his chamber music was held in
Garmisch Town Hall. At eighty-five, Richard Strauss was once again a
star. Munich University conferred on him the title of Honorary
Doctor of Law and the city set up a Strauss foundation in his honour.
The previous evening, he found the strength to go to Munich for a
dress rehearsal of *Der Rosenkavalier*. Once there he asked if he could
conduct the finales of Acts II and III. The young Georg Solti, the

Strauss conducting the
'Moonlight' interlude from
Capriccio with the Bavarian
Radio Orchestra in July
1949. It was the last time
he ever conducted.

Opera's new music director, handed him the baton, cameras began to
roll and his performance became the basis of a film, *A Life for Music*.
The film also contains footage of Strauss playing the piano; the work,
significantly, is the final scene from *Daphne*. The Bavarian authorities
had asked him to select one of his own works for a celebratory
performance. He chose *Der Bürger als Edelmann* and the play was
accordingly staged at the Gärtnerplatztheater on 13 June. 'It's a pity
Hofmannsthal couldn't see it too,' he commented. A month later, he
returned to Munich to conduct the Bavarian Radio Orchestra. He
chose the 'Moonlight' interlude from *Capriccio*. His usual gesture at
the end of a performance was to close the score. On this occasion he
left it lying open. He would never conduct again.

Shortly after he returned to Garmisch his health began to fail,
though he remained mentally active and continued to receive guests.
Solti was among his visitors. He wanted to talk about Strauss's own
music, but the composer excitedly began to chatter about *Tristan und
Isolde* until Pauline, stroppily devoted as always, appeared and
terminated the visit on the grounds that Strauss was becoming tired.
In August he had a series of minor heart attacks and took to his bed.
He wanted to see Hartmann, who arrived at the villa on 29 August
and later wrote an affecting account of their last meeting:

'In the room, which seems to be filled with light, the white bed
stands with its head facing the doorway. Richard Strauss has turned his
head a little, he reaches out his right hand to me and greets me …

Then he says: "Death has dealt me the first hard blow, has given me the first sign." … I hear the deep, rather hoarse voice speaking about his ever-recurring anxiety for the continuance of European Theatre … After a while he goes on in a different tone of voice: "Grüss mir die Welt" ("Greet the world for me"). He stops, asks "Where does that come from?" I think of the similar words from *Walküre* and say so, but he shakes his head: "No, no, it's not that, this occurs somewhere else." … He remains silent for a long time. I see that his face is showing signs of fatigue and that it is time to leave … I turn hesitantly away. He once more grasps my right hand in both of his and holds me back: "Perhaps we'll see each other again." … A last vehement grip, his hands release me, and I quickly leave the room. On my way out I hear Richard Strauss give a suppressed sob, then call loudly for his son.' *Grüss mir die Welt* is a quote from Act I of *Tristan*; Isolde, believing she is going to die, dismisses her faithful servant Brangäne.

His condition began to deteriorate rapidly. A catheter, inserted during his bladder operation, gave him considerable pain. 'Funny thing, Alice,' he told his daughter-in-law, 'dying is just the way I composed it in *Tod und Verklärung*.' When the end came, however, it was far from being the moment of abrupt, terrifying suddenness depicted in the tone-poem. On the afternoon of 8 September 1949, he died peacefully in his sleep.

Strauss's funeral service, at the Ostfriedhof, Munich, 12 September 1949

His body was cremated three days later in Munich. There were so
many mourners that the funeral service was held in the open air. Solti
conducted the Trio from *Rosenkavalier*, at which point Pauline,
distraught and broken, slid from her seat sobbing 'Richard! Richard!'
The urn containing his ashes was placed in the bedroom at Garmisch.
Four days later, democracy was finally established in West Germany
with the founding of the Bonn Republic. Konrad Adenauer was
elected Chancellor.

Pauline Strauss de Ahna survived her husband by less than a year.
Her indomitable spirit was shattered. 'I never realized that a person
could cry so much,' was Alice's comment. Strauss had requested that
Pauline should go back to Montreux after his death, and she returned
to the Palace Hotel, where she shut herself off from the world and
remained a recluse. In March 1950 Alice took her back to Garmisch
where she died on 13 May at the age of eighty-eight. Towards the end,
Alice frequently found her weeping alone in the room where her
husband had died.

Classified List of Works

Works are listed in the following order: opera, ballet, other stage works, film music, lieder, other vocal, choral (with instruments or orchestra), choral (unaccompanied), orchestral, solo instruments with orchestra, chamber, solo instrumental and, finally, adaptations. Incomplete works and works known to be lost, unless important, have not been included. Orchestral suites drawn by Strauss or other composers from stage works are listed under the work in question.

Works with opus numbers are designated accordingly. Users should be warned that Strauss's system of opus numbering, particularly in his earlier works, can be confusing and does not necessarily indicate chronological order of composition – Op. 23 (*Macbeth*), for instance, predates Op. 20 (*Don Juan*). Some opus numbers were allotted posthumously.

'fp' denotes first public performance, and details have been given where known.

Opera

Guntram, Op. 25, opera in three acts, libretto by Richard Strauss (1892–3). fp Weimar, 10 May 1894. Revised version (1934–9). fp Weimar, 29 October 1940

Feuersnot ('Fire Famine'), Op. 50, song-poem in one act, libretto by Ernst von Wolzogen (1900–1). fp Dresden, 21 November 1901

Salome, Op. 54, drama in one act, libretto by Strauss, adapted from Hedwig Lachmann's translation of Oscar Wilde's play (1903–5). fp Dresden, 9 December 1905

Elektra, Op. 58, tragedy in one act, libretto by Hugo von Hofmannsthal, based on his own play (1906–8). fp Dresden, 25 January 1909

Der Rosenkavalier ('The Rose Bearer'), Op. 59, comedy for music in three acts, libretto by Hofmannsthal (1909–10). fp Dresden, 26 January 1911 [*Walzerfolge* ('Waltz Sequence'); subsequently retitled 'No. 2' (1911). *Erste Walzerfolge* ('First Waltz Sequence', 1944). fp London, 4 August 1946. The many other orchestral arrangements of sections from the opera are not by Strauss.]

Ariadne auf Naxos ('Ariadne on Naxos'), Op. 60. First version: play *Der Bürger als Edelmann* ('Le Bourgeois Gentilhomme') by Molière [with incidental music] and opera in one act, libretto by Hofmannsthal (1911–12). fp Stuttgart, 25 October 1912. Second version: opera in a prologue and one act, libretto by Hofmannsthal (1916). fp Vienna, 4 October 1916

Die Frau ohne Schatten ('The Woman without a Shadow'), Op. 65, opera in three acts, libretto by Hofmannsthal (1914–17). fp Vienna, 10 October 1919 [*Sinfonische Fantasie* (arrangement by Strauss, 1946). fp Vienna, 6 June 1947]

Intermezzo, Op. 72, bourgeois comedy with symphonic interludes in two acts, libretto by Strauss (1917–23). fp Dresden, 4 November 1924 [*Vier sinfonische Zwischenspiele aus Intermezzo*, arrangement by Strauss (1932)]

Die ägyptische Helena ('The Egyptian Helen'), Op. 75, opera in two acts, libretto by Hofmannsthal (1923–7). fp Dresden, 6 June 1928. Revised version, with sections of the text of the second act rewritten by Lothar Wallerstein (1932–3). fp Salzburg, 14 August 1933

Arabella, Op. 79, lyrical comedy in three acts, libretto by Hofmannsthal (1929–32). fp Dresden, 1 July 1933

Die schweigsame Frau ('The Silent Wife'), Op. 80, comic opera in three acts, libretto by Stefan Zweig freely adapted from *Epicoene, or The Silent Woman* by Ben Jonson (1933–4). fp Dresden, 24 June 1935

Friedenstag ('Peace Day'), Op. 81, opera in one act, libretto by Josef Gregor (1935–6). fp Munich, 24 July 1938

Daphne, Op. 82, bucolic tragedy in one act, libretto by Gregor (1936–7). fp Dresden, 15 October 1938

Die Liebe der Danae ('The Love of Danae'), Op. 83, cheerful mythology in three acts, libretto by Gregor after a sketch by Hofmannsthal (1938–40). fp Salzburg, 14 August 1952

Capriccio, Op. 85, conversation piece for music in one act, libretto by Clemens Krauss (1940–1). fp Munich, 28 October 1942
[Harpsichord Suite (1944?). fp Vienna, 6 November 1946]

Des Esels Schatten ('The Donkey's Shadow'), Singspiel in one act, libretto by Hans Adler (1947–8); left incomplete by Strauss, finished by Karl Haussner. fp Ettal, 6 June 1964

Ballet

Josephslegende ('The Legend of Joseph'), Op. 60, ballet in one act, scenario by Count Harry Kessler and Hofmannsthal (1913–14). fp Paris, 14 May 1914
[*Sinfonische Fragment*, arrangement by Strauss (1946–7). fp Cincinnati, March 1949]

Schlagobers ('Whipped Cream'), ballet in two acts, scenario by Strauss (1921–2). fp Vienna, 9 May 1924
[Orchestral Suite (1932). fp Mannheim, 8 November 1932]

Verklungene Feste ('Faded Festivals'), dance vision from two centuries with music after François Couperin (1940–1); consists of 1923 *Tanzsuite aus Klavierstücken nach François Couperin* with six new numbers which eventually formed the basis of the Op. 86 Divertimento. fp Munich, 5 April 1941

Other Stage Works

Romeo und Julia ('Romeo and Juliet'), incidental music, attributed to Strauss, for William Shakespeare's play, date of composition uncertain, possibly unfinished. fp Munich, 23 October 1887

Der Jäger, fanfare for play by August Iffland (1891). fp Weimar, 7 May 1891

Lebende Bilder ('Living Pictures'), tableaux vivants for the celebration of the golden wedding of the Grand Duke and Duchess of Weimar (1892). Four movements only by Strauss; also included music by Franz Liszt, Eduard Lassen and Hans von Bronsart. fp Weimar, 8 October 1892. Strauss's third movement, also included in *Der Rosenkavalier* film music, revised 1931 as *Kampf und Sieg* ('Battle and Victory'). fp Vienna, 2 March 1931

Zwei Lieder aus 'Der Richter von Zalamea' ('Two Songs from "The Judge of Salamea"'), play by Pedro Calderón de la Barca, translated by Rudolf Presber (1904). fp Berlin, 7 February 1904: 1. *Liebesliedchen* ('Little Love Song'), for tenor, guitar, harp; 2. *Lied der Chispa* ('Chispa's Song'), for mezzo-soprano, male chorus, guitar, two harps

Der Bürger als Edelmann ('Le Bourgeois Gentilhomme'), incidental music to play by Molière, freely adapted by Hofmannsthal (1917); incorporates music from the first version of *Ariadne auf Naxos*. fp Berlin, 19 April 1918
[Concert Suite (1919). fp Vienna, 31 January 1920]

Film Music

Der Rosenkavalier ('The Rose Bearer'), music for silent film with titles by Hofmannsthal directed by Robert Wiene; music arranged by Otto Singer and Karl Alwyn; includes sections of the Couperin *Tanzsuite* and the *Lebende Bilder* revised by Strauss (1925). fp Dresden, 10 January 1926

München, ein Gelegenheitswalzer ('Munich, an Occasional Waltz'), music for a planned documentary film (1938–9). fp Munich, 25 May 1939. Revised as *München, ein Gedächtniswalzer* ('Munich, a Memorial Waltz') (1945)

Lieder

Strauss's lieder exist in many different versions. Many were originally written for voice and piano, then later orchestrated, though it was not unknown for Strauss to write the orchestral version first and then prepare a piano reduction. On occasion orchestral versions were prepared by other composers. Some of the songs were grouped together under opus numbers for the convenience of publication, and were not intended to be sung as cycles.

This list follows published groupings of songs as ordered by Strauss, with the exception of the early songs which follow the Boosey & Hawkes edition of 1964. Uncollected songs are placed chronologically: indication is given of the spurious opus numbers and grouping under which some of the later songs were posthumously published.

A number of manuscripts of Strauss's unpublished early songs were given to his aunt Johanna Pschorr. Their whereabouts remain unknown; they are believed to be lost and are not included in this list.

Jugendlieder ('Songs of Youth') (1870–83), collected and published 1964: 1. *Weihnachtslied* ('Christmas Carol'), text by Christian Schubart (1870); 2. *Einkehr* ('Reflection'), text by Ludwig Uhland (1871); 3. *Winterreise* ('Winter's Journey'), text by Uhland (1871); 4. *Der müde Wanderer* ('The Tired Wanderer'), text by August Heinrich Fallersleben (1873); 5. *Husarenlied* ('Hussar's Song'), text by Fallersleben (1876); 6. *Der Fischer* ('The Fisherman'), text by Johann Wolfgang von Goethe (1877); 7. *Die Drossel* ('The Thrush'), text by Uhland (1877); 8. *Lass ruhn die Toten* ('Let the dead rest'), text by Adalbert von Chamisso (1877); 9. *Lust und Qual* ('Pleasure and Pain'), text by

Goethe (1877); 10. *Spielmann und Zither* ('The Minstrel and his Zither'), text by Theodor Körner (1878); 11. *Wiegenlied* ('Cradle Song'), text by Fallersleben (1878); 12. *Abend und Morgenrot* ('Evening and Dawn'), text by Fallersleben (1878); 13. *Im Walde* ('In the Forest'), text by Emanuel Geibel (1878); 14. *Nebel* ('Mist'), text by Nikolaus Lenau (1878); 15. *Soldatenlied* ('Soldier's Song'), text by Fallersleben (1878); 16. *Ein Röslein zog ich mir im Garten* ('I picked a rose in the garden'), text by Fallersleben (1878); 17. *Alphorn*, with horn obbligato, text attributed to Justinus Kerner (1878); 18. *Waldesgesang* ('Forest Song'), text by Geibel (1879). fp Munich, 16 March 1881; 19. *In Vaters Garten* ('In Father's Garden'), text by Heinrich Heine (1880); 20. *Die erwachte Rose* ('The Awakened Rose'), text by Friedrich von Sallet (1880). fp New York, 30 November 1958; 21. *Begegnung* ('Meeting'), text by Otto Friedrich Gruppe (1880). fp New York, 30 November 1958; 22. *John Anderson, mein Lieb* ('John Anderson, My Love'), text by Robert Burns translated by Ferdinand Freiligrath (1880); 23. *Rote Rosen* ('Red Roses'), text by Stieler (1883). fp New York, 30 November 1958

Zwei Orchesterlieder ('Two Orchestral Songs') (1878): 1. *Aria der Almaide* ('Almaide's Aria'), text by Goethe; 2. *Der Spielmann und sein Kind* ('The Minstrel and His Child'), text by Fallersleben

Acht Lieder aus 'Letzte Blätter' ('Eight Songs from "Last Pages"'), Op. 10, texts by Hermann von Gilm (1885): 1. *Zueignung* ('Dedication'), orchestral versions by Robert Heger (1932) and Strauss [with one additional line of text] (1940). fp (Strauss's orchestral version) Rome, 7 July 1940; 2. *Nichts* ('Nothing'); 3. *Die Nacht* ('Night'); 4. *Die Georgine* ('Georgina'); 5. *Geduld* ('Patience'); 6. *Die Verschwiegenen* ('People with Secrets'); 7. *Die Zeitlose* ('The Woman beyond Time'); 8. *Allerseelen* ('All Soul's Day'), orchestral version by Robert Heger (1932)

Wer hat's gethan? ('Who Did It?'), text by Gilm (1885). Omitted from the above set

Fünf Lieder ('Five Songs'), Op. 15, texts by Adolf Friedrich von Schack unless otherwise stated (1884–6): 1. *Madrigal*, text by Michelangelo, translated by Sophie Hasenclever; 2. *Winternacht* ('Winter's Night'); 3. *Lob des Leidens* ('In Praise of Suffering'); 4. *Aus den Liedern der Trauer*, No. 1 ('From the Songs of Mourning'); 5. *Heimkehr* ('Return Home')

Sechs Lieder ('Six Songs'), Op. 17, for high voice and piano, texts by Schack (1887). fp Weimar, 18 October 1889: 1. *Seitdem dein Aug' in meines schaute* ('Since your eyes met mine'); 2. *Ständchen* ('Serenade'), orchestral version by Felix Mottl (1912), transcription for solo piano by Walter Gieseking (1923); 3. *Das Geheimnis* ('The Mystery'); 4. *Aus den Liedern der Trauer*, No. 2 ('From the Songs of Mourning'); 5. *Nur Mut* ('Just Have Courage'); 6. *Barcarolle*

Sechs Lieder aus 'Lotosblätter' ('Six Songs from "Lotus Leaves"'), Op. 19, texts by Schack (1888): 1. *Wozu noch, Mädchen* ('What for, girl'); 2. *Breit über mein Haupt* ('Far above my head'); 3. *Schön sind, doch kalt die Himmelssterne* ('The stars in Heaven are beautiful but cold'); 4. *Wie sollten wir geheim sie halten* ('How should we keep it secret'); 5. *Hoffen und wieder verzagen* ('To hope and then again despair'); 6. *Mein Herz ist stumm* ('My heart is silent')

Vier Mädchenblumen ('Four Girl-Blossoms'), Op. 22, texts by Felix Dahn (1888–9): 1. *Kornblumen* ('Cornflowers'); 2. *Mohnblumen* ('Poppies'); 3. *Efeu* ('Ivy'); 4. *Wasserrose* (Water-Rose)

Schlichte Weisen ('Simple Tunes'), Op. 21, texts by Dahn (1889–90): 1. *All mein Gedanken* ('All My Thoughts'); 2. *Du meines Herzens Krönelein* ('You, the crown of my heart'); 3. *Ach Lieb, ich muss nun scheiden* ('My love, I now must leave you'); 4. *Ach weh mir unglückhaften Mann* ('What an unlucky man I am'); 5. *Die Frauen sind oft fromm und still* ('Women are often pious and quiet')

Zwei Lieder ('Two Songs'), Op. 26, for high voice and piano, texts by Lenau (1891): 1. *Frühlingsgedränge* ('The Rushing of Spring'); 2. *O wärst du mein* ('Oh, were you mine')

Vier Lieder ('Four Songs'), Op. 27, for high voice and piano (1894): 1. *Ruhe, meine Seele* ('Rest, my soul'), text by Karl Henckell, orchestral version by Strauss (1948); 2. *Cäcilie*, text by Heinrich Hart, orchestral version by Strauss (1897); 3. *Heimliche Aufforderung* ('A Clandestine Invitation'), text by John Henry Mackay, orchestral version by Heger (1932); 4. *Morgen!* ('Tomorrow!'), text by Mackay, orchestral version by Strauss (1897)

Drei Lieder ('Three Songs'), Op. 29, for high voice and piano, texts by Otto Julius Bierbaum (1895): 1. *Traum durch die Dämmerung* ('A Dream at Twilight'), orchestral version by Heger (1932); 2. *Schlagende Herzen* ('Beating Hearts'); 3. *Nachtgang* ('A Walk at Night')

Vier Lieder ('Four Songs'), Op. 31, for high voice and piano, texts by Carl Busse unless otherwise stated (1895–6): 1. *Blauer Sommer* ('Blue Summer'); 2. *Wenn …* ('When …'); 3. *Weisser Jasmin* ('White Jasmin'); 4. *Stiller Gang* ('A Silent Walk'), with violin/viola obbligato, text by Richard Dehmel

Fünf Lieder ('Five Songs'), Op. 32 (1896). fp Munich, 9 November 1896: 1. *Ich trage meine Minne* ('I bear my desire'), text by Henckell; 2. *Sehnsucht* ('Yearning'), text by Detlev von Liliencron; 3. *Liebeshymnus* ('Hymn to Love'), text by Henckell, orchestral version by Strauss (1897); 4. *O süsser Mai* ('Oh Sweet May'), text by Henckell; 5. *Himmelsboten* ('Heaven's Messengers'), text by Clemens Brentano and Achim von Arnim, from *Des Knaben Wunderhorn* ('The Child's Magic Horn')

Wir beide wollen springen ('We would both leap'), text by Bierbaum (1896)

Vier Gesänge ('Four Songs'), Op. 33, for voices and orchestra (1896–7): 1. *Verführung* ('Seduction'), for soprano or tenor, text by Mackay. fp Brussels, 6 February 1896; 2. *Gesang der Apollopriesterin* ('Song of the Priestess of Apollo'), for soprano, text by Emanuel von Bodman. fp Brussels, 6 February, 1896; 3. *Hymnus* ('Hymn'), for baritone or mezzo-soprano, text attributed to F. Schiller. fp London, 5 June 1903; 4. *Pilgers Morgenlied* ('Pilgrim's Morning Song'), for baritone, text by Goethe. fp Elberfeld, 13 November 1897

Vier Lieder ('Four Songs'), Op. 36 (1897–8): 1. *Das Rosenband* ('The Rose Garland'), text by Friedrich Gottlieb Klopstock, orchestral version by Strauss (1897); 2. *Für fünfzehn Pfennige* ('For Fifteen Pfennigs'), text by Arnim and Brentano, from *Des Knaben Wunderhorn*; 3. *Hat gesagt – bleibt's nicht dabei* ('As he said – nothing lasts'), text by Arnim and Brentano, from *Des Knaben Wunderhorn*; 4. *Anbetung* ('Adoration'), text by Friedrich Rückert

Sechs Lieder ('Six Songs'), Op. 37 (1896–8): 1. *Glückes genug* ('Enough Happiness'), text by Liliencron; 2. *Ich liebe dich* ('I Love You'), text by Liliencron, orchestral version by Strauss (1943); 3. *Meinem Kinde* ('For My Child'), text by Falke, orchestral version by Strauss (date uncertain, possibly 1900); 4. *Mein Auge* ('My Eye'), text by Dehmel, orchestral version by Strauss (1933). fp (orchestral version) Berlin, 13 October 1933; 5. *Herr Lenz* ('Lord Spring'), text by Bodman; 6. *Hochzeitlich Lied* ('Wedding Song'), text by Anton Lindner

Fünf Lieder ('Five Songs'), Op. 39, texts by Dehmel unless otherwise stated (1898). 1. *Leises Lied* ('Gentle Song'); 2. *Jung Hexenlied* ('Young Witch's Song'), text by Bierbaum; 3. *Der Arbeitsmann* ('The Workman'), orchestral version by Strauss (1941); 4. *Befreit* ('Freed'), orchestral version by Strauss (1933). fp Berlin, 13 October 1933; 5. *Lied an meinen Sohn* ('Song to My Son')

Fünf Lieder ('Five Songs'), Op. 41 (1899): 1. *Wiegenlied* ('Cradle Song'), text by Dehmel, orchestral version by Strauss (1900). fp (orchestral version) Elberfeld, 8 June 1900; 2. *In der Campagna* ('In the Campagna'), text by Mackay; 3. *Am Ufer* ('On the Bank'), text by Dehmel; 4. *Bruder Liederlich* ('Brother Dissolute'), text by Liliencron; 5. *Leise Lieder* ('Gentle Songs'), text by Christian Morgenstern

Drei Lieder ('Three Songs'), Op. 43 (1899): 1. *Muttertändelei* ('A Mother's Games'), text by Gottfried August Bürger, orchestral version by Strauss (1900). fp (orchestral version) Berlin, 3 December 1900; 2. *An Sie* ('To You'), text by Klopstock; 3. *Die Ulme zu Hirsau* ('The Elm Tree at Hirsau'), text by Uhland

Zwei grössere Gesänge für tiefe Stimme mit Orchesterbegleitung ('Two Large Songs for Low Voice with Orchestral Accompaniment'), Op. 44 (1899). fp Berlin, 3 December 1900: 1. *Notturno* ('Nocturne'), text by Dehmel; 2. *Nachtlicher Gang* ('Nightly Walk'), text by Rückert

Weihnachtsgefühl ('Christmas Emotion'), text by Martin Greif (1899)

Fünf Gedichte von Friedrich Rückert ('Five Poems by Friedrich Rückert'), Op. 46 (1899–1900): 1. *Ein Obdach gegen Sturm und Regen* ('A Shelter against Storm and Rain'); 2. *Gestern war ich Atlas* ('Yesterday I Was Atlas'); 3. *Die sieben Siegel* ('The Seven Seals'); 4. *Morgenrot* ('Dawn'); 5. *Ich sehe wie in einem Spiegel* ('I look as if in a mirror')

Fünf Lieder ('Five Songs'), Op. 47, texts by Uhland (1900): 1. *Auf ein Kind* ('On a Child'); 2. *Des Dichters Abendgang* ('The Poet's Evening Walk'), orchestral version by Strauss (1918); 3. *Rückleben* ('Living Backwards'); 4. *Einkehr* ('Reflection'); 5. *Von den sieben Zechbrüdern* ('About the Seven Drunks')

Fünf Lieder ('Five Songs'), Op. 48 (1900): 1. *Freundliche Vision* ('Friendly Vision'), text by Bierbaum; 2. *Ich schwebe* ('I Hover'), text by Henckell; 3. *Kling!* ('Ring!'), text by Henckell; 4. *Winterweihe* ('Consecration to Winter'), text by Henckell, orchestral version by Strauss (1918); 5. *Winterliebe* ('Love in Winter'), text by Henckell

Acht Lieder ('Eight Songs'), Op. 49 (1900–1): 1. *Waldseligkeit* ('Forest Happiness'), text by Dehmel, orchestral version by Strauss (1918); 2. *In goldner Fülle* ('In Golden Plenty'), text by Paul Remer; 3. *Wiegendliedchen* ('Little Cradle Song'), text by Dehmel; 4. *Lied des Steinklopfers* ('Song of the Stone-Breaker'), text by Henckell; 5. *Sie wissen's nicht* ('You don't know it'), text by Oscar Panizza; 6. *Junggesellenschwur* ('The Oath of Young Companions'), text by Arnim and Brentano, from *Des Knaben Wunderhorn*; 7. *Wer lieben will, muss leiden*

('Who wants to love must suffer'), text by Curt
Mündel, from *Elsässische Volkslieder* ('Folk Songs from
Alsace'); 8. *Ach, was Kummer, Qual und Schmerzen*
('Oh, what sorrow, torment and pain'), text by Mündel,
from *Elsässische Volkslieder*

*Zwei Gesänge für eine tiefe Bass-stimme mit
Orchesterbegleitung* ('Two Songs for Low Bass and
Orchestra'), Op. 51 (1902–6): 1. *Das Thal* ('The Valley'),
text by Uhland. fp Berlin, 7 April 1903; 2. *Der Einsame*
('The Solitary Man'), text by Heine. fp Leipzig,
5 March 1906

Sechs Lieder ('Six Songs'), Op. 56 (1902–6): 1. *Gefunden*
('Found'), text by Goethe; 2. *Blindenklage* ('The Plaint
of the Blind'), text by Henckell; 3. *Im Spätboot* ('In the
Last Boat'), text by C. F. Meyer; 4. *Mit deinen blauen
Augen* ('With Your Blue Eyes'), text by Heine;
5. *Frühlingsfeier* ('The Rite of Spring'), text by Heine,
orchestral version by Strauss (1933). fp Berlin,
13 October 1933; 6. *Die heiligen drei Könige aus
Morgenland* ('The Three Kings from the East'), for
soprano and orchestra, text by Heine (piano reduction
by Strauss for publication as a set)

Der Graf von Rom ('The Count of Rome'), vocalise for
voice and piano (1906)

Krämerspiegel ('The Tradesman's Mirror'), Op. 66, texts
by Alfred Kerr (1918). fp (private performance) Berlin,
1 November 1925: 1. *Es war einmal ein Bock* ('Once
there was a goat'); 2. *Einst kam der Bock als Bote* ('The
goat once came as messenger'); 3. *Es liebte einst ein Hase*
('A hare was once in love'); 4. *Drei Masken sah ich am
Himmel stehen* ('I saw three masks in Heaven'); 5. *Hast
du ein Tongedicht vollbracht* ('Once you've completed a
tone-poem'); 6. *O lieber Künstler sei ermahnt* ('Be
warned, dear artists '); 7. *Unser Feind ist, grosser Gott,
wie der Brite so der Schott* ('A Scotsman is our enemy
like a British man, dear God'); 8. *Von Händlern wird
die Kunst bedroht* ('Art is under threat from tradesmen');
9. *Es war mal eine Wanze* ('Once there was a bug');

10. *Die Künstler sind die Schöpfer* ('Artists are creators');
11. *Die Händler und die Macher* ('Tradesmen and
doers'); 12. *O Schröpferschwarm, O Händlerkreis* ('O
swarm of fleecers, circle of tradesmen')

Sechs Lieder nach Gedichte von Clemens Brentano ('Six
Songs after Poems by Clemens Brentano'), Op. 68, for
high voice and piano (1918), orchestral version of No. 6
(1933), of Nos. 1–5 (1940). fp (Nos. 1–5) Berlin, 30 May
1919; (No. 6) Dresden, 29 September 1920; (No. 6,
orchestral version) Berlin, 13 October 1933; (complete
orchestral version) Düsseldorf, 9 February 1941: 1. *An
die Nacht* ('To Night'); 2. *Ich wollt' ein Sträusslein
binden* ('I wanted to make a posy'); 3. *Säusle, liebe
Myrthe* ('Whisper, Beloved Myrtle'); 4. *Als mir dein
Lied erklang* ('When your song rang out'); 5. *Amor*
('Eros'); 6. *Lied der Frauen* ('The Song of Women')

Sechs Lieder ('Six Songs'), Op. 67 (1918): A. *Drei Lieder
der Ophelia* ('Three Songs for Ophelia'), texts by
Shakespeare, translated by Karl Simrock: 1. *Wei erkenn'
ich mein Treulieb* ('How should I your true love know');
2. *Guten Morgen, s'ist Sankt Valentinstag* ('Tomorrow is
Saint Valentine's Day'); 3. *Sie trugen ihn auf der Bahre
bloss* ('They bore him barefaced on the bier'); B. *Drei
Lieder aus den Büchern des Unmuts des Rendsch Nameh*
('Three Songs from the Book of Ill-Humour of
Rendsch Nameh'), texts by Goethe, from the
Westöstlicher Divan; 4. *Wer wird von der Welt verlangen*
('Whoever desires worldly things'); 5. *Hab' ich euch
denn je geraten* ('Did I ever advise you'); 6. *Wanderers
Gemütsruhe* ('Wanderer's Peace of Mind')

Fünf kleine Lieder ('Five Little Songs'), Op. 69 (1918):
1. *Der Stern* ('The Star'), text by Arnim; 2. *Der Pokal*
('The Goblet'), text by Arnim; 3. *Einerlei* ('Sameness'),
text by Arnim; 4. *Waldesfahrt* ('Forest Journey'), text by
Heine; 5. *Schlechtes Wetter* ('Bad Weather'), text by Heine

Sinnspruch ('Saying'), text by Goethe (1918)

Drei Hymnen für eine hohe Singstimme und grosses Orchester ('Three Hymns for High Voice and Large Orchestra'), Op. 71, texts by Friedrich Hölderlin (1921). fp Berlin, 9 November 1921: 1. *Hymne an die Liebe* ('Hymn to Love'); 2. *Rückkehr in die Heimat* ('Return to the Homeland'); 3. *Die Liebe* ('Love')

Erschaffen und Beleben ('Creation and Animation'), text by Goethe (1922). fp Berlin, 1957. Later published spuriously as Op. 87, No. 2

Durch allen Schall und Klang ('Through every sound and tone'), text by Goethe (1925)

Gesänge des Orients ('Songs of the East'), texts by Hans Bethge (1928). fp Berlin, 5 June 1929: 1. *Ihre Augen* ('Her Eyes'); 2. *Schwung* ('Sweep'); 3. *Liebesgeschenke* ('Love's Gifts'); 4. *Die Allmächtige* ('Allmighty Powers'); 5. *Huldigung* ('Homage')

Zwei Gesänge ('Two Songs'), for bass and piano, texts by Rückert (1929). fp Vienna, 9 June 1964: 1. *Vom künftigen Alter* ('Of future old age'); 2. *Und dann nicht mehr* ('And then no more'). Later published spuriously as Op. 87, Nos. 1 and 3

Wie etwas sei leicht ('How easy it can be'), text by Goethe (1930)

Das Bächlein ('The Brook'), text anonymous, attributed to Goethe (1933), orchestral version (1935). fp Berlin, 19 June 1942. Later published spuriously as Op. 88, No. 1

Im Sonnenschein ('In the Sunshine'), for bass and piano, text by Rückert (1935). fp Vienna, 9 June 1964. Later published spuriously as Op. 87, No. 4

Zugemessne Rhythmen ('Allotted Rhythms'), text by Goethe (1935)

Hab Dank, du gütger Weisheitsspender ('Receive my thanks, thou good Giver of Wisdom'), for bass voice unaccompanied, text by Strauss (1939)

Notschrei aus den Gefildern Laplands ('Cry for Help from the Fields of Lapland'), for soprano or tenor unaccompanied, text by Strauss (1940)

Zwei Lieder ('Two Songs'), texts by Josef Weinheber (1942). fp Vienna, 9 March 1942: 1. *Sankt Michael* ('Saint Michael'); 2. *Blick vom oberen Belvedere* ('View from Upper Belvedere')

Xenion, text by Goethe (1942)

Wer tritt herein? ('Who Came in?'), for unaccompanied soprano or tenor, text anonymous (1943)

Vier letzte Lieder ('Four Last Songs'), for high voice and orchestra (1946–8). fp London, 22 May 1950. In order of composition: 1. *Im Abendrot* ('At Twilight'), text by Joseph von Eichendorff; 2. *Frühling* ('Spring'), text by Hermann Hesse; 3. *Beim Schlafengehen* ('Going to Sleep'), text by Hesse; 4. *September*, text by Hesse. Published and usually performed in the order 2, 4, 3, 1. Strauss is said to have preferred the order 3, 4, 2, 1 and possibly wanted the orchestral version of *Ruhe, meine Seele* as a fifth song. The title of the collection is not by Strauss.

Malven ('Mallows'), for soprano and piano, text by Betty Knobel (1948). fp New York, 10 January 1985

Other Vocal

Der weisse Hirsch ('The White Stag'), for alto, tenor, bass and piano, text by Uhland (1871)

Four Scenes from a Singspiel (text anonymous, possibly by Strauss), voices and piano (1876)

Utan Sfafvel och fosfor ('From a Swedish Matchbox'), for two tenors, two basses, text anonymous (1889). fp Weimar, 1 February 1889

Enoch Arden, Op. 38, melodrama for speaker and piano, text by Alfred Tennyson (1897). fp Munich, 24 March 1898

Das Schloss am Meere ('The Castle by the Sea'), melodrama for speaker and piano, text by Uhland (1899). fp Berlin, 23 March 1899

Hans Huber in Vitznau sei schönstens bedankt ('My Heartfelt Thanks to Hans Huber in Vitznau'), four-part canon, text by Strauss (1903)

Skatcanon ('Skat Canon'), canon for four voices, text by Strauss (1904)

Hymne auf das Haus Kohorn ('Hymn to the Kohorn House'), for two tenors, two basses, text by Strauss (1925)

Choral (with Instruments/Orchestra)

Chorus from Electra, for male voices and small orchestra, text by Sophocles (1881). fp Munich, 1881

Wandrers Sturmlied ('Wanderer's Storm Song'), Op. 14, for six-part choir and full orchestra, text by Goethe (1884–5). fp Cologne, 8 March 1887

Licht, du ewiglich Eines ('Light, thou eternal One'), hymn for female chorus and orchestra (1897). fp Munich, June 1897

Taillefer, Op. 52, for soprano, tenor and baritone soloists, chorus and orchestra, text by Uhland (1903). fp Heidelberg, 26 October 1903

Bardengesang aus der 'Hermannsschlacht' ('Song of the Bards from the "Hermann's Battle"'), Op. 55, for three male choruses and orchestra, text by Klopstock (1905). fp Dresden, 6 February 1906

Die Tageszeiten ('Times of the Day'), Op. 76, for male voices and orchestra, text by Eichendorff (1927). fp Vienna, 21 July 1928: 1 *Der Morgen* ('Morning'); 2. *Mittagsruh* ('Midday Rest'); 3. *Der Abend* ('Evening'); 4. *Die Nacht* ('Night')

Austria, Op. 78, for male chorus and orchestra, text by Anton Wildgans (1929). fp Vienna, 1 January 1930

Olympische Hymne ('Olympic Hymn'), for mixed chorus and orchestra, text by Robert Lubahn (1934–5). fp Berlin, 1 August 1936

Choral (Unaccompanied)

Zwei Lieder ('Two Songs'), for mixed chorus, texts by Eichendorff (1876): 1. *Morgengesang* ('Morning Song'); 2. *Frühlingsnacht* ('Spring Night')

Kyrie, Sanctus, Agnus Dei, for mixed chorus (1877)

Sieben Lieder ('Seven Songs'), for mixed chorus (1880): 1. *Winterlied* ('Winter Song'), text by Eichendorff; 2. *Spielmannsweise* ('Minstrels Tune'), text by Genischen; 3. *Käferlied* ('Beetle's Song'), text by Robert Reinick; 4. *Pfingsten* ('Whitsun'), text by Bottger; 5. *Waldgesang* ('Forest Song'), text by Bottger; 6. *Schneeglockchen* ('Snowdrop'), text by Bottger; 7. *Trüb blinken nur die Sterne* ('The stars only glimmer faintly')

Schwäbische Erbschaft ('Swabian Legacy'), for four-part male chorus, text by Loewe (1884?). fp Mönchengladbach, 7 October 1950

Zwei Gesänge ('Two Songs'), Op. 34, for sixteen-part mixed chorus (1897): 1. *Der Abend* ('Evening'), text by Schiller; 2. *Hymne* ('Hymn'), text by Rückert

Soldatenlied ('Soldiers Song'), text by August Kopisch, for male chorus (1899)

Zwei Männerchore ('Two Men's Choruses'), Op. 42, texts by Johann Gottfried Herder, from *Stimmen der Völker in Liedern* ('The Voices of Nations in Song') (1899). fp Vienna, 8 December, 1899: 1. *Liebe* ('Love'); 2. *Altdeusches Schlactlied* ('Old German Battle Song')

Drei Männerchöre ('Three Men's Choruses'), Op. 45, texts by Herder, from *Stimmen der Völker in Liedern* (1899): 1. *Schlachtgesang* ('Battle Song'); 2. *Lied der Freundschaft*; 3. *Der Brauttanz* ('Bridal Dance')

Sechs Volksliedbearbeitungen ('Six Folk Song Arrangements'), for male-voice choir, texts traditional (1905): 1. *Geistliche Maien* ('Clerical May Celebrations'); 2. *Misslungene Liebesjagd* ('The Unsuccessful Hunt for Love'); 3. *Tummler* ('Tumbler'); 4. *Hüt' du dich* ('Be on your guard'); 5. *Wächterlied* ('Watchman's Song'); 6. *Kuckuck* ('Cuckoo')

Deutsche Motette ('German Motet'), for soprano, alto, tenor and bass soloists and mixed chorus, text by Rückert (1913). fp Berlin, 2 December 1913

Cantata, for male chorus, text by Hofmannsthal (1914)

Die Göttin im Putzzimmer ('The Goddess in the Boudoir'), for eight-part mixed chorus, text by Rückert (1935). fp Vienna, 2 March 1942

Drei Männerchöre ('Three Men's Choruses'), texts by Rückert (1935): 1. *Vor den Türen* ('Before the Doors'); 2. *Traumlicht* ('Ideal Light'); 3. *Fröhlich in Maien* ('Happy in May'). fp Cologne, 29 March 1936

Durch Einsamkeiten ('Solitude'), for four-part male chorus, text by Wildgans (1938). fp Vienna, 1 April 1939

An den Baum Daphne ('To the Tree Daphne'), for nine-part unaccompanied mixed chorus, text by Gregor (1943). fp Vienna, 7 November 1947

Orchestral

Hochlands Treue ('Highland Loyalty'), overture (1872–3). Unfinished, in short score only

Concert Overture in B minor (1876)

Festmarsch ('Festival March'), in E flat major, Op. 1 (1876). fp Munich, 26 March 1881

Serenade in G major (1877). fp Munich, 1878

Overture in E major (1878)

Overture in A minor (1879)

Symphony in D minor (1880). fp Munich, 30 March 1881

Serenade in E flat major, for 13 wind instruments, Op. 7 (1882). fp Dresden, 27 November 1882

Lied ohne Worte ('Song without Words') (1883)

Overture in C minor (1883). fp Munich, 8 November 1883

Symphony in F minor (1883–4). fp New York, 13 December 1884

Suite in B flat major, for 13 wind instruments, Op. 4 (1884). fp Munich, 18 November 1884

Festmarsch ('Festival March') in D major (1884, revised 1888). fp Munich, 8 January 1885

Aus Italien ('From Italy'), Symphonic Fantasy in Four Movements, Op. 16 (1886). fp Munich, 2 March 1887

Macbeth, Op. 23, tone-poem after Shakespeare (first version, 1886–8; revised 1890, second revision 1891). fp (first revised version) Weimar, 13 October 1890; (second revised version) Berlin, 28 February 1892

Don Juan, Op. 20, tone-poem after Lenau (1887–9?). fp Weimar, 11 November 1889

Festmarsch ('Festival March') in C major (1889). fp Munich, 1 February 1889

Tod und Verklärung ('Death and Transfiguration'), Op. 24 (1888–9). fp Eisenach, 21 June 1890

Till Eulenspiegels lustige Streiche, nach alter Schelmenweise in Rondeauform für grosses Orchester gesetzt ('Till Eulenspiegel's Merry Pranks, after an old rogue's tune, set in rondo form for large orchestra'), Op. 28 (1894–5). fp Cologne, 15 November 1895

Also sprach Zarathustra ('Thus Spake Zarathustra'),
Op. 30, tone-poem freely after Friedrich Nietzsche
(1895–6). fp Frankfurt, 27 November 1896

Don Quixote, Fantastic Variations on a Theme of
Knightly Character, Op. 35, after Cervantes (1896–7).
fp Cologne, 8 March 1898

Ein Heldenleben ('A Hero's Life'), Op. 40, tone-poem
(1897–8). fp Frankfurt, 3 March 1899

Sinfonia Domestica, Op. 53 (1902–3). fp New York,
21 March 1904

Königsmarsch für Wilhelm II ('Royal March for Wilhelm
II') (1905). fp Berlin, 3 March 1907

Zwei Militärmarsche ('Two Military Marches') (1906).
fp Berlin, 3 March 1907: No. 1 *Militärmarsch* ('Military
March'); No. 2 *Kriegsmarsch* ('War March')

De brandenburgsche Mars ('The Brandenburg March')
(1907). fp Berlin, 3 March 1907

Königsmarsch ('Royal March') (1907). fp Berlin,
3 March 1907

Feierlicher Einzug der Ritter des Johanniter-Ordens
('Solemn Entrance for the Knights of the Order of
St John'), for brass and timpani (1909)

Eine Alpensinfonie ('An Alpine Symphony'), Op. 64
(1911–15). fp Berlin, 28 October 1915

Festliches Präludium ('Festival Prelude'), Op. 61, for
orchestra and organ (1913). fp Vienna, 19 October 1913

Tanzsuite aus Klavierstücke von François Couperin
('Dance Suite from Piano Pieces by François Couperin'),
for small orchestra (1922–3). fp Vienna, 17 February
1923. Later incorporated in *Verklungene Feste*

Wiener Philharmoniker Fanfare ('Vienna Philharmonic
Fanfare'), for brass and timpani (1924). fp Vienna,
4 March 1924

Fanfare, for brass and timpani (1924). fp Vienna,
14 September 1924

*Festmusik zur Feier des 2600 jährigen Bestehens des
Kaisserreichs Japan* ('Music to Celebrate the 2600 Years
of Existence of the Empire of Japan'), Op. 84; usually
called *Japanische Festmusik* ('Japanese Festival Music')
(1940). fp Tokyo, 7 December 1940

Divertimento for small orchestra, Op. 86 (1940–1);
contains music from *Verklungene Feste*, together with
further Couperin arrangements. fp Vienna,
31 January 1943

Festmusik der Stadt Wien ('Festival Music for the City of
Vienna'), for brass and timpani, two versions (1943).
fp Vienna, 9 April 1943

Sonatina No. 1 in F major, 'Aus dem Werkstatt eines
Invaliden' ('From an Invalid's Workshop'), for 16 wind
instruments (1943). fp Dresden, 18 June 1944

München, ein Gedächtniswalzer ('Munich, a Memorial
Waltz'), based in part on abandoned film music.
(1945). fp Vienna, 31 March 1951

Metamorphosen ('Metamorphoses'), study for 23 solo
strings in C minor (1944–5). fp Zurich, 25 January 1946

Sonatina No. 2 in E flat major, 'Fröhliche Werkstatt'
('The Happy Workroom'), for 16 wind instruments
(1944–5). fp Winterthur, 25 March 1946

Instrumental with Orchestra

Romanze in E flat, for clarinet and orchestra (1879)

Violin Concerto in D minor, Op. 8 (1880–2).
fp Vienna, 8 December 1882

Horn Concerto No. 1 in E flat, Op. 11 (1882–3).
fp Meiningen, 4 March 1885

Romanze in F major, for cello and orchestra (1883)

Der Zweikampf ('The Duel'), polonaise in B flat for flute, bassoon and orchestra (1884)

Burleske for piano and orchestra (originally Scherzo for Piano and Orchestra) (1885–6). fp Eisenach, 21 June 1890

Parergon zur Sinfonia Domestica ('Offshoot of the Sinfonia Domestica'), Op. 73, for piano (left hand) and orchestra (1924). fp Dresden, 16 October 1925

Panathenäenzug ('Procession for the Festival of Panathenea'), Op. 74, for piano (left hand) and orchestra (1925–7). fp Vienna, 11 March 1928

Horn Concerto No. 2 in E flat (1942). fp Salzburg, 8 August 1943

Oboe Concerto (1945–6, revised 1948). fp Zurich, 26 February 1946

Duett-Concertino, for clarinet and bassoon with strings and harp (1947). fp (Swiss Radio broadcast) 8 April 1948

Chamber

Piano Trio No. 1 in A major (1877)

Introduction, Theme and Variations in E flat major, for horn and piano (1878)

Piano Trio No. 2 in D major (1878)

Introduction, Theme and Variations in G major, for flute and piano (1879)

Five Part Fugue, for violin and piano (1880)

String Quartet in A major, Op. 2 (1880). fp Munich, 14 March 1881

Sonata in F major, Op. 6, for cello and piano (1880–3). fp Nuremberg, 8 December 1883

Piano Quartet in C minor, Op. 13 (1884). fp Weimar, 8 December 1885

Sonata in E flat major, Op. 18, for violin and piano (1887). fp Elberfeld, 3 October 1888

Andante for horn and piano (1888). Probably from an incomplete sonata

Hochzeitspräludium ('Wedding Prelude') (1924). fp Vienna, 15 January 1924

Allegretto in E major for violin and piano (1948)

Solo Instrumental

(piano unless otherwise stated)

Schneiderpolka ('Tailors' Polka') (1870); orchestral version by Strauss (date unknown). fp (orchestral version) Munich, 2 February 1873

Moderato in C Major (1871?)

Panzenburg Polka ('Beer-Barrel Polka') (1872); orchestral version by Franz Strauss (1872). fp (orchestral version) Munich, 31 May 1872

Five Little Pieces (1873?)

Two Études: No. 1 for horn in E flat; No. 2 for horn in E (1873?)

Three Sonatinas (1874): No. 1 in C major; No. 2 in F major; No. 3 in B flat major

Fantasia in C major (1874?)

Sonata No. 1 in E major (1877)

Twelve Variations in D major (1878)

Aus alter Zeit: eine kleine Gavotte ('From Olden Times: a Little Gavotte') (1879?)

Andante in C minor (1879)

Grosse Sonata ('Great Sonata'; Sonata No. 2 in C minor) (1879)

Scherzo in B minor (1879)

Skizzen ('Sketches'), five pieces (1879)

Two Little Pieces (1879–80)

Double Fugue in B flat major (1880)

Fugue in C major (1880)

Fugue on Four Themes in C major (1880)

Five Pieces, Op. 3 (1880–1)

Sonata in B minor, Op. 6 (1880–1)

Largo in A minor (1883?)

Stiller Waldespfad ('Quiet Forest Path') (1883)

Stimmungsbilder ('Mood Paintings'), Op. 9 (1882–4):
1. *Auf stillen Waldespfad* ('On a Silent Forest Path');
2. *An einsamer Quelle* ('By a Solitary Fountain');
3. *Intermezzo*; 4. *Träumerei* ('Reverie'); 5. *Heidebild* ('Heath Landscape')

Parademarsch des Regiments Königs-Jäger zu Pferde ('Parade March for the Mounted Royal Hunting Regiment') (1905)

Parade-Marsch Cavallerie ('Cavalry Parade March') (1905)

Königsmarsch ('Royal March') (1905)

Daphne-Étude, for violin (1945)

Adaptations

Cadenzas for W. A. Mozart's Piano Concerto K. 491 (1885). fp Meiningen, 20 October 1885

Iphigénie en Tauride ('Iphigenia in Tauris'), opera by Christoph Willibald Gluck, additional texts adapted from Goethe by Strauss (1899). fp Weimar, 9 June 1900

Die Ruinen von Athen ('The Ruins of Athens'), incidental music by Ludwig van Beethoven for a play by Kotzebue, text revised by Hofmannsthal (1924); also includes music from Beethoven's *Die Geschöpfe des Prometheus* ('The Creatures of Prometheus'). fp Vienna, 20 September 1924

Idomeneo, opera by Mozart, text revised by Lothar Wallerstein (1930). fp Vienna, 16 April 1931

Further Reading

Literature on Strauss is extensive, both in English and German, though a number of individual works are widely recognized as constituting the kernel of Strauss scholarship and make essential reading. Norman Del Mar's *Richard Strauss: A Critical Commentary on his Life and Works* (three volumes, London, Barrie & Rockliffe, 1962, 1969, 1972; reissued London, Faber & Faber, 1986) remains the definitive analysis of his music. The principal biographies in English are Michael Kennedy's *Richard Strauss* (London, Dent, 1976, revised edition Oxford, Oxford University Press, 1995) and George R. Marek's controversial *Richard Strauss: The Life of a Non-Hero* (London, Victor Gollancz, 1967). The principal studies in German are Ernst Krause's *Richard Strauss, Gestalt und Werk* (Leipzig, Breitkopf & Härtel, 1955, revised edition 1963, English edition, as *Richard Strauss, the Man and his Work*, translated by John Coombs, London, Collett's, 1964) and Walter Panofsky's *Richard Strauss, Partitur eines Lebens* (Munich, Piper, 1965, sadly never translated into English). Kurt Wilhelm's *Richard Strauss persönlich* (Munich, Kindler, 1985, English edition, as *Richard Strauss, An Intimate Portrait*, translated by Mary Whittall, London, Thames and Hudson, 1989) is an important and impressive collection of letters and photographs from the Strauss archive in Garmisch, many of which are not available elsewhere. The operas have tended to attract more critical attention than the rest of Strauss's output and are dealt with extensively in William Mann's *Richard Strauss: A Critical Study of the Operas* (London, Cassell, 1964) and Charles Osborne's *The Complete Operas of Richard Strauss* (London, Victor Gollancz, 1988).

The following list of related material is by no means exhaustive, and for reasons of space I have largely confined myself to works which are available in English, with the exception of a number of major texts, notably Strauss's own writings, some of which have only appeared in German.

Writings by Strauss

Betrachtungen und Errinerungen, edited by Willi Schuh (Zurich, Atlantis Verlag, 1949); English edition, as *Recollections and Reflections*, translated by L. J. Lawrence (London, Boosey & Hawkes, 1953)

Richard Strauss und Joseph Gregor: Briefwechsel, edited by Willi Schuh (Salzburg, Otto Müller Verlag, 1954)

Richard Strauss und Hugo von Hofmannsthal Briefwechsel, edited by Willi Schuh (Zurich, Atlantis Verlag, 1952; revised edition 1978); English edition, as *The Strauss Hofmannsthal Correspondence*, translated by H. Hammelmann and E. Osers (London, Collins, 1961, reissued Cambridge, Cambridge University Press, 1980)

Richard Strauss – Clemens Krauss Briefwechsel, edited by Willi Schuh and G. K. Kende (Munich, C. H. Beck Verlag, 1964)

Gustav Mahler – Richard Strauss Briefwechsel 1888–1911, edited by Herta Blaukopf (Munich, Piper, 1980); English edition translated by Edmund Jephcott (London, Faber, 1984)

Romain Rolland – Richard Strauss: Correspondence et Fragments de Journal, edited by Gustave Samazeuilh (Paris, Albin Michel, 1951); English edition, *Richard Strauss and Romain Rolland: Correspondence, Diary and Essays*, edited and translated by Rollo H. Myers (London, Calder and Boyars, 1968)

Richard Strauss – Stefan Zweig Briefwechsel, edited by Willi Schuh (Frankfurt, Fischer Verlag, 1957); English edition, as *A Confidential Matter*, translated by Max Knight (Berkeley, CA, University of California Press, 1977)

Biographies

Jefferson, A. *The Life of Richard Strauss* (Newton Abbott, David and Charles, 1973)

Jefferson, A. *Richard Strauss* (London, Novello, 1975)

Kennedy, M. 'Richard Strauss' in S. Sadie (ed.) *The New Grove Dictionary of Music and Musicians* (London, Macmillan, 1980); reprinted, with revisions, in *The New Grove Turn-of-the-Century Masters*, The New Grove Biography Series (London, Macmillan, 1985)

Nice, D. *Richard Strauss* (London, Omnibus, 1993)

Schuh, W. *Richard Strauss: Jugend und frühe Meisterjahre Lebenschronik 1864–1898* (Zurich, Atlantis-Musik-Verlag, 1976); English edition, as *Richard Strauss: A Chronicle of the Early Years, 1864–1898*, translated by Mary Whittall (Cambridge, Cambridge University Press, 1982)

Splitt, G. *Richard Strauss 1933–1945: Aesthetik und Musikpolitik zu Beginn der nationalsozialistischen Herrschaft* (Pfaffenweiler, Centaurus Verlagsgesellschaft, 1987)
A much disputed study of Strauss's work with the Reichsmusikkammer.

Stage Works

Dusek, P. and Koller, H. *Elektra, Rache ohne Erlösung* (Monaco, Editions Tomek, 1982)

John, N. (ed.) *Arabella* (English National Opera Guide, London, Calder, 1981)

John, N. (ed.) *Der Rosenkavalier* (English National Opera Guide, London, Calder, 1981)

John, N. (ed.) *Salome/Elektra* (English National Opera Guide, London, Calder, 1981)

Hartmann, R. *Die Bühnenwerke von der Uraufführung bis heute* (Fribourg, Office du Livre SA, 1980); English edition, as *Richard Strauss, the Staging of his Operas and Ballets*, translated by Graham Davis (Oxford, Oxford University Press, 1982/London, 1983)

Jefferson, A. *The Operas of Richard Strauss in Britain, 1910–1963* (London, Putnam, 1963)

Jefferson, A. *Der Rosenkavalier* (Cambridge, Cambridge University Press, 1985)

Milnes, R. 'Somewhere between Moscow and New York: Strauss's Helena', *Opera*, July 1997

Orchestral Works

Armstrong, T. *Strauss's Tone Poems* (Oxford, Oxford University Press, 1931)

Kennedy, M. *Strauss Tone Poems* (London, BBC Publications, 1984)

Williamson, J. *Also sprach Zarathustra* (Cambridge, Cambridge University Press, 1993)

Lieder

Jefferson, A. *The Lieder of Richard Strauss* (London, Cassell, 1971)

Petersen, B. A. *Ton und Wort: The Lieder of Richard Strauss* (Ann Arbor, MI, UMI Research Press, 1977)

Schlotterer, R. (ed.) *Texte der Lieder von Richard Strauss* (Munich, Pfaffenhafen Ludwig, 1988)
An invaluable critical edition of the complete texts of the songs.

Collections of Essays about Strauss

Gilliam, B. (ed.) *Richard Strauss: New Perspectives on the Composer and his Work* (Durham and London, Duke University Press, 1992)

Gilliam, B. (ed.) *Richard Strauss and his World* (Princeton, Princeton University Press, 1992)
Also contains Rudolf Hartmann's memoir of his last meeting with Strauss, important critical works by Theodor W. Adorno and Paul Bekker, and the only available selections in English of Strauss's correspondence with Thuille and Gregor.

Jaacks, G. and Jahnke, A. W. *Richard Strauss, Musik des Lichts in dunkler Zeit* (Mainz, Schott, 1980)

Other Related Material

Bracher, K. D. *Die deutsche Diktatur: Entstehung, Struktur, Folgen des Nationalsozialismus* (Cologne and Berlin, Kiepenhauer & Witsch, 1969); English edition, as *The German Dictatorship: The Origins, Structure and Consequences of National Socialism*, translated by Jean Steinberg (London, Weidenfeld & Nicolson, 1971)

Carr, W. *A History of Germany 1815–1990* (London, Edward Arnold, 1969, revised edition 1991)

Conrad, P. *A Song of Love and Death: The Meaning of Opera* (London, Chatto & Windus, 1987, revised edition New York, Graywolf Press, 1996)

Gay, P. *Weimar Culture, The Insider as Outsider* (London, Secker & Warburg, 1969)

Hugo von Hofmannsthal: Gesammelte Werke, edited by Herbert Steiner (fifteen volumes, Frankfurt, Fischer, 1945–58, reissued in ten volumes 1979)
The standard German edition of Hofmannsthal's works.

Kaes, A., Jay, M. and Dimendberg, E. (eds.) *The Weimar Republic Source Book* (Berkeley, CA, University of California Press, 1994)

Kater, M. H. *The Twisted Muse: Musicians and their Music in the Third Reich* (New York and Oxford, Oxford University Press, 1997)

Levi, E. *Music in the Third Reich* (London, Macmillan, 1994)

Mann, G. *Deutsche Geschichte des 19. und 20. Jahrhunderts* (Frankfurt, 1958); English edition, as *The History of Germany since 1789*, translated by Marian Jackson (London, Chatto & Windus, 1968)

Müller, H. *Stefan Zweig* (Hamburg, Rohwolt, 1988)

Richie, A. *Faust's Metropolis: A History of Berlin* (London, Harper Collins, 1998)

Rolland, R. *Jean Christophe* (ten volumes, Paris, Albin Michel, 1904–1912); English edition, as *John Christopher*, translated by Gilbert Cannan (London, Calder and Boyars, 1913, reprinted 1962)

Ross, A. 'The Devil's Disciple', *New Yorker*, 21 July 1997

Tambling, J. *Opera and the Culture of Fascism* (Oxford, Clarendon, 1996)

Volke, W. *Hugo von Hofmannsthal* (Hamburg, Rohwolt, 1967)

Selective Discography

Strauss's works have been extensively recorded, although some are not available at the time of writing, and the absence of *Guntram*, *Feuersnot* and *Die Liebe der Danae* is much to be regretted. Major versions of operatic highlights, recorded independently of complete performances, are given when the musical quality is particularly exemplary.

In compiling this selection, excellence of performance has taken precedence over sound recording quality. A recording may be listed more than once, if its contents fall into two or more categories.

Opera

Salome
Montserrat Caballé, Regina Resnik, Richard Lewis, Sherrill Milnes, James King, London Symphony Orchestra conducted by Erich Leinsdorf
RCA GD8644 (2CDs)

Salome
Cheryl Studer, Leonie Rysanek, Horst Hiestermann, Bryn Terfel, Clemens Bieber, Orchestra of the Deutsche Oper Berlin conducted by Giuseppe Sinopoli
DG 431 810–2HG2 (2CDs)

Salome (Closing Scene)
Ljuba Welitsch, Orchestra of the Metropolitan Opera House New York conducted by Fritz Reiner; with arias and lieder by Welitsch
SONY MHK 262866 (2CDs)

Elektra
Birgit Nilsson, Marie Collier, Regina Resnik, Gerhard Stolze, Tom Krause, Vienna State Opera Chorus, Vienna Philarmonic Orchestra conducted by Georg Solti
DECCA 417 345–2DH2 (2CDs)

Elektra
Alessandra Marc, Deborah Voigt, Hanna Schwarz, Siegfried Jerusalem, Samuel Ramey, Vienna State Opera Chorus, Vienna Philharmonic Orchestra conducted by Giuseppe Sinopoli
DG 453 429–2GH2 (2CDs)

Der Rosenkavalier
Christa Ludwig, Edith Mathis, Tatiana Troyanos, Anton de Ridder, Otto Wiener, Theo Adam, Vienna State Opera Chorus, Vienna Philharmonic Orchestra conducted by Karl Böhm
DG 445 338–2GX3 (3CDs)

Der Rosenkavalier
Anna Tomowa-Sintow, Janet Perry, Agnes Baltsa, Vinson Cole, Gottfried Hornik, Kurt Moll, Vienna State Opera Chorus, Vienna Philharmonic Orchestra conducted by Herbert von Karajan
DG 423 850 2GH3

Ariadne auf Naxos (1912 version)
Margaret Price, Sumi Jo, Gosta Winbergh, Thomas Mohr, Ernst Theo Richter, Lyon Opera Orchestra conducted by Kent Nagano
VIRGIN CLASSICS VCD 5 45111 2 (2CDs)

Ariadne auf Naxos (1916 version)
Maria Reining, Irmgard Seefried, Alda Noni, Max Lorenz, Erich Kunst, Paul Schöffler, Vienna State Opera Orchestra conducted by Karl Böhm
PREISER 90217 (2CDs)

Ariadne auf Naxos (1916 version)
Gundula Janowitz, Teresa Zylis-Gara, Sylvia Geszty, James King, Hermann Prey, Theo Adam, Dresden Staatskapelle conducted by Rudolf Kempe
EMI CMS 7 64159 2 (2CDs)

Die Frau ohne Schatten
Leonie Rysanek, Christa Ludwig, Grace Hoffman, Jess Thomas, Walter Berry, Walter Kreppel, Chorus and Orchestra of the Vienna State Opera conducted by Herbert von Karajan
DG 457 678–2 (3CDs)

Die Frau ohne Schatten
Leonie Rysanek, Birgit Nilsson, Ruth Hesse, James
King, Walter Berry, Peter Wimberger, Chorus and
Orchestra of the Vienna State Opera conducted by
Karl Böhm
DG 445 325–2GX3 (3CDs)

*Die Frau ohne Schatten (Highlights: The Empress's
Awakening Scene; Act III, Scenes 3 and 4)*
Eleanor Steber, Christl Goltz, Set Svanholm, Otto
Wiener, Orchestra and Chorus of the Bavarian State
Opera conducted by Karl Böhm; with *Vier letzte Lieder*
and Beethoven's *Ah, Perfido!*
VAI VAIA 1012

Intermezzo
Lucia Popp, Alfred Dallapozza, Dietrich Fischer-
Dieskau, Bavarian Radio Symphony Orchestra
conducted by Wolfgang Sawallisch
EMI CDS7 49337–2 (2CDs)

Die ägytpische Helena
Gwyneth Jones, Barbara Hendricks, Matti Kastu,
Willard White, The Jewell Chorale, Detroit Symphony
Orchestra conducted by Antal Dorati
DECCA 430 381–2DM2 (2CDs)

Arabella
Lisa della Casa, Hilde Gueden, Mimi Coertse, Ira
Malaniuk, Anton Dermota, George London, Otto
Edelmann, Vienna State Opera Chorus, Vienna
Philharmonic Orchestra conducted by Georg Solti
DECCA 430 387–2DM2 (3CDs)

Die schweigsame Frau
Jeannette Scovotti, Trudeliese Schmidt, Anneliese
Burmeister, Eberhard Büchner, Wolfgang Schöne,
Theo Adam, Dresden State Opera Chorus, Dresden
Staatskapelle conducted by Marek Janowski
EMI CMS5 66033–2 (3CDs)

Friedenstag
Arabella (Highlights)
Ariadne auf Naxos (1916 version) (Highlights)
Viorica Ursuleac, Hans Hotter, Vienna State Opera
Orchestra and Chorus conducted by Clemens Krauss
KOCH SCHWANN 3–4165–2 (2CDs; recorded at the 1939
Vienna première)

Daphne
Lucia Popp, Otrun Wenkel, Peter Schreier, Rainer
Goldberg, Kurt Moll, Bavarian Radio Symphony
Orchestra and Chorus conducted by Bernard Haitink
EMI CDS7 49309–2 (2CDs)

Capriccio
Gundula Janowitz, Tatiana Troyanos, Peter Schreier,
Hermann Prey, Dietrich Fischer-Dieskau, Karl
Ridderbusch, Bavarian Radio Symphony Orchestra
conducted by Karl Böhm
DG 445 347–2GX2 (2CDs)

Des Esels Schatten
Bodil Arnesen, Mette Ejsing, Eberhard Büchner, Oskar
Hillebrand, Andreas Kohn, Berlin Radio Choir, Berlin
Radio Symphony Orchestra conducted by Karl Anton
Rickenbacher
KOCH SCHWANN 3–6548–2

Ballet

Josephslegende
Tokyo Metropolitan Symphony Orchestra conducted
by Hiroshi Wakasugi
DENON 33CO 2050/EX

Other Stage Works

Der Bürger als Edelmann
Academy of Saint Martin in the Fields conducted by
Neville Marriner; with *Tanzsuite aus Klavierstücken von
François Couperin*
PHILIPS 446 696 2PH

Lieder

There have been a large number of recordings of
Strauss's songs, but singers have tended to be extremely
selective and very few of the published groups have
been recorded complete, with the obvious exceptions of
the *Brentano Lieder*, the *Ophelia Lieder*, *Krämerspeigel*,
the Op. 71 *Hymnen* and the *Vier letzte Lieder*. In the
early 1970s, however, Fischer-Dieskau and the pianist
Gerald Moore recorded all the songs suitable for a male
voice; it remains the most extensive selection of the
lieder available, including Opp. 10, 15, 17, 19, 21, 22, 26,
27, 29 (nos. 1 & 3), 31, 32, 36 (nos. 1 & 4), 37 (nos. 1, 2,
3, 5 & 6), 39, 41 (nos. 2, 3, 4 & 5), 43 (nos. 1 & 3), 46,
47, 48, 49 (nos. 1, 2, 4, 5 & 6), 56, 67 (nos. 4, 5 & 6), 68
(nos. 1 & 4), 69, 77, 88, *Krämerspiegel, Liebesliedchen,
Vom künftigen Alter, Und dann nicht mehr, Im
Sonnenschein, Rote Rosen, Wir beide wollen springen,
Sinnspruch, Durch allen Schall und Klang, Zugemessne
Rhythmen* and *Xenion*
EMI CMS7 63995-2 (6CDs)

Jugendlieder
Charlotte Morgiono, Bernd Weikl, Friedrich Haider
(piano), Wolfgang Vladar (horn)
NIGHTINGALE CLASSICS NC017260-2

Notturno
Linda Finnie, Royal Scottish National Orchestra
conducted by Neeme Järvi; with *Macbeth* and
Rosenkavalier Waltzes
CHANDOS CHAN 8834

Ophelia Lieder
Elisabeth Schwarzkopf, Glenn Gould; with *Enoch
Arden*, Piano Sonata in B minor, Five Piano Pieces
SONY SM2K 52657

Brentano Lieder
Eileen Hulse, Royal Scottish National Orchestra
conducted by Neeme Järvi; with Symphony in F minor
CHANDOS CHAN 9166

Brentano Lieder
Vier letzte Lieder
Zueignung
Meinem Kinde
Müttertändelei
Frühlingsfeier
Die heilige drei Könige aus Morgenland
Edita Gruberova (*Brentano Lieder*), Lucia Popp
(*Vier letzte Lieder*), Karita Mattila (others), London
Symphony Orchestra conducted by Michael
Tilson Thomas
SONY SK 48242

Vier letzte Lieder
Eleanor Steber, Cleveland Orchestra conducted by
James Levine; with highlights from *Die Frau ohne
Schatten* and Beethoven's *Ah, Perfido!*
VAI VAIA 1012

Vier letzte Lieder
Gundula Janowitz, Berlin Philharmonic Orchestra,
conducted by Herbert von Karajan; with *Tod und
Verklärung* and *Metamorphosen*
DG 447 422-2GOR

Krämerspiegel
Knut Skram, Eva Knardahl; with Cello Sonata
BIS BIS-CD049

Drei Hymnen
Karita Mattila, Berlin Philharmonic Orchestra
conducted by Claudio Abbado; with Hölderlin settings
by Brahms, Reger and Rihm
SONY SK 53975

Other Vocal

Enoch Arden
Claude Rains, Glenn Gould; with *Ophelia Lieder*, Piano
Sonata in B minor, Five Piano Pieces
SONY SM2K 52657

Choral

Wandrers Sturmlied
Taillefer
Die Tageszeiten
Felicity Lott, Johan Botha, Michael Volle (all *Taillefer*),
Ernst-Senff Chorus Berlin, Dresden Philharmonic
Orchestra conducted by Michel Plasson
EMI 724 3 5 56572 2 0

Deutsche Motette
Die Göttin im Putzzimmer
An den Baum Daphne
Tina Kiberg, Randi Stene, Gert Henning Jensen (all
Deutsche Motette), Danish National Radio Chorus
conducted by Stefan Parkman
CHANDOS CHAN 9223

Orchestral

Any discography of the orchestral music must
inevitably be dominated by two musicians who still
represent the pinnacle of Strauss conducting – Rudolf
Kempe and Fritz Reiner (the latter, sadly, never made a
complete commercial recording of any of the operas,
though 'bootlegs' and 'live' performances can be
obtained through specialist dealers). Kempe recorded
the major orchestral works and concertos with the
Dresden Staatskapelle in the 1970s and his
performances are now available in three sets from EMI.
This is the most complete cycle of Strauss's non-
operatic work on disc and for anyone wishing to
explore his orchestral music *in toto*, they remain
essential purchases:–

Volume 1: *Horn Concerto No. 1* (Peter Damm), *Horn
Concerto No. 2* (Peter Damm), *Duett Concertino*
(Manfred Wise, clarinet and Wolfgang Liebscher,
bassoon), *Oboe Concerto* (Manfred Clement), *Burleske*
(Malcolm Frager, piano), *Parergon zur Sinfonia
Domestica* (Peter Rösel, piano), *Panathenäenzug* (Peter
Rösel, piano), *Till Eulenspiegel, Don Juan, Ein
Heldenleben*
EMI CMS7 64342–2 (3CDs)

Volume 2: *Violin Concerto* (Ulf Hoelscher), *Sinfonia
Domestica, Also sprach Zarathustra, Tod und Verklärung,
Rosenkavalier Waltzes, Dance of the Seven Veils from
Salome, Der Bürger als Edelmann Concert Suite,
Schlagobers Waltzes, Josephslegende Symphonic Fragment*
EMI CMS7 64346–2 (3CDs)

Volume 3: *Metamorphosen, Eine Alpensinfonie, Aus
Italien, Macbeth, Don Quixote* (Paul Tortelier, cello and
Max Rostal, viola), *Tanzsuite aus Klavierstücken von
François Couperin*
EMI 3CKs CMS7 64350–2

Fritz Reiner, a conductor much admired by Strauss,
recorded the major orchestral works (with the exception
of *Till Eulenspiegel*) along with extracts from the operas
with the Chicago Symphony Orchestra in the 1950s and
60s. Though his discography is less extensive than
Kempe's, his performances remain definitive. The
reader could do no better than purchase the collected
edition released by RCA:–

Burleske (Byron Janis, piano), *Also sprach Zarathustra*
(two performances, recorded 1954 and 1962),
Rosenkavalier Waltzes, Don Juan, Don Quixote (Antonio
Janigro, cello and Milton Preves, viola), *Sinfonia
Domestica, Der Bürger als Edelmann, Ein Heldenleben*,
Salome (Dance of the Seven Veils, Closing Scene, soloist
Inge Borkh), *Elektra* (Elektra's Soliloquy, Recognition
Scene, Closing Scene, soloists Inge Borkh, Frances
Yeend, Paul Schöffler)
RCA 09026 68635 2 (5CDs)

Serenade for Thirteen Wind Instruments
Suite in B flat for Thirteen Wind Instruments
Sonatina No. 1 for Wind Instruments
Sonatina No. 2 for Wind Instruments
Netherlands Wind Ensemble conducted by Edo de
Waart; with Oboe Concerto
PHILIPS 438 733 2PM2

Symphony in F Minor
Royal Scottish National Orchestra conducted by
Neeme Järvi; with *Brentano Lieder*
CHANDOS CHAN 9166

Aus Italien
Macbeth
Aarhus Symphony Orchestra conducted by Norman
Del Mar
ASV CD DCA 750

Macbeth
Royal Scottish National Orchestra conducted by
Neeme Järvi; with *Rosenkavalier Waltzes* and *Notturno*
CHANDOS CHAN 8334

Don Juan
Ein Heldenleben
Berlin Philharmonic Orchestra conducted by Herbert
von Karajan
DG 429 717–2GGA

Don Juan
Till Eulenspiegel
Berlin Philharmonic Orchestra conducted by Claudio
Abbado; with *Burleske*
SONY SK5265

Tod und Verklärung
Metamorphosen
Berlin Philharmonic Orchestra conducted by Herbert
von Karajan; with *Vier letzte Lieder*
DG 447 422–2GOR

Tod und Verklärung
Also sprach Zarathustra
New York Philharmonic Orchestra conducted by
Giuseppe Sinopoli
DG 423 576–2GH

Don Quixote
Jacqueline Du Pré (cello), Herbert Downes (viola),
Philharmonia Orchestra conducted by Adrian Boult;
with music by Lalo
EMI 5 55528 2

Sinfonia Domestica
Vienna Philharmonic Orchestra conducted by André
Previn; with *Parergon zur Sinfonia Domestica*
DG 449–188–2GH

Eine Alpensinfonie
Concertgebouw Orchestra conducted by Bernard
Haitink
PHILIPS 416 156–2PH

Instrumental with Orchestra

See Orchestral for recordings conducted by Rudolf
Kempe and Fritz Reiner as part of their EMI and RCA
Strauss cycles.

Violin Concerto
Oboe Concerto
Duett Concertino for Clarinet and Bassoon
Boris Belkin (violin), Gordon Hunt (oboe), Dmitri
Ashkenazy (clarinet), Kim Walker (bassoon), Berlin
Radio Symphony Orchestra conducted by Vladimir
Ashkenazy
DECCA 436 415–2DH

Oboe Concerto
Heinz Holliger, New Philharmonia Orchestra
conducted by Edo de Waart; with *Serenade for Thirteen
Wind Instruments, Suite for Thirteen Wind Instruments,
Sonatinas Nos. 1 & 2*
PHILIPS 438 733 2PM2

Concerto for Horn and Orchestra No. 1
Concerto for Horn and Orchestra No. 2
Barry Tuckwell, Berlin Radio Symphony Orchestra
conducted by Vladimir Ashkenazy
DECCA 430 370–2DH

Burleske for Piano and Orchestra
Martha Argerich, Berlin Philharmonic Orchestra
conducted by Claudio Abbado; with *Till Eulenspiegel*
and *Don Juan*
SONY SK52565

Parergon zur Sinfonia Domestica
Gary Graffman (piano), Vienna Philharmonic
Orchestra conducted by André Previn; with *Sinfonia
Domestica*
DG 449 188–2GH

Chamber

Sonata for Cello and Piano
Elemér Lavotha, Kerstin Åberg; with *Krämerspiegel*
BIS BIS–CD049

Violin Sonata
Ginette Neveu, Gustaf Beck; with music by Chausson,
Debussy and Ravel
EMI CDH7 63493–2

Piano

Five Piano Pieces
Piano Sonata in B minor
Glenn Gould; with *Enoch Arden, Ophelia Lieder*
SONY SM2K 52657

Recordings by Strauss

Strauss made a good number of recordings, both of his
own works and those of other composers, though by no
means all of them are currently available. The most
important issue consists of the two Preiser sets which
contain the 1944 recordings of his major works:–

Volume 1: *Don Quixote, Ein Heldenleben* (first
recording), *Eine Alpensinfonie, Japanische Festmusik,
Rosenkavalier Waltzes*
Bavarian State and Vienna Philharmonic Orchestras
PREISER 90205 (2CDs)

Volume 2: *Don Juan, Till Eulenspiegel, Also sprach
Zarathustra, Ein Heldenleben* (second recording), *Der
Bürger als Edelmann, Tod und Verklärung, Sinfonia
Domestica*
Vienna Philharmonic Orchestra
PREISER 90216 (3CDs)

*Gluck: Iphigénie en Aulide Overture; Mozart: Die
Zauberflöte Overture; Weber: Euryanthe Overture;
Cornelius: Der Barbier von Bagdad Overture; Wagner:
Der fliegende Holländer Overture, Prelude to Tristan und
Isolde*
Berlin State Opera and Berlin Philharmonic Orchestras
KOCH 37119–2

Mozart: Symphony No. 40 and Symphony No. 41 'Jupiter'
Berlin State Opera and Berlin Philharmonic Orchestras
KOCH 37076–2

Index

Page numbers in italics refer to
picture captions.

Photographic Acknowledgements

The author and publisher would like to give special thanks to Dr Christian Strauss for his kind help in providing photographs from the Richard Strauss Archiv and for granting us permission to reproduce them in this book.

AKG London: 14, 21, 29, 46, 49, 55, 67, 70, 80, 115, 133, 147
Corbis, London: 100
Deutsches Theatermuseum, Munich/R. Betz: 148, 179
The Hulton Getty Picture Collection/Corbis, London: 37, 159
Imperial War Museum, London: 113
© Kranichphoto, Berlin: 98
Photograph courtesy of the Metropolitan Opera Archives, New York: 154
Nationalarchiv der Richard-Wagner-Stiftung Bayreuth: 15, 45
Salzburger Festspiele: 120, 194
Reproduced with permission of the Richard Strauss Archiv, Garmisch-Partenkirchen: 13, 17, 19r, 23, 24, 25, 33, 53, 58, 60, 65, 89, 131, 139, 141, 143, 161, 163, 201, 205, 211
Süddeutscher Verlag Bilderdienst, Munich: 19l, 44, 71, 73, 91, 110, 117, 156, 173, 186, 190, 193, 199, 210
Theaterwissenschaftliche Sammlung, Universität zu Köln: 77, 125, 174
© Sabine Toepffer/Deutsches Theatermuseum, Munich: 2
Ullstein, Berlin: 52, 85, 104, 140, 142, 168, 178, 180
Courtesy Unitel Film- und Fernseh-Produktionsgesellschaft mbH & Co., Ismaning, Germany: 93
Werner Volke, *Hugo von Hofmannsthal*, Reinbek bei Hamburg, 1967: 129
© Roger Wood: 87

Text Acknowledgements

Every effort has been made to trace copyright holders for the quoted textual material contained within this book. We apologise to those whom we have so far failed to find.

Extracts from the librettos of *Guntram, Feuersnot, Der Rosenkavalier, Ariadne auf Naxos, Die Frau ohne Schatten, Intermezzo, Arabella, Friedenstag, Die Liebe der Danae* and *Capriccio* are reprinted by kind permission of Boosey & Hawkes Music Publishers Ltd.

Extracts from *Richard Strauss & Romain Rolland: Correspondence, Diary and Essays*, edited and annotated with a preface by Rollo H. Myers (Calder Publications, 1968), are reprinted by permission of the publisher.

Acknowledgements are due to Thames and Hudson for their permission to quote from K. Wilhelm, *Richard Strauss: An Intimate Portrait*, translated by M. Whittall (Thames and Hudson, 1989); original German edition © Kindler Verlag GmbH, Munich; English translation © 1989 Mary Whittall

Thanks are also extended to Mr Richard Marek for his kind permission to reprint extracts from *Richard Strauss: The Life of a Non-Hero* by George R. Marek.